Writing the Dream

A Serenity Press anthology

Edited, compiled and published by Serenity Press

Serenity Press books may be ordered through online booksellers or by contacting:
www.serenitypress.org
publisher@serenitypress.org

Because of the dynamic nature of the Internet, any web addresses or links contained in this book may have changed since publication and may no longer be valid. The views expressed in this work are solely those of the authors and do not necessarily reflect the views of the publisher and the publisher hereby disclaims any responsibility for them.

Although the author/s and publisher have made every effort to ensure that the information in this book was correct at press time, the author and publisher do not assume and hereby disclaim any liability to any party for any loss, damage, or disruption caused by errors or omissions, whether such errors or omissions result from negligence, accident, or any other cause.

ISBN: (sc) 978-0-9946337-3-6

ISBN: (e) 978-0-9946337-4-3

Table of Contents

Introduction

NO two writers are the same, but they have one thing in common: they are storytellers at heart and their deepest desire is to be heard. Like oral storytellers of old, who travelled from village to village, writers today have unique, creative and inspirational voices that travel the world sharing stories in digital and print forms.

Writing the Dream shares the stories of twenty-five Australian writers, from established and well-known authors like Anna Jacobs, Juliet Marillier, Natasha Lester and Jenn J McLeod, to emerging and aspiring authors who are only beginning to make their mark. Some are traditionally published, while others have taken the self-publishing route. Some have faced rejection after rejection, while others have had a dream path. Some have had agents, while others are yet to send out their first query. But, while their writing journeys are different, all of them strive to create, entertain, inspire and inform.

Writing the Dream grew from a desire to inspire and encourage those who, like us, dream of writing and being published. We wanted to create a book that would give hope when a writer's fragile heart is tested. And so, we put the call out for submissions, and we were blown away by the quality and honesty of the pieces we received.

The stories we selected for *Writing the Dream* are set to strike a chord in every hopeful writer's heart. You'll connect with some more than others, because you will identify with elements of their journey. But, it's our hope in putting together this collection, that *each* story will inspire, encourage and motivate you to start telling *your* stories.

Rather than rank authors by number of books sold or published, we compiled the stories in *Writing the Dream* by listing the authors in alphabetical order. We've also included a short list of five writing tips at the end of each contribution.

For gender neutrality, the word 'they' has been used in place of 'he or she'. Although some argue that 'they' is not a third-person singular pronoun, evidence shows that it is commonly accepted to be so, and the word has long been used by authors, including Jane Austen. We're sticking to that ... or 'they'.

Eagle-eyed readers will also note that some specific writers' centres mentioned by authors have an apostrophe after the word 'writers', while others do not. We have used the name each centre prefers — some use the apostrophe and others don't.

KAREN MC DERMOTT & MONIQUE MULLIGAN,

SERENITY PRESS

Foreword

AS I write this foreword, I pause and look to the bookshelf on my right. There they are: Lajos Egri's *The Art of Dramatic Writing*. Booth, Colomb and Williams' *The Craft of Research*. Stephen J Pyne's *Voice & Vision: A Guide to Writing History and Other Serious Nonfiction*. Helen Sword's *Stylish Academic Writing*. There are numerous other similar titles next to them — all, to a staff writer such as myself working for a large metropolitan daily, invaluable.

But one never stops learning, and there is always room for another 'how to' book on writing. One such is this present volume, which, like the wonderful New York Times' column Writers on Writing (its archive is available free on the internet), conveys something of the pleasures and pains of the writing life – straight from the horse's mouth, so to speak – while preserving its essential mysteries.

That's not to say the advice offered by these writers from various backgrounds working in various genres isn't pure gold: it is. Rather, it's the individuality and intimacy of their personal narratives which will touch and inspire you in less obviously practical but equally valuable ways. The effect is of an informal conversation among friends; and indeed, it comes as no surprise that one of the most frequent tips offered here is 'Join a writers' group'.

Then there is that other conversation, the one between writer and reader, which doubly ensures writing is never the solitary pursuit it's made out to be. Perhaps that's the overriding message of *Writing the Dream*: you're never alone.

WILLIAM YEOMAN, BOOKS EDITOR,
THE WEST AUSTRALIAN

Am I a Writer?

by Louise Allan

IF someone had asked me a decade ago what I might be doing in ten years' time, 'Writing a novel' wouldn't have been on the list. At that time, it wasn't a dream of mine, nor had it ever been, not even a pipe dream.

I'd never entertained the possibility of being a writer, mainly because I didn't believe I was creative or that I could write. At the time we chose our careers, I believed writers belonged to another world, an almost mythical one, and they possessed qualities that had not been bestowed upon me:

- Writers had fanciful imaginations and could create whimsy out of the ordinary, whereas I only saw what was around me: a bed to be made, a meal to be eaten, homework to be completed.

- Writers loved reading nineteenth century Classics and quoted from them at length. I, on the other hand, was bored by most of the Classics, skipped pages at a time, and from them, could only remember two quotes, both by Shakespeare, and both known by everyone in the English-speaking world.

- Writers started writing as soon as they could hold a pen, and kept diaries in which they wrote about the sky and how flowers smelled and what birdsong they'd heard. As a teenager I made two attempts to keep a diary, both of which failed after a couple of entries, and neither of which still exist, nor would I want them to. They certainly contained no descriptions of skies or flowers or birds.

- Writers had unlimited memories where they stored every conversation they'd ever had, including witticisms uttered by shopkeepers or bus drivers. They also remembered exactly what people looked like and what they wore. I remembered the gist of conversations if I was interested in them. Like, if I couldn't afford a Lime Split and had to buy an icy pole instead. As for what people wore, unless they sported a ballet tutu at a footy game, I was unlikely to notice.

- Writers possessed vast vocabularies with which they peppered their sentences, and their stories spilled onto their pages whole and complete. My vocabulary was narrow and simple, and every word I penned was a chore to find.

- Writers were either British or American, and I was Australian. Importantly, they were prepared to live in tiny garrets and be penniless, whereas I wanted a house and a job for which I'd be paid.

You see, I possessed none of the qualities needed to be a writer.

Before I started school, my sister and I spent our days playing with dolls. We fed and dressed our babies, and popped them in their prams and visited each other, where we sipped raspberry cordial from a tea cup and discussed the funny things our 'children' did.

Sometimes, we played 'shops'. My sister owned the 'grocery store', and we kept old packets of Fiesta bleach and OMO, and jars and bottles to line the shelves of the store. Each time we went to the swimming pool, we dipped our hands into the bin of discarded tickets, and used them as 'money'. I owned the post office, and made my own envelopes and stamps; I ruled up a sheet of paper and drew the Queen's head in each tiny square, then perforated the lines between each for easy separation. I couldn't glue their backs, but I discovered that saliva alone was sticky enough.

If we weren't playing those games, we played 'schools'. We were both teachers, and cut up paper and stapled it together to make exercise books for our 'students'. We set our pupils homework and tests, which *we* had to complete, of course, in different handwriting for each student. Then we marked them and gave comments, before handing them back to our imaginary pupils.

At school, I enjoyed writing stories. In Year Three, I was chosen to write one for the local Young Writers' Awards. The story was about Flossy, a mare, and Andy, her foal. Andy was gored by a bull, and the story was a will-he-or-won't-he-make-it, tear-jerking cliff hanger. Despite that, it didn't win.

I dabbled in poetry, too, like this one for my school yearbook in 1978:

For those who can't read the topsy-turvy words, they are:

> *How many whales are left?*
> *Not enough.*
> *Anyway, there's other stuff*
> *That could be used.*
> *I won't have the whale abused.*
> *Through sun, wind, rain or hail,*
> *I will SAVE THE WHALE.*

Not long after that, something happened, and between primary and high school, I lost my imagination and ability to write.

It might have had something to do with being told we had to write maturely now we were in high school. Or it may have been the topics we were meant to write about, or the structures and constraints within which we had to fit our words. It may even have had something to do with being marked, or with English becoming more about reading literature and writing essays than having fun.

Whatever it was, I lost my confidence, and became self-conscious about my writing. I had difficulty finding the right words. Each time I wrote a story or essay, I ground out four or five drafts, and with the deadline looming or gone, I handed it in, never satisfied and never feeling as if I had conveyed what I'd wanted to say.

At the same time, I had no problems with maths or science. I 'got' these subjects, and for a fraction of the effort, I achieved much higher marks. I found it incredibly rewarding to solve problems, but also, it was straightforward and objective – right or wrong, black or white, and so impersonal. I didn't have to give away anything of myself. I could keep my private thoughts private. I didn't have to risk digging deep for an opinion, only for it to be wrong. These subjects were less risky, less scary, and much, much safer.

I decided English wasn't my thing. I wasn't creative after all. I dropped English in Year Eleven, and again in Year Twelve, and I stayed with the rational and logical me – that seemed to be my calling.

Although I loved art and music and literature, I thought that world was for people more creative than me, and as I had the right marks in the right subjects, and I was good at solving problems, I decided to become a doctor.

I remember sitting in my first lecture at university and feeling as if I'd travelled to a different country, or even a different world. A world of delicious Latin and voluminous texts that taught us about the intricacies and workings of the human body. It was a hallowed world, a world with a history as long and respected as that of literature.

I completed my degree and began work as a doctor. During these years, I bore witness to the many vulnerable and intimate moments of people's lives: to the joy of birth, the finality of death, and all the shades of life in between. For sixteen years, I had the privilege of sharing these moments with my patients. I haven't forgotten any of them, and they're precious keepsakes tucked away inside my mind.

During these years, I married and had four children. When my children were little, I sometimes made up stories to keep them entertained. I'd say the first idea that came into my head, and keep going, sometimes even surprising myself with the fantastical stories I concocted.

I made up songs, too, silly ditties that made my kids laugh. Again, I surprised myself with what came out of my mouth, especially for someone like me, someone who wasn't creative.

My kids started school and I expected they'd be like me – good at maths and science, and lousy at English and the arts.

To my surprise, they were avid writers, and a couple of their stories were commendable enough to win Young Writer awards. When people asked me where they got their ability to write from, I laughed and said, 'Definitely not from their mother. I haven't a creative bone in my body.'

Gradually over the years, though, I grew less and less happy. I've since realised there were many reasons for this, but at the time, I thought it was the busyness of life as a working mother of four, and, eventually, I stopped work.

But through the stories I'd made up for my children, and the songs I'd sung to them, I'd glimpsed my childhood self again.

That unguarded, unhindered, creative spirit I'd once been. I'd also sighted my children's creativity, and I sometimes wondered if, maybe, some of that *did* come from me. If, buried somewhere inside me, I did have an imagination.

Despite not having written a single creative thing since high school, as soon as I stopped work, I enrolled in an online writing course.

Our first assignment was to write a quick biography, a summary of our lives to date. Mine was about four sentences long and it took me four hours to complete as I agonized over every word – write, delete, rewrite, delete, over and over again.

Our second exercise was to light a candle and describe it. We had an old, fat candle that sat on an ornate cast iron holder. I lit it and started writing, and about fifteen minutes later, I had a poem:

THE CANDLE
You're fat, frumpy, opaque. Not transparent, but might as well be.
You're used but you still have hours of light left in you, thanks to your girth.
Tonight you dust off and don your thin-stemmed, elegantly curved stilettos for a night out.
You love the height. Already more confident.
And now alight. Wow, you're transformed. Radiant.
You've cast away the frumpy you. Begone!
You're someone else.
You're the brightest light in the room.
Alluring. Spellbinding. Your tongue erect.
Kiss me, kiss me, you whisper to passers-by.
Feel my heat, you sing, temptingly.
Moisture pools, glistening in your little well.
Someone notice me, please, please, your tears cry.
Before I die again.

As soon as I'd started to write, I felt something open and I let it spill onto the page uncensored. Listening to a voice telling my fingers what to type was liberating. I had no idea where that voice came from, but I left the poem largely as it was – unedited, unhindered.

With a pounding heart, I clicked 'send'. My writing, the first words from my creative self in decades, was out there for others to see, and not just see, but to assess. I felt exposed and vulnerable. And frightened. Really frightened. What if the teacher hated it? What if she was critical? What if she judged me because of it? Worst of all: What if she laughed?

Fear gets a lot of bad press, particularly when it comes to creativity. But it's there for a reason. As a teenager, it kept me emotionally safe. It shielded the most fragile parts of me, the tender fragments I needed to keep tucked away and hidden because they were too personal, too intimate, too close to my core to cope with criticism. Fear had kept that part of me safe.

But the time had come when I no longer needed to keep that side of me safe. I could take risks I couldn't take as a teenager. I could take this tender self out and show it to people – safe people, kind people. I could write those parts of me down and put them out there for others to read.

Still, it took me a long time to tell people I was writing. It felt strange to say that I, the ultimate science nerd, wanted to write. It felt weird even telling my husband and I didn't tell anyone else for a long time. I was too frightened – I didn't want anyone to laugh at me, or say something like, 'You? You can't write. You were hopeless at English.' So I kept it to myself, until I felt confident enough to survive any ridicule or criticism.

Ever since then, slowly, the real me has emerged. That girl who'd played make-believe with her sister, and who'd written stories about horses gored by bulls and poems about saving whales. That weird but funny mother who made up stories and songs to make her children laugh. That carefree girl who'd gone into hibernation in her teenage years, who'd hidden among the practical and logical because of fear. She was coming out again, and, my goodness, she was having fun. I'd had to protect her for many, many years, until it was safe for her to show herself once more.

I still spend hours honing each word I write and although sometimes it's hard, it's never a grind. In the mornings, my feet slide into my slippers and I race to my computer, eager to become lost in the world of my story.

At the time I wrote the words to my candle poem, I didn't know it would be the beginning of finding myself again. Writing has been my pathway out of hiding, and every piece of writing I do is my small gift to myself.

FIVE TIPS FROM LOUISE ALLAN

1. If you want to write, honour your wishes and write. Only good can come of it.
2. Don't use your marks in English at school as a guide for whether you should write or not. They are no indication whatsoever of your ability to write now.
3. Writing is frightening, and showing your writing to others is even more scary, so your feelings aren't foolish. Acknowledge them because they're present for a reason, and they're just trying to keep you 'safe'.
4. Acknowledge your fear, and then write anyway, and let the discomfort sit beside you as you do. Believe me, after a while it passes.
5. If you're new to writing, only show your work to 'safe' people, people who won't be too critical, and who won't cut you off at the knees.

Dream, Act, Create

by Sonia Bellhouse

'All the things we achieve are things we have first imagined and then made happen.'
David Malouf.

A DREAM usually means 'a night-time vision' but I'd like you to consider its other meanings. Dream is also defined as 'the time to allow oneself **to** believe'. Additionally, it can mean 'to wish'. Consider the significance of those words, that in order to achieve, you have to allow yourself to believe. Believe – *in yourself.*

Everyone is a beginner sometime. I wasn't a prodigy, or gifted, or even a doyenne of an ancient and respected literary family. I didn't know anyone who was a writer or anybody who believed that I could become one. Yet I believed that one day I'd write and not just any old thing. I'd write books.

To turn a dream like this into reality you must begin to write. Even if your ambition is to write novels, I'd suggest that you begin by writing something easier. Try a letter to the editor, or flash fiction, or a book review. Starting small with frequent submissions allows you to build your writing abilities, your confidence and belief in yourself – that you are a writer and can actually write.

HOW DO I BECOME A WRITER?

So how do you begin? You can go to classes, take up online courses, read books and articles on writing, and listen to published authors, but I didn't know any of these opportunities were available to learn to write when I began. In hindsight, maybe that was a good thing.

My profound love of reading fuelled my passion to write. To me there is an obvious connection, you love to read, so why wouldn't you want to write? It seems as natural as breathing, to transfer those ideas onto paper and to wish to share them with others.

HOW IT BEGAN

I grew up in England and spent some of my childhood living by the wild and beautiful Cornish coast. The Cornish villagers whispered their tales of the old days and smugglers; to me they seemed thrilling adventures. My imagination was also fired by the tales of the pixies, who the villagers said played tricks on the unwary. One particular local legend said you should never tell the pixies where you were going. I always kept that in mind, but one day I was so excited I blurted out our destination. Although Dad drove the car in the correct direction and followed a sign posted road, we never did get there. That reinforced in my young mind that the pixies' magic was powerful.

In that ancient place it was easy to believe in magic. It was sad to leave, but as a young child I had no choice. The beauty and mystery of the Cornish coast, infused as it was in folklore, has always remained in my heart. I think my imagination, with its love of stories, magic and secrets sparked into existence then.

I realised my first storytelling ambitions when I was about six. I wrote and illustrated my own stories inspired by Enid Blyton. I loved reading her stories, especially *The Magic Faraway Tree*. I sent her a fan letter with an illustrated story; to my surprise I received a reply. It was a postcard from Green Hedges with the magical words, 'One day perhaps, you will write a book' on it and signed 'With love from Enid Blyton' in the familiar handwriting. I treasured it for years in the hope I could do as she had suggested and one day write a book.

As an only child I spent a lot of time alone and my imaginary friends and story ideas were born during those times. I was always scribbling away at something. English was my favourite subject at school and I was thrilled when I won essay prizes for two consecutive years. The prizes were books I could choose myself. Each time I picked an historical novel and an art book, another one of my interests.

As I do now, I preferred strong female heroines, selecting books about Elizabeth I, and Katherine de Roet (Katherine Swynford), mistress to John of Gaunt. The school did not vet my book choices too closely, but if they had, I doubt they would have been impressed. Neither would the teachers have been impressed with my out-of-school activities, which included writing and illustrating a satirical take on my school, classmates and teachers. It's still in my files and as the adult me, I am rather proud of that early writing.

A TIME TO PUT AWAY CHILDISH THINGS?

Work, marriage, grown-up-living all took over my life. My ambitions were banked down but not stifled. The flame of my writing dream flickered within me, a burning sense inside that whispered I *can* and *must* do this.

Not having a typewriter, I wrote by hand. The connection between hand writing and generating ideas is an enduring linkage. New research suggests that if children do not learn cursive writing and move onto typing they are missing a significant part of their brain development processes. Neuroscientists say the more complicated process of writing by hand activates three centres of the brain: visual, motor and cognitive.

Their argument is simple: those who write by hand are better able to retain knowledge.

I still revert to handwriting when I need to work out connections and complexities. When I write by hand the words are not as 'fixed' in my mind as they are when they appear on my computer screen.

I combined my desire to write with voracious reading by researching background information for a historical novel I'd decided to write. I called it *Loyalty Binds Me* after King Richard III's motto. The book was about him and written long before his cause became a popular one. That handwritten, part-completed novel is in my files still waiting. Maybe I will revisit it one day.

FIRST PUBLICATION

Writing letters to local papers or magazines and getting them published were challenges that spurred me on and also taught me some things. I learnt the sort of prose that worked, and whether it should be argumentative, opinionated or conciliatory. My first paid publication was a letter to the British magazine, *Woman's Own*. What a thrill! Someone liked my work enough to pay for it. It might only have been a small amount of money but it kept the writing flame alive.

A FORK IN THE ROAD

Sadly, my personal life imploded; once again I took refuge in writing. What I wrote was never to be published. I confided my feelings to paper and tore them up afterwards. Writing my way through pain was my way of coping and of making sense of life. It was cathartic to rip my troubles up, and to consign them to the fire's blaze. If only I could have handled the real life problems as easily.

Emigration offered me a new beginning, I'd often dreamt of going to Australia; partly fuelled by a long ago primary school workbook provided by the Australian sugar industry. Such small things can have such large and life-changing consequences.

It took a while to settle into a new way of life, and find my way in a new country. Eventually, I joined a writing group. It seemed such a big step, announcing that I was serious about becoming a writer. It was gratifying to find the people who understood my passion. I enjoyed their company. After a while I realised that I wanted to do much more than simply write pieces to be read out each week to fellow writers.

My dream to be a published writer wouldn't go away. I enjoyed reading magazines and decided to submit articles and stories to them. I studied the magazines — their format and how they used words. Eventually it paid off. My first paid and published article appeared in *Today's Bride*. To write it I reconnected with the romantic young woman I once had been and wrote to appeal to her.

BACK TO SCHOOL

Another challenge presented itself; a chance to go to university, even though I was in my fifties. I was told that no one would take you seriously as a writer unless you had a degree. It isn't true, lots of successful writers haven't; but at the time I believed it and anyway, I'd always wanted to get a degree.

Some of the best times of my life followed, with time spent researching and writing essays, and the additional bliss of an entire university library to browse. My marks gave me the confidence to believe in myself and trust my judgement. Some might say I wasted time, but I don't think so, because I gained so much perspective and self-assurance from completing that English degree. I now believe that I am doing as Nietzsche suggested and becoming who I am.

Before I went to university I could barely use the library computer catalogue. Fortunately, I had taken a typing course when I came to Australia as a career-enhancing skill. Now that I needed to learn how to use a computer to submit my assignments, the long-ago typing course proved invaluable.

While I was at university my writing was published in the student paper. Later on I was invited to contribute a chapter to *The Revolution Won't be Downloaded* (edited by Professor Tara Brabazon). My experience was a rarity in that environment — by having virtually no computer skills, I was the ideal person to write about a beginner's fear of using computers. Rereading the chapter now, I'd love the chance to rewrite it, although I am glad I accepted the challenge. I wrote and re-wrote over again, learning that much of writing is rewriting.

Achieving the degree took six years of part-time study, but it felt tremendously satisfying. I knew that my much-loved Dad would have been proud of me, the first in our family to achieve a degree. We had shared a birth date and he had died much too soon, just prior to my twenty-first and his sixtieth birthday. It would have meant so much to me if he could have been there to cheer me on. Perhaps he was, in spirit.

During my studies I maintained my links with my writing group, attending when I could through semester breaks and holidays. I also coordinated a monthly library-based book group as a way of contributing to my community. This gave me a sense of how various readers reacted to the same book and it made me more aware that I needed to keep readers in mind when I was writing.

PUBLICATION

While still studying, I wrote more letters, articles, and stories, determined to see my name in print and be paid for it. I had some success with articles and stories being published. Additionally, several true-life experience pieces I'd written were acknowledged and then re-written by staff at *Take Five* magazine. Although I was paid I didn't feel the same sense of pride in these pieces, because they were my ideas but I hadn't written them.

The rejections came thick and fast. For each heart-stopping moment when I opened the mail, I dared to believe there was an acceptance.

Some publishers offered feedback, but most did not. I consoled myself that at least I wasn't an actor or a model; they got rejected to their face and I wasn't dependent on my writing to put food on the table.

After a few days I would look at the piece and then consider if the publisher had a point and whether it was worth sending out again with changes. 'Know the market' is wise advice, so if they sent guidelines I studied them to see what I needed to do differently.

One of the writing challenges set at my writing group was to write and submit a book review to *The West Australian* newspaper. I had read and enjoyed Kate Morton's *The Forgotten Garden* and submitted a review. A few weeks later it was published and I was sent six current books as payment.

We never know when and in what form our luck is going to take. Mine came in an unexpected email one January. I'd been submitting stories to various magazines without success. So it was a surprise to get an email from an editor I didn't know, asking if I had any book reviews. Isn't it said that luck is when preparation meets opportunity? You never know when an opportunity will present itself and I hesitated briefly before choosing to be brave. Since he'd asked for book reviews I duly sent off a copy of my review of *The Forgotten Garden*. It was accepted by return email and he asked if I had any more.

I'd received books by Matthew Reilly and Maeve Binchy for Christmas and fortunately, I had just read them both. The editor suggested that I write reviews and in return he'd pay me and send me more books. A few days later a parcel of four books arrived.

That began my time as a book reviewer for *That's Life Fast Fiction Special.* I reviewed books for them for several years, a job that I relished. Sadly, an editorial change brought that to an end, with the new editor preferring to use people that she knew. It was my dream job, being paid to read books plus receiving regular parcels of books. It taught me to write to a deadline.

National Novel Writing Month (NaNoWriMo) is an international initiative which is held every November. Completing the required 50,000-plus words in a month is categorised as 'winning'. I've managed it several times, finding it good discipline. It taught me that while you are immersed in writing, you are not the best judge of it. Usually I only wrote when I felt inspired; but with NaNoWriMo I had to write when I could to meet the daily word count of close to 1700 words per day. Later, re-reading my words, I could not tell which pages were written when I had felt enthusiastic and which were written when I felt no motivation. It was a valuable lesson which showed me that writing quickly and allowing first thoughts onto the page could be freeing. I had produced something that was worth working further on, the bones of a novel.

In 2012 the City of Rockingham launched a short fiction contest. It offered cash prizes and was open to all, nationally and internationally. The stories had to be inspired by a painting from the council's art collection. Called 'Spring Breakers at Trigg', it showed a coastal scene. I admired the picture and thought long and hard to find my themes. Eventually I submitted two stories in different categories. By the time I submitted I was quite sick of them, of fiddling with them and altering them; self-doubt crept in and I almost did not send them off. A few weeks later when I got the mail, there was a letter of congratulations telling me that my story 'Driftwood' had placed first for Western Australia and second overall. My husband pointed out another letter I hadn't noticed. It was also from the City of Rockingham and it said my story 'Uncharted Territory' had also placed first for Western Australia and second nationally. Wow! I was an award-winning writer, not just in my local area but a winner in Western Australia and a runner-up nationally.

At the award presentation I learnt there had been one hundred and ninety-two entries, including ones from the USA and Canada. Winning in two categories was a huge boost to my writing confidence.

Encouraged by these wins, I sent off more stories and articles. A few were accepted. Among them was a tender story of love, "The Night Gate", which featured a vampire. It was picked up by *That's Life!* Another story was selected for their *Fast Fiction Special*. Called "Holiday Horror", it also featured a vampire. The story was, as its name suggests, a horror story. I found it creatively challenging to use the same basic idea in each story and produce a different effect.

Currently I am writing my third novel, *Starting Over*, even though my first and second novels are unfinished. I am okay with this, because I know that resting works is a good thing to do.

Starting Over is contemporary women's fiction. It's the first book in a series set in Herons Bay, a fictional West Australian seaside community with golden sandy beaches, the swell of surf and a salty tang in the air. Like most coastal communities it has a summer influx of people – some who stay and some who move on, like Bev, who runs the popular Mermaids cafe where the food is good and the coffee hot, and disillusioned British expat Chris, who is facing more trouble than he thought possible. Then there's sad teenager Zack and Lauren, a police officer with an instinct that something is about to happen, and the mysterious, Iris who drove into town at the start of the summer. It's a sleepy town but the report of an abandoned yacht shakes everything up.

IDENTIFYING AS A WRITER

It's a big step to identify yourself as a writer. When you do, you're sending a message to yourself and to others that you take your writing seriously. It's something that matters to you.

---

*Dismissing yourself as a scribbler, or saying nervously
that you write a bit, is not acknowledging your passion,
your ambition.*

It may feel safer, but it's soul destroying, and a betrayal of yourself.

My writing life, as you can see, has been an unplanned journey. No doubt it might have been easier if I had intentionally planned and mapped it all out. Nevertheless, I'm comfortable saying I am a writer. Being published has made it easier to say this, but really what made me a writer was simply that I wrote, rewrote and kept on writing. I braved rejection, and kept alive the belief that I could do it. For me, I am a writer, but I'm not yet comfortable with calling myself an author. That will happen when a book of mine is published.

To those of you, who also aspire to write and be published, keep in mind that writing and creativity is a function of the brain's right hemisphere. Creativity is unpredictable, playful, adventurous and messy. It colours outside the lines; it turns the page sideways. It can be scary, and when it is, perhaps that's a hint you're breaking through to something with potential. Go with that creative flow, take the risks, play, and enjoy it. The time for editing, which is a left brain activity, is later. That's when you engage the analytical, critical part of the brain. If you edit before you have finished writing it will cramp your style, leaving you hesitant and reluctant to complete your work.

To me, finishing prior to editing is important. Doing so gives a huge sense of personal satisfaction. Others don't feel the same way, but I feel that unfinished pieces clutter the mind, and can even 'haunt' you in a morass of mental confusion. However, novels are a different category as they are 'in the vault', so to speak, and may or may not be worked on again.

Remember that nothing is set in stone. You get to decide what to keep, and what to discard. You can choose to feed what Margaret Atwood calls 'The Muse of Oblivion' – the handy waste paper basket. You can afford to be fearless, safe in that knowledge.

It's not possible or helpful to offer absolutes as far as writing and getting published is concerned. This is what has worked for me and perhaps you can take something from my journey that may also work for you.

We are all individuals and nowhere is this more apparent than in our writing. We should write what excites us, engages us or even enrages us. Unless you are passionate about a topic it's hard to keep going to the finish line. As writers we need passion and persistence. A great idea is not going to move anyone else but yourself if it remains unexpressed.

Unless you write, you cannot call yourself a writer. You are a dreamer, a thinker, a would-be writer, a wannabe. You need to be brave and take the pen, or the computer mouse or the pointer and begin. As Marsha Alderson aka The Plot Whisperer said: 'You imagine yourself into being a writer'. These words continue to inspire me. I have imagined myself as a writer and acted accordingly.

FIVE TIPS FROM SONIA BELLHOUSE

1. **Read**: Read voraciously. Analyse why you did/didn't like a book. Was it predictable? An unconvincing plot or flat characters?
2. **Write:** Show up, give yourself a time limit; write daily. Get up earlier or stay up later.
3. **Criticism:** Don't ask family or friends. Find writers, ones who will be honest with you. Ignore your Inner Critic, that insidious voice which whispers, 'Who will want to read that?' The saddest words in the English language are, 'What might have been'.
4. **Stretch!** You don't want writer's slump, so stretch at your desk, swim, or walk the dog. Stretch mentally, too: Attend writing events, go to a play, a concert, or visit a museum or gallery.
5. **Luck:** Luck is often the result of risks taken, entering a contest, speaking to an editor, or thanking an author. The media loves an 'overnight' success, but probe a bit deeper and you'll find most writers have been quietly working away for years.

Breathing Life Into a Dream

by Sandi Bowie

ONE of my earliest and most vivid memories is the day my grandmother was accused of beating me. It was a warm summer's day in Perth and I was lying on a pile of pillows, loudly protesting while Gran took me through my physiotherapy. In the 1970s, cystic fibrosis (CF), a genetic disease which primarily affects the lungs and digestive system, was still relatively unknown; physio tables had not been invented so I was lying on the pillow mound, my chest and head tipped downwards while Gran performed 'percussion'.

Percussion, where hands are cupped and repeatedly clapped against the chest to vibrate mucous and loosen it from the lungs, sounds far more violent than it is. I endured physio twice a day every day, and on this afternoon it was hot and I was wriggly. Moments after I yelled, 'Just stop hitting me!' there was a knock on the door. Through the open window, two door-to-door salesmen had heard my loud protests and what suspiciously sounded like a child being beaten. It took an awful lot of convincing for them to go away, but my respite didn't last long because Gran still made me finish my physio.

Reading took me away from the reality of living with a chronic illness. Books became a mainstay in my life; I could read while sitting at the hospital waiting for appointments or drift away for another adventure up Enid Blyton's *Magic Faraway Tree* while I did the endless grind of twice-daily physio. By the time I reached high school, there was no doubt in my mind that one day I would write a book and see my name on the cover.

My writing at the time was eclectic, highly influenced by what I was reading, and my English grades seemed to depend on how my various teachers viewed my creative writing skills. On one occasion, I was given a D for what I had considered an amazing story, but I had misspelt the same word eight different ways, and *that* apparently was far more important. I thought my perseverance deserved more credit – I had known the word was misspelt but hadn't quit. Instead I'd kept trying to spell the word correctly and get the story written.

In Year Ten I found *Robyn's Book: A True Diary* by Robyn Miller. Like me, Robyn had CF. The disease was so little known in the community that I had to explain it to every new person I met. Finally, I had found a book about someone who not only had CF, but had dreamt of being a writer. Her book contained a mix of diary entries and fictional stories that I read and reread until my copy was tattered and torn. After this book, I discovered *Alex: The Life of a Child* by Frank Deford, which was considered *the* go-to book by the CF community. I had a tattered extract from Reader's Digest which contained the pertinent sections and I thumbed through it as much as *Robyn's Book*.

Throughout my high school years, I suffered from the misconception that writers were either old, dead or Stephen King. It's possible this belief had been influenced by the bittersweet ending of *Robyn's Book*, which culminated in her death. However, I can't pinpoint why Stephen King was special, except perhaps that his books came out with such regularity it suggested he couldn't be *that* old, and each new publication attested to the fact he certainly wasn't dead yet. Regardless, I had this notion writing was something I would do when I was older.

In my early twenties, although not actively writing, I became aware that if I wanted to be a writer I needed to practise my writing skills. Keeping a diary was bandied about as an option but it didn't resonate with me. I already knew what I had done all day and couldn't fathom why I would need to keep a record of it. When I attended a talk about developing writing habits, one thing that did strike a chord was the speaker's alternative to diary writing that used the same skill set – she used an exercise book to write a long letter to a friend. When the book was complete, she would then post her finished book/letter to an overseas friend. And so my journal writing commenced.

In time it evolved to include badly drawn pictures and the odd joke or two; plagiarism abounded with some truly hideous efforts at mimicking other writers' styles and ideas. I didn't have an overseas friend, but I did have a best friend with whom I could share my thoughts and feelings without censorship. That we lived together seemed insignificant. Night after night I would sit at the table writing to Julie, sometimes while she sat next to me. In this strange bubble of writing madness, topics that were deemed notable enough to write about were off limits to talk about. As a bonus, this meant that if something was written and needed to be discussed, there was a pressing urgency to fill the book with words to remove the taboo on the subject.

Time marched on, as it inevitably does, and I married and had a son. My exercise book activities had gone so well with Julie, that I wanted to continue the tradition, this time addressing them to my son, Jarryn, but the days seemed to slip through my fingers, and any writing time was nibbled away composing essays on librarianship as I studied.

By the time Jarryn was in primary school, my studies were complete and I took over the management of a specialised library which housed resources for classroom use. Inclusivity was the new buzzword in education, so I allocated a specific shelf to house those books. The library collection had all the big names covered, with cancer and asthma being the most prominent, but it was apparent that orphan diseases, those that only affect a small number of the population, were clearly under-represented. With the demands of the curriculum, teachers were time poor and if resources were not readily accessible it was easy for them to move to teaching about the more common diseases, which had an abundance of resources available.

Having CF, this lack of educational resources and literature concerned me. At some level, I had been aware growing up that none of the characters I read about in books were quite like me until Robyn. Over the weekend I compiled details of CF in literature, noting that this wasn't just a problem in my library, but there was an overall shortage. The strongest section by far was the biographies, still dominated by parents writing about their dead children – and most online references still pointed to *Alex: The Life of a Child* as the pick of the bunch. A few books had been written specifically for children, but they seemed focused on education, with *Taking Cystic Fibrosis to School* highlighted as being useful for teachers. In Australia, Cystic Fibrosis Queensland had recently published *Monty*, featuring the life of a family, including a child with CF, as seen through the eyes of the family dog.

I invited myself to a meeting with Karen O'Neil, who was at the time the Cystic Fibrosis Western Australia (CFWA) education officer, and presented her with a teaching program and resource kit designed by the Asthma Foundation as my model. The package included a fictional story along with teaching notes.

'This,' I told her, 'is what we need to do. We need to educate through literature.'

Karen was enthusiastic about the project and didn't need much convincing, but there was one slight problem.

'Who will write it for us?' she asked.

'I will,' I said.

I didn't have an idea, let alone a single word on paper, and CFWA had never published a book before, but that meeting started us on the six-year journey to publish my first children's book, *The Mystery of the Sixty-Five Roses*.

In preparation, I read many books for children that included diseases or disabilities. A common thread wove through many of them, resulting in a clearly identifiable teaching agenda. *The Smell of Chocolate* by Barbara McGuire was different. It focused on the relationship between Ben and his grandfather and how they enjoyed baking a cake for the Queen in the middle of the night. Ben's grandfather had Alzheimer's, but instead of trying to cram facts into the story and explain them, the story stood alone. A section called 'Pog's Alzheimer's Fact File!' at the end of the book explained pertinent facts about Alzheimer's and memory loss, along with helpful suggestions. This, I decided, was how I was going to model my story. It would be a story first, with facts and information delegated to the rear.

But, while I had the structure, I still needed an idea. 'Write what you know' is perhaps the most common and most misunderstood advice writers can receive. I knew what it was like to live with CF, and I had a ten-year-old son who liked to sneak and spy, but it wasn't until I combined those two ideas that I found inspiration. What would happen if a ten-year-old child, who liked to sneak and spy, saw someone having treatments for CF? What would they think? I already knew the answer, because on that hot day long ago, Gran had been accused of child abuse.

From this real-life event, I researched the different medications and treatments for CF, imagining a myriad of terrible conclusions that my character, Jeremy, could jump to. I explored some crazy theories including the use of Agent Orange and alien abduction. But finally, I settled on the most logical idea. Jeremy would see something that made him believe the woman next door was abusing her daughter.

Originally, I was looking at writing a chapter book, however the vivid image of Jeremy with big googly eyes, peering through a window, wouldn't leave me. Sometimes it's the characters who lead the story, because it is, after all, their tale, and they know best how it should be told.

I pared the text back, and twenty-five drafts later I delivered it to CFWA. Natalie Amos had taken over the role of education officer, including the management of my book. While working on another project, Natalie had a chance encounter with illustrator Stacey Hutton, and mentioned my project. Stacey submitted a picture the following week and as soon as I saw it, I knew we had found the person to bring Jeremy to life.

Stacey took on the project pro bono, so she worked in her spare time. However, in the two years it took her to complete the illustrations my health took a sudden downturn. When people asked the progress of my writing I had a pre-prepared answer: 'One project at a time is enough for me.' But the truth was, the additional demands on my health were exhausting. I was in respiratory failure, with a bilateral lung transplant my only option for survival. Words ran through my head, but there was nothing left to allow them to be released. All my energy was required just to keep breathing.

While waiting for the phone to ring with news of a possible transplant match, I clung to the thought that my book was significantly advanced enough to continue without me, yet there was a terrible sense of loss for all those words I had yet to write, and for those characters whose voices tumbled around inside my head. I decided that if I survived, if I were lucky enough to be matched with another person's lungs, then writing would be a priority.

Towards the end of May 2011, as hope was rapidly fading, that call did come. The first six months after a transplant are incredibly hard. A new medication regime needed to be learnt, along with physical rehabilitation. I used part of my recovery time to do an online writing course. In addition, I worked on the final stages of the publication of *The Mystery of the Sixty-Five Roses* with Natalie. With neither of us having publishing experience, we muddled along, learning on the go. Google was our friend, from figuring out how to purchase an ISBN to researching legal deposit requirements. On more than one occasion we photocopied printouts from the graphic designer, manually cut them up and physically pasted them onto another section to experiment with the layout. Then Natalie presented our cut-and-paste booklets to the graphic designer for him to recreate our vision in a printable format. *The Mystery of the Sixty-Five Roses* went to the printer in late December 2012 and arrived back in all its technicolour glory in early January.

Marketing was another learning curve, and I came to appreciate how time-consuming promoting writing can be.

Designed to be a fundraiser for CFWA, copies sold well and received pleasing reviews. But the best review came via Katrina Wellborn, who as part of her final year studies compiled *37 is Just a Number, Stories of Living with Cystic Fibrosis*. She interviewed four people, but it was the words from seven-year-old Lara that touched my heart. Lara said: 'My favourite book to read is called *The Mystery of the Sixty-Five Roses* … I don't get to hang out with other kids that have CF because it can make me sick. That's why I like to read this book. It gives me other people I can relate to. I'm not the only girl with cystic fibrosis.'

Starting in the early 1990s the issue of cross infection had started to raise its head. I'd grown up in a community, surrounded by other people with CF; there had been camps and various social activities, but new guidelines suggested reasonable precautions were not enough to prevent cross infection and it was recommended that all contact between people with CF should cease. I couldn't imagine how isolating it would be to grow up like this. Not only did today's generation lack a support base to share common experiences, but there was little in literature for them to identify with. On the other hand, not only had I shared experiences with friends who also suffered from CF, I'd also had the fortune to find *Robyn's Book*. It was a lightning bolt moment for me, as I realised although my intent had not been clear, I'd also been aiming to provide today's children with their own version of *Robyn's Book*.

I tipped all the publishing rules upside down on *The Mystery of the Sixty-Five Roses'* journey to publication. While it's acceptable to pitch ideas for non-fiction books, traditionally, fiction is written and polished before presentation. However, when I pitched to CFWA, not only had I not written a single word of my story, I didn't even have an idea to present to them; in addition, I was an inexperienced writer, with no publication history. Essentially, I identified a gap in the book industry and presented such a persuasive argument that between us, despite no publishing experience, we would be the best people to solve this problem. I knew my book was going to be published before I even wrote a word. I was involved in the choice of Stacey as illustrator, and I was able to collaborate closely with her. I know better now, but as a complete rookie I had delivered the text to her along with comprehensive illustration notes. We tossed out the thirty-two-page rule for picture books and I even stuck my nose into the placement of the text on the page.

While there were some similarities, much of the experience of writing my second book was vastly different. Throughout 2013, I continued attending writing courses, but my blue heeler, Pepsi Parsons, kept intruding into my thoughts. Phrases my husband and I were saying about our dog's behaviour bounced around: 'Pepsi Parsons pounced', 'Pepsi Parsons went past fast' and the dreaded, 'Pepsi Parsons peed!'

The alliteration appealed to me, and I tried several times to write another picture book based on this. But as much as I fiddled with the words and rearranged them, they didn't feel right. Once again, the character had interfered and this time, the fictional Pepsi Parsons demanded far more words than a picture book text would allow.

By this time, I had started working in a school library, so I made use of the inbuilt beta readers and tested my first chapter on a class of Year 3 students. Their response was overwhelmingly positive and several students asked if I would read the next chapter the following week.

'Of course,' I said.

My smile disappeared as they exited the room.

There was no next chapter.

Each week I frantically wrote another chapter to keep up with the demand. This pressure resulted in the fastest first draft I have ever completed.

I received valuable feedback from the students, mainly based on watching their reactions as I read. While Pepsi was in the middle of mischief and mayhem, they were engaged. However, scenes that didn't contain Pepsi resulted in mutterings and rustling of library bags, clearly identifying the need for some other sort of intriguing stimulus to hold their attention. This helped me identify gaps where my writing hadn't quite succeeded.

Writing the traditional way hasn't always been easy for me. It is nerve-racking to send your stories off into the great unknown, with fingers crossed in anticipation. The journey behind each story I've written has been unique, and I wouldn't change a thing. Except maybe those copious illustration notes …

FIVE TIPS FROM SANDI BOWIE

1. Don't add illustration notes to picture book manuscripts. EVER. Your illustrator will have their creative interpretation of the story. Let them do their thing.
2. If a great sentence springs into your head, don't delude yourself that you'll remember it. You won't. Write it down.
3. First drafts are often compared to shovelling sand into a sandbox to build a sandcastle later on. You're going to need a lot of sand.
4. Sometimes, your characters will have their ideas about how their story should be told, so let them tell it their way.
5. If you are tempted to add illustration notes to a picture book manuscript, see Tip 1.

Two Paths to Publication

by Andi Bremner

MY journey to publication began a long time ago. Or just a few months ago, depending on perspective. You know the line about the fork in the road in the Robert Frost poem, "The Road Not Taken"? Well, I took one fork and it took me on a wonderful, exciting, nerve-wracking journey only to bring me *back* to the same fork so I could take the other road. Let me explain.

As a little girl I loved to write. I loved to make up stories. I spent hours lying on my bed or bedroom floor daydreaming of princesses and castles, handsome princes and evil witches. I took the stories I knew, such as *Sleeping Beauty* or *Beauty and the Beast*, and elaborated on them, building fantastical worlds and adding depth to the characters. I wanted to know *more* about the characters so I gave them hobbies, and I wanted more interaction between my hero and heroine before and after their happily ever after.

In primary school I had a teacher who encouraged my love of storytelling. He took his time and patiently explained the proper structural ways for setting out my ideas and creating worlds to share with others. Throughout my primary and high school years I had three teachers who believed in my writing abilities, even though they were all male and I was writing impossibly romantic and nostalgic tales of love, heartbreak, and happily ever afters. It must have been tedious for them to read, but I will be forever grateful that they took their time to foster my love of writing. It would be another twenty years before I returned to writing.

When high school was over I shelved my writing ambitions. This was the pre-Internet era and my stories were typed on an electric typewriter. To submit a manuscript required a lot more work and quite simply, I had no idea where to begin. Plus, I had discovered boys and I soon found that the real thing was way more fun to indulge in.

Fast forward to my mid-thirties, when the boys in my life amounted to a husband and three sons. I began to think about my dreams of writing and publishing a novel again. No one – not my husband, my close friends nor my three children – knew about the deep feelings I had harboured over the years of achieving this. Writing a book and publishing a book were number one on my bucket list, and with forty looming in my near future I decided it was now or never.

So I wrote a book.

Actually, I wrote three chapters. I was so excited that I googled 'what to do to get published'. I had a blockbuster, I knew it, and I just had to get it into the hands of readers. Good old Google told me what I needed to do, and it seemed that first and foremost, I needed to find an agent. So, I googled again, and found an agency in the UK which appeared a perfect fit for my young adult romance novel that was only a teeny, tiny bit completed. Excited, inspired, motivated, and naïve, I typed up a query letter (yes, I googled how to do that), attached my three chapters and sent it off. While I waited, I googled some more, joined the Romance Writers of Australia group, and found myself a marvellous critique partner.

Three days later I had a response from the UK agent. She loved it! Could she have more?

Oops. I didn't have any more. I replied and politely thanked her for her kind words and explained I hadn't finished the manuscript (even now I cringe as I type this). She was very kind though, and said to send the rest of it through to her as soon as I finished it. She would wait.

So I got busy and I typed, typed, typed. It was easy to finish the manuscript: I had thirty years of making up stories, voracious reading and daydreaming to fuel my imagination. I wanted something that transcended time; a time-travel crossover, something with a gothic twist set in the early 1800s, and something young and funky with a tortured teenager for a protagonist. My critique partner worked with me and we spent a little while polishing and polishing the manuscript before I sent it to the agent on the other side of the world. She replied saying she was looking forward to reading it while she was on her few weeks' leave.

Again I waited. I was beginning to realise that patience was an important virtue for writers. While I waited, I began work on another young adult manuscript, with loose ideas I had yet to tie together. Although I had the themes of time crossover, witchcraft, reincarnation and star-crossed lovers, I had no idea where I was going with it all apart from the opening few chapters. I figured it would work itself out as I wrote, which it kind of did. But more on that later.

Eventually the London-based agent got back to me. I heard my phone ping with an incoming message in the middle of the night and sprang out of bed. I clearly remember seeing her name in the inbox, and clicking on the link, holding my breath. Her first words were: 'I think this is fabulous.'

I started to cry.

I don't really remember much of the email after that, but I know she wanted to speak to me on the phone, despite the eight-hour time difference between London and Perth. That whole day I walked around in a daze, smiling at random people in my elation. My husband bought home a bottle of Moet & Chandon to celebrate.

I spoke to my lovely agent later that night and she explained that while she loved the novel and the characters, she thought there were some elements that didn't quite work. There were a few loose ends, but she was happy to work with me on them before submitting to publishers. And she offered to represent me.

I had an agent. I had to pinch myself. I had an agent who believed in me and my writing ability, which at that stage was pretty raw and unrefined. I was in my mid-thirties and hadn't written anything since I was sixteen years old.

For the next couple of months, I worked hard at rewriting and polishing the manuscript and when it was ready, she submitted it to a range of publishers: Simon & Schuster, Pan Macmillan, Random House, Penguin, Scholastic … all powerhouses in the publishing world. Then we waited.

After a few days she sent me some feedback from the editor at Pan Macmillan. The editor loved it. I wanted to pinch myself. I was scared and excited at the same time, although I couldn't explain the scared part. Maybe it was instinct knowing what was to come.

Slowly, over the next few weeks, the rejections started to come. That editor at Pan Macmillan? She loved it but the ending didn't quite work for her. Other publishers? Loved parts of the manuscript, loved certain characters, but not enough. Some enjoyed the manuscript and had nothing negative to say other than that their rejection (such a horrid word) was based on the fact they had recently acquired or published something similar. This was the post-*Twilight* era and paranormal romances were big business.

Eventually all the publishers on the initial submission list passed. Except one.

One editor at a fairly large publishing house enjoyed my story and wanted to work with me to refine it further. At this stage I had read the manuscript so many times that I really, really didn't want to pass my eyes over it again. But I agreed, and over the next couple of months he and I worked quite closely on tightening the manuscript. He was new to this publishing house and was keen for my story to be his first acquisition. His assistant also worked with us and was a huge champion of the story. Eventually the day came and he took the manuscript to the acquisitions team.

They passed.

It wasn't unanimous and there was quite a lot of positive feedback — nothing really negative, they just passed. It was frustrating and disheartening. All that work, all that time and attention, all that blood and sweat (because it truly started to feel like that) into one manuscript only for them to just say 'no thanks', without any plausible reason.

The editor I had worked with? He was so angry and frustrated that he ended up resigning and going back to his old job.

Maybe, I decided, it just wasn't meant to be.

I shelved the manuscript and finished my new one – the one about witches and destiny and time-travelling romance with no plot, no ending and no direction. Yeah. My agent didn't like it. Not at all. She didn't even finish reading it and I don't blame her. I was too impulsive and eager. I should have taken my time with it, nutted out all the problems, tidied up loose ends, and spent time on character development.

I was devastated and started to doubt I was a writer.
Was I deluded? Had I got lucky with the few people
who had liked my story?

Maybe being a writer was what *other* people did and I should just focus on being a wife, mother and a teacher …

Self-doubt is crippling and I kick myself now for every second I wasted indulging in it. If I don't believe I can do it, how can I expect anyone else to?

I spent the next few months reading and there were other things going on in my life that distracted me from writing. While I still dabbled, writing some steamier romances that I didn't finish, I didn't do much else. I had rushed in before and fallen flat on my face. My emotional roller coaster ride had taken its toll and I was nervous to get back on it. The highs, when someone liked what I had written were amazing, but the lows when they didn't like my work were awful.

I kept in loose contact with my critique partner, and joined a local, face-to-face writers group. It was through them I learnt about an online e-publisher of romance and young adult fiction. They were Australian-based but linked to a bigger publishing house. By this time, about two years had passed since I'd first submitted to my agent and I'd recovered somewhat from my disappointment. *Why the hell not?* I thought. *I will submit and see what they think.*

In my mind I had already talked myself into rejection. The publisher would provide me with limited, unhelpful feedback along with a simple 'pass', like most of the other publishers.

A few weeks later I received an email from the editor. She thoroughly enjoyed my manuscript and wanted to acquire it for her publishing house. I could hardly believe it. I contacted my agent in the

UK (who had since moved publishing houses and therefore no longer represented me) to tell her the good news. She kindly offered to go over the contract for me, and I accepted, thinking that since she had put so much time and effort into the story she should receive some of the royalties.

She nearly cost me the contract. Having never worked with e-publishers before, she had many demands and insisted on many changes. Her world of publishing, I soon came to realise, was very different to how things worked in the online world of publishing. There were times when I wanted to cut her out. I had a publishing contract and someone was willing to put my book out there and finally, finally readers would be able to read it. I didn't care about movie rights (I was being realistic here) or who had rights to any follow-up stories (I had already decided that I was done with these characters). But she did her thing, she insisted, and they eventually agreed. Finally, my contract was signed.

Then things got exciting! There were covers to design and edits (groan) to be done, but eventually on April 1, 2014 (yes, I kept wondering if the whole thing was an April Fool's joke) my very first novel, *Time After Time*, was launched. My first review was pretty awful, but luckily most of them weren't so scathing and on the whole I received some good reviews. It wasn't a big seller and I haven't made enough money to throw in my day job as a teacher, but that's okay. That was never what it was about, although I have a hard time explaining that to people.

For me writing, and publishing, was never about money.
It was more about getting the stories out of my head,
losing myself in another world for a little while, and
seeing something I created out there for readers to enjoy.

Since *Time After Time* (cute title right?) was published I have continued to write, but my writing has changed. *Time After Time* was a young adult novel and although it had romantic elements, it was decidedly 'sweet'. My stories since then have moved along and would more likely be described as 'not sweet' or even 'erotic'. My heroes are darker and more dangerous, and my heroines more adventurous … and everything is sexier. I enjoy taking risks with my stories and characters now.

Now, I should remind you that I am a mother of three teenage boys. Teenage boys do not want it known that their mother is writing erotic novels. So, for a while I just wrote the stories. I went through so much heartache with *Time After Time* that I was reluctant to put myself out there and possibly get hurt again. Writing is kind of like dating in a way. You are taking risks, putting your heart, almost literally, on the line, and you are definitely going to get rejected in your search for 'the one'.

But nearly two years after my debut novel, I felt like I was ready to take a risk again. So, early this year I submitted the first in a series of books about an all-girl rock band to a few select, online publishers under a pseudonym. I waited for the heartache and the rejection to start again, but my first response was positive and I had an offer of publication! Inspired, I finished another novel I had been working on, edited and polished it, and sent it off, only to receive another offer of publication less than twenty-four hours later! I am busy polishing and editing a fifth manuscript for this year and have another couple of stories nutted out in my head (they always spend quite a bit of time in my head before I put them onto paper).

I feel like I have two 'road to publishing' stories here. One, the dream that happened so suddenly and felt like a whirlwind; and the other, a slow, up-and-down road to publication that evolved over time.

Over the last few years my writing has developed and grown, and I am more comfortable with the type of romance writer I have become. It's who I am and I am not trying to fit anyone else's formula of what should be included in my novel. With so many small, independent, and online publishers opening up there are plenty of options for writers. Boundaries are being pushed and things are changing. When I started on this journey four years ago, self-publishing was a huge no-no. Also called vanity publishing, it was something that no self-respecting writer would do. Now, with the success of writers like Jamie McGuire, it is a plausible avenue for publication and I would never discount it as an option (although it seems like a lot of work and I am a little lazy).

The road to publication is never easy. Or at least, it isn't for the most part. I remember at a writers' conference a few years ago, a publisher stood up and said, 'To all writers, there is only one J.K. Rowling and Stephenie Meyer and you aren't either one of them.' Those writers are the anomaly. Every writer I know works damn hard and writes, writes, writes. They build an online brand and they deal with rejections and successes constantly. They have had to learn to guard their hearts against the harsh world of publishing (or at least I know I have).

But if you love to write, like I do, then it is all very much worth it.

FIVE TIPS FROM ANDI BREMNER

1. Read in your genre – and read a lot!
2. Guard your heart. Some of the rejections can hurt like hell.
3. Be patient. You might be able to stay up all night reading your manuscript, but agents and editors have hundreds to read and they also have a life away from your story.
4. Build an online brand. I am still working on this one and know that it is strongly linked to book sales.
5. Write because you love it, not because you want to make a lot of money.

Historical Fiction

by Deborah Burrows

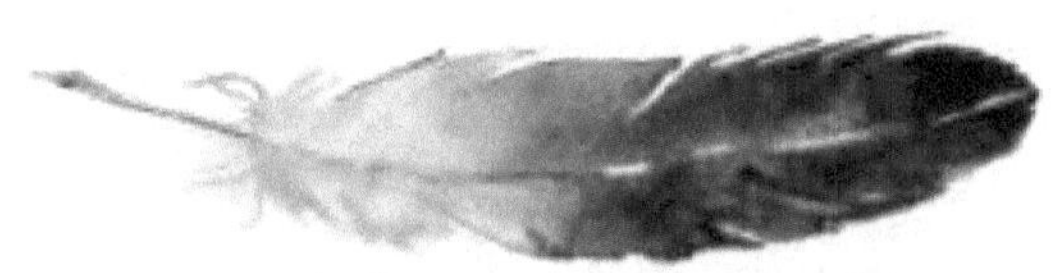

SOMEONE once wrote that reading historical fiction is the closest we can come to time travel. And it is true that a novel set in another period can give the reader a sense of how it must have been to live then, what it was like to be a twelfth-century monk, a nineteenth-century doctor, a flapper in 1920s America, a Japanese geisha in the early twentieth century, or an Australian typist in World War II. With this power to send readers back in time, however, comes responsibility.

When readers set out on the time-travelling journey they place their trust in the author, but this trust is easily broken if there are glaring historical errors in the novel. A writer of historical fiction needs not only to write a good story, but also to ensure that the background has been well researched and that it is, as far as possible, historically correct. As the historian and author, Antony Beevor, stated: 'The power of historical fiction for bad and for good can be immense in shaping consciousness of the past.'

And yet the purpose of historical fiction is not to attempt to supplant literature from the period it describes, or to write a historical treatise fully annotated and footnoted. Few novelists nowadays would attempt to write a Regency romance using the language and descriptive techniques of Jane Austen, but rather they seek to write a window into Austen's time to help a reader in the early twenty-first century try to understand how it felt to live in England in the early nineteenth.

That does not mean that an author should make up history to suit the story; rather, it means that a writer of historical fiction must be prepared to work out what history to include, what history to ignore and – perhaps – what history to amend. The Pulitzer Prize winning author, Geraldine Brooks, has said: 'The thing that most attracts me to historical fiction is taking the factual record as far as it is known, using that as scaffolding, and then letting imagination build the structure that fills in those things we can never find out for sure.'

This problem of how to mesh reality with imagination has been grappled with by writers for centuries. In his introduction to the fourth volume of *War and Peace* (1868), Tolstoy stated:

> *'The divergence between my description of historical events and the accounts of historians … is not accidental but inevitable. A historian and an artist, describing a historical epoch, have two completely different objects. As a historian would be wrong if he*

> *should try to present a historical figure in all his entirety, in all the complexity of his relations to all sides of life, so an artist would not fulfil his task by always presenting a figure in his historical significance.'*

Getting the history 'right' can be difficult. Sometimes there is simply no information, and it is then that the writer's imagination must wholly come into play. According to Hilary Mantel, who wrote the critically acclaimed *Wolf Hall* about Thomas Cromwell in the time of Henry VIII of England: 'For a novelist, this absence of intimate material is both a problem and an opportunity.'

A reader will excuse much if a story is engaging and at least appears to properly represent the period in which the novel is set. But if the historical information is available (and easily discovered) then it should be used as accurately as possible *within the confines of the story being told*. That proviso is important, because an author of historical fiction is, first and foremost, writing a work of entertainment. If, in a particular work, it is the 'feel' of a historical period that is important rather than the specifics, then historical facts may need to be changed or ignored.

To quote Hilary Mantel again: 'Unlike the historian, the novelist doesn't operate through hindsight. She lives inside the consciousness of her characters for whom the future is blank.'

It is perfectly acceptable for a character in a novel to 'get things wrong', because they cannot see their world with hindsight.

> *The novelist, however, must be aware of what she is doing and in my view, if she constructs a story in a way that is at odds with the historical 'truth', she should let the reader know.*

Otherwise she risks breaking faith with the reader.

And yet, sometimes the cold facts simply do not fit a cool story. If an author feels that the story justifies changing or ignoring historical facts, I suggest that this should be acknowledged in the Preface or Afterword. Otherwise the author has been party to a knowing deception of the readers and this would be a breach of the readers' trust.

And this advice can apply even to very small details. A writer I admire wrote a book based around the tragic bombing of the Café de Paris nightclub in London in 1941. Throughout the book he kept referring to the tune being played by the dance orchestra when the bombs hit as "Body and Soul". I knew, from my own research, that the song 'Snake Hips' Johnson was playing when he died was "Oh Johnny. Oh Johnny. Oh!" The error annoyed me as I read the book and I wondered if he had simply not bothered to check this one fact, when so much else in the novel was (as far as I could tell) entirely accurate. In the Afterword he acknowledged that he had changed the title of the song because "Body and Soul" had more resonance to his story than did the other song. He was right: "Body and Soul" fitted the story better and I forgave him the 'error' because he had come clean about it.

This need to 'come clean' with the reader becomes much more important where an author introduces real historical figures as characters – imposes her own consciousness onto a person of the past – because then the reader will be unable to determine what has been taken from recorded fact and what has been invented. If an author is not prepared to make this clear, then she should at least change the names of her characters to emphasise that her version is based on imagination and not historically verifiable reality.

There is an element of self-preservation in this advice. I give fair warning that any author who 'bends' the truth or 'gets it wrong' becomes fair game for informed readers (and nowadays this means any reader who has access to the internet). We live in a Wikipedia world, and the accuracy or otherwise of historical facts is very easy to check nowadays. Readers of historical fiction are often very sensitive to factual errors and will make their annoyance clear on Amazon or Goodreads, or other public forums.

Another issue that should be of concern to writers of historical fiction is anachronism. One instance is where historical characters use language that is identifiably modern. I was gently criticised in a newspaper review of my third novel, *A Time of Secrets*, because a character – an American army officer – used the word 'lifestyle'. The reviewer pointed out that the word was not used in 1943. I am scrupulous about trying to make sure that my characters use the language of the 1940s, and it was upsetting to find, when I checked the *Oxford English Dictionary*, that the reviewer was correct; the word was not widely used in Australia or America until the 1970s, and not used at all before 1946. The fact that the reviewer mentioned such a small matter (and the review was in fact very favourable) shows the dangers in not getting your facts right.

Another form of anachronism is where characters think and act in ways that are inappropriate for the time in which the book is set. Often this occurs when the past is presented in terms of a writer's own present experience. An example would be where women of an earlier era are written so they act with the freedom that a women of 2016 living in our developed western society takes for granted, but which was simply not possible in many earlier periods.

Rather than have characters think and act like twenty-first century people running around on a carefully constructed mid-twentieth century set, I find it is more interesting and challenging to devise ways in which my characters can act appropriately for their time, but perhaps challenge the social mores, or at least recognise the problems. For instance, I might write a scene where a female character considers the dangers she faces in engaging in sexual activity in a time of unreliable contraception.

I write historical fiction because I love historical research, and it is second nature for me to begin the process of writing a novel by collecting or arranging historical evidence so that that my dates are correct and, as far as I can ensure, my characters speak, think and act appropriately for the time in which they live. Balancing these elements is a difficult task. Too much 'history' can produce a novel that reads more like a cut-and-paste job from Wikipedia and it quickly loses its narrative momentum. Too little history, on the other hand, can make the setting seem perfunctory and lacking in believability.

For this reason, any author of historical fiction faces a major challenge in selecting and including just enough historical detail to ensure there is enough historical accuracy without the facts swamping the story.

The way an author finds historical evidence can take many forms. The Internet has made historical research much more accessible, and it is relatively easy to find newspapers, novels, music, letters and photographs from many periods. In preparing to write my novels I watched many films and newsreels of the 1940s, read novels published in that period and combed newspaper articles for interesting facts. I found the advertisements to be particularly useful. And, of course, an author will need to read at least a few textbooks, articles and websites, or watch film documentaries about that period of history.

I like to be able to use verifiable facts in my books. Before I began writing *Taking a Chance* I read newspaper reports about the WA Children's Court in the 1940s. There were many sad stories of girls aged fifteen, sixteen, seventeen or so who would stay out all night, drink too much, keep undesirable company and get in too deep. Apparently it was as much a problem in 1943 as it appears to be now. I used some of those stories in the novel.

Those articles were easily accessible because over the past few years the National Library has been quietly arranging for the digitization of Australian newspapers and magazines, from the nineteenth century to the 1980s. They are all there: *The West Australian*, the *Daily News*, *The Argus*, the *Army News*, *The Australian Women's Weekly* and many more. As of February 2016 there were 19,940,893 pages consisting of 194,417,217 articles available to search in Trove Digitised Newspapers. It is a goldmine for an author who wants to give a sense of true Australian history in her novels, but I have also found it invaluable for researching British and American history, as so many articles were imported verbatim from British and American newspapers.

I write about World War II, and that is a time still within living memory. My mother was born in 1920 and she loved to tell stories. As I grew up I heard her speak about life in Perth in World War II, about coping with blackouts, and casualty lists, rationing and identity cards, and censorship of private letters and news. From my mother I had a sense of what it was like to *be* a young woman living an ordinary life in those extraordinary times. She told me of the thousands of allied troops who flooded into a city without its own men, who had left to fight. 'We danced with Americans,' she said, 'because there weren't any Australians to dance with.'

In fact, the idea for *A Stranger in My Street* came from my mother's account of returning home each night from work when she was nineteen, and her terror as she ran through a pocket of scrubland in the blackout to get to her house. I imagined her fear in that dark and deserted bit of urban bush, and I thought how easy it would be to murder someone there in the darkness ...

Like any human being, a well-rounded character has to have a backstory. Mum's stories were useful there, too, as she was from the same generation as my characters. That meant I was able to draw upon her stories of her childhood in Kalgoorlie during the Great Depression, when she lived in straitened circumstances with a widowed mother. World War I cast a deep shadow over the life of any person who was – as my characters are – an adult in the 1940s. My mother's father fought in World War I and her uncle had been killed at Gallipoli. She grew up hearing stories of the Great War, and had school friends whose fathers had been gassed and maimed on the battlefields of France and Belgium. She had met shell-shocked ex-soldiers of World War I. Such experiences may not be directly mentioned in a novel set in World War II, but as my characters had grown up in the shadow of the Depression and the Great War, in my own mind those experiences affected their actions in World War II.

In my first novel, *A Stranger in My Street*, I wanted to include a sense of this 'long history' and I incorporated a family story told by my mother, but put the story into the words of Meg, my heroine:

'My father was a casualty of the Great War, even though he didn't actually die until 1922. He'd joined the Australian Army in 1916, after he'd learned of the death of his younger brother in France. He said it was his duty to go off to war, but it meant leaving a wife and two small daughters behind in Kalgoorlie. On the sideboard in the dining room was a photograph, taken just before he left, of my father standing stiffly in his uniform next to his wife and daughters. My sisters Joan and Mary, who were five and three, regarded the camera with blank, confused stares, and Father appeared grimly determined, like a man who was tired of arguing the point of why he had to go away to war. Ma hated that photograph. "I look so sad," she always said when she saw it. "Because I was so sad."' (pp. 9-10)

That is the story almost exactly as my mother told it to me when we looked at the photograph, except that her father was a forty-three-year-old accountant who had lied about his age to join up, his younger brother had died at Gallipoli, not in France, and he had left behind him in Kalgoorlie four young daughters, not two.

Many little details in my novels about living on the 'home front' in Australia were taken from my mother's stories. My mother took a trolley bus or a parlour car into Perth city (she preferred the parlour car). She joined the Red Cross and learnt first aid, and she packed comfort parcels for the troops. She described the horror Perth people felt on learning of the sinking of the HMAS Sydney, the fear caused by the surrender of Singapore and the bombing of Darwin, and the bitter joy that came with the Japanese attack on Pearl Harbor, because it meant that the USA would be fighting with Australia against the Japanese Empire. These details are in my novels and I think they add an extra layer of 'truth' to the stories.

As part of my research I also spoke to other people who had lived through World War II. They and my mother told me of fears for friends who were fighting, but also admitted it was a time of challenges, of excitement, and sometimes of love and great joy. That sense of excitement is something that I try hard to include in my novels.

My mother told me stories about my father's war. He was one of the group of Australian Commandos who fought a guerrilla campaign on Timor. In trying to understand his experiences I was able to use my mother's stories and I was lucky enough also to have the invaluable resource of his war diary. After the war he suffered what we now know as post-traumatic stress, and he died young. My mother told me of his terrible bouts of malarial fever, which caused uncontrollable sweating and shaking, and how he would wake up screaming, night after night, re-living his experiences in the war. It is no coincidence that in all of my novels the male characters suffer, to a lesser or greater extent, because of their fighting experiences.

When writing I also rely to a fairly large extent on my own personal experience of the places or events that form the backdrop to my books. I have always set my novels in places I have visited and know quite well. The first two novels were set in Perth, the third in Melbourne, and the latest is set in London. I like to walk where my characters walk and to imagine I am looking at what they see. I know exactly what view of the Swan River you get from various points on Stirling Highway and these are the views Meg sees in *A Stranger in My Street*. I know the route taken by her trolleybus as it winds along Mounts Bay Road towards Perth.

The house where Meg lives is the house where my mother lived in 1939 with her mother and sisters. I wandered down Violet Grove in Shenton Park, where Nell lives in *Taking a Chance*, and noted each house as I passed and I tried to get a sense of the 'feel' of the street. I strode around South Yarra, where my third novel, *A Time of Secrets*, is set, and visited the mansions that housed various branches of the Allied Intelligence Bureau during the war. My latest novel is set in the London Blitz, and I have walked those streets with a bomb map, working out exactly which buildings were hit.

I shamelessly use my friends, relatives, even strangers on the street to obtain background I can use in my novels. Authors are like magpies: we pick up shiny pieces of information for our books and hide them away until needed. We call in favours and ask friends, colleagues and professionals for information if they have knowledge that may be of use in our writing. At a friend's birthday afternoon tea, I cornered a man I hadn't seen for a while who had been a policeman in Sydney in the 1980s. I spent an hour interrogating him about his memories of those days, about cases he'd been involved with, the methodologies used in solving crimes, the means used to calm violent situations, and how he would defend himself – or attack – when necessary. Interesting facts emerged from this conversation, not least of which was that the large torches the policemen carried were much better in a scrap than the smaller, lighter coshes.

The first chapter of *Taking a Chance* begins with a judge putting on the black cap and pronouncing the sentence of death. The death sentence wasn't actually abolished in Western Australia – the last state to do so – until 1984. So although I have not heard the words spoken myself, I know people who have been in court when the death sentence was pronounced. I asked them how it made them feel, and then I used my imagination to feel the horror for myself.

I store up interesting little stories. How being taken to Kings Park was a Sunday treat in wartime, because you could watch the American Catalina flying boats take off and land in the river. How to wheedle chocolates and chewing gum out of the nice Americans who arrived to take out your sister. How it felt, at the age of six, to run into your mother's room and find her in bed with a strange man who she introduced as your father, who had not been home for four years.

A woman who came to one of my talks told me about living in Wales in the war. Her older sister loved to dance with Americans and, like Meg in *A Stranger in My Street*, painted her legs in a time of shortage of nylons. One evening her sister painted her legs beautifully, drew the line up the back of the calf with an eyebrow pencil for the seam, and slipped on her lovely white dancing shoes. Only it rains a lot in Wales, so by the time she arrived at the dance those white shoes were a muddy brown.

My own life experiences also add verisimilitude to my novels. In the 1970s I ate hamburgers at the now long gone Bernie's Hamburger Bar and I used that memory in *A Stranger in My Street*. I have sat through trials in the Perth Criminal Court, that grand old Number 2 Court in the Supreme Court building. I've seen it from the viewpoint of a barrister. I know how it looks, smells and feels. And I used that personal knowledge in the first chapter of *Taking a Chance*. Later in the novel Nell visits Fremantle Prison. In 1982 I visited the prison to take a statement from a prisoner. It was then still a working prison. In the novel I tried to invoke the sense of desperation I felt when the heavy doors were locked behind me, that irrational panic and the feeling that the sun shone less brightly in that ghastly place.

I have even used my own health issues to add a sense of truth to the novels. Stella, the heroine of *A Time of Secrets*, is asthmatic. I was at my doctor's surgery when I was writing the book and as my GP took my blood pressure I asked her about treatments for asthma in the 1940s. She laughed and said: 'In your first novel the heroine had a migraine. You get migraines. Now you're writing about asthma and you're asthmatic. I suppose it's a good idea to write what you know.'

She was right, of course, but only to a certain extent. The small details add the icing on the cake and so enhance the reader's enjoyment of your novel. There is 'truth' when I write about what it's like to gasp for breath during an asthma attack and to experience the dentist's drill-like pain of a migraine, but I have never been assaulted. I have never been a soldier or a secretary or a journalist or driven an ambulance in the London Blitz.

Personal experience can only get an author so far. Imagination is the tool of a writer and at the end, it is the story that is the most important thing. A writer of historical fiction must find a greater 'truth' than simply a slavish adherence to the facts, but she must also work out how to best use those facts to enhance her story, and in so doing, how she can keep faith with her reader.

I have tried in my novels to recreate what it was like to be a young woman in 1943, living in Australia when the world was at war, a time of excitement and fear, when there was a real sense of 'living for the moment'. I have tried to do so in a way that is historically accurate but which also gives a sense of that time to a reader in 2016. And that is possibly the most difficult part of writing historical fiction – balancing historical plausibility with an engaging story.

FIVE TIPS FROM DEBORAH BURROWS

1. Read widely, and not just in your area. You will pick up ideas from seeing how other writers deal with characterisation and thorny plot problems. Don't plagiarise, of course, but allow yourself to appreciate other writers' techniques and see if you can adapt those techniques to enhance your own writing.
2. Get up from your desk, get out and exercise! Many of my best ideas come when I'm simply putting one foot in front of the other in the open air.
3. Write every day. Writing is a skill and must be honed by doing.
4. If you've nothing specific to write, then 'shoot film'. By that, I mean write scenes to get your imagination going. Set up the background of a character, whether or not that character is in your current novel. Describe scenery. Write a fight scene or an emotional scene. Basically, write whatever takes your fancy and store it in a special folder. I regularly open my 'film' folder to read what's there and I often find that it contains exactly what I need for my current novel or to get me started on a new one.
5. Copy edit. Then copy edit again. There is never any excuse for sloppy grammar or spelling mistakes. Never!

Rejection-

Acceptance

by Deborah Disney

ONE of the obstacles to publication for many, I believe, is the torrent of anecdotal evidence supporting the notion that rejection is a necessary step (or in some cases, a necessary double-storey staircase!) on the road to acceptance. Rejection after rejection after rejection, that's what we should expect. Even brilliant and successful authors regale us with their tales of multiple rejections before they opened that coveted letter of acceptance from the publisher who would take them from weeknight-word-wrangler to published author. Think J.K. Rowling …

These rejection stories are so widespread, I am sure many a magnificent and potentially enormous profit-making manuscript sees out its eternity in the bottom drawer of its creator's desk. Perhaps it resurfaces intermittently during moments of optimistic conviction before being returned to the bottom drawer, maintaining the risk-free existence of its ever-hopeful, but ultimately self-preserving owner. Because, really, *who likes rejection?*

I don't know how much rejection I would have been able to handle. I may have survived one rejection. When I sent off the first three chapters of my first novel, *Up and In*, to a publisher, I did so with the accompanying self-coaching: 'Rejection is part of the process, and the sooner I start the rejections rolling in, the sooner my work will get to the point of acceptance.' It sounds like I was very resigned to rejection, doesn't it? Like I had rejection-acceptance?

To a large extent, rejection-acceptance is a state a writer must achieve before they hit the send button.

But how long that rejection-acceptance would have lasted for me, how many publishers could have said no to me before I would have given up on the idea entirely, I will never know.

What I can tell you, though, by sharing my publication story, is that rejection doesn't *have* to be part of the process. Sometimes, *some*times, there is no rejection before acceptance. Before I proceed, please understand this is not a gloating story. I share this because I think that while rejection-acceptance is important for aspiring authors (even for established authors), so too is an underlying optimism for every author as they hit the send button that 'this might just be it'.

My publication story started, of all places, in the school pick-up line, late in 2013. I had been working freelance for a couple of years, writing copy for an advertising firm and articles for various magazines.

Prior to having children, I had practised as a solicitor, which involved a lot of writing, but I think it was the creativity that came with working out how to use the written word to flog everything from bus tours to kids' yoga classes that set the cogs in motion for novel writing. The absolute, honest-to-universe truth is that I had not engaged in any form of creative story-telling since finishing school many years prior. No short stories, no poems, not even embellished journal writing. Suddenly, here I was, waiting for a school bell to ring, creating characters, dialogue and funny scenes on the Notes app on my iPhone. I had often heard people tell stories and I'd say to them, 'There's a book in that!' but when I set upon my new school pick-up zone hobby, I had absolutely no concrete plan about where it was going or what I intended to do with it.

Later that week, I met a friend for lunch. As our conversation turned to some of her recent experiences with fellow mums at her children's school, I pulled out my iPhone and said, 'Here, have a read of this.' *This*, as it turned out, was the first chapter of *Up and In*, my novel about school gate politics. I just didn't know it yet. As she was reading, she was nodding and laughing. This is good, I thought, I'm amusing my friend as well as myself.

'You should send this to a publisher,' she said. With those seven words she lit a flicker of passion within me that has yet to be snuffed out.

'Really?' I tried to stifle the exhilaration that now filled me – the idea that a publisher might find my writing interesting.

'Really. It's great. It reminds me of Liane Moriarty,' she continued.

As much as I would like to say I was so far across the world of Australian publishing at that time (or even that I was sufficiently up with the latest must-reads) that I immediately knew who she was talking about, I must confess that I did *not* immediately know who she was talking about. In my defence, this particular friend has relatives with the surname Moriarty, so I was a little thrown by that. I was far less chuffed than I ought to have been, as I sipped wine and tried to work out which distant cousin of hers wrote as compellingly and wittily as her laughs had convinced me that *I* could.

'You know, the author? She's one of my favourites. She wrote *The Husband's Secret*? *Three Wishes*?'

'Ah. Yes,' I said. '*Three Wishes*, I think I read that.' And, as was established when I spied it in my bookcase later that day, I had read it. Years earlier. Back when reading for relaxation had been a viable option for me. I kind of remembered it. I was pretty sure I liked it. So this was good. This was a compliment.

Feeling quite buoyed by her strokes and the two glasses of wine I'd consumed over lunch, I went home and googled 'Liane Moriarty Publisher'. (No, it didn't occur to me to get the book down from the shelf and look inside the front cover for that information.) About three links down the page of Google results, there was a heading that included Liane Moriarty and HarperCollins. I went straight to googling HarperCollins, without looking any further or even clicking on that result. It turns out (as I discovered much later) that Liane Moriarty is not published by HarperCollins. But, I believe, fate was working its wonderful magic, and when I 'mistakenly' googled HarperCollins, I found they had just started an online submissions portal called The Wednesday Post. I just needed to submit the first three chapters for them to consider. My iPhone was already sporting what could easily be one chapter, and I spent the next couple of weeks madly typing away, so that by two Wednesdays later, I had enough to submit.

Other than my husband and two of my friends (including the well-read one who had pointed me in HarperCollins's direction … kind of), I didn't tell anyone about submitting. I think there was part of me – a big part of my logical self – that believed there was no way this would ever come to anything, and I didn't want to look like a goose when I got rejected. But as much as I steeled myself for rejection, there was also a part of me that really believed from the moment I hit send, that something *was* going to come of it.

From the information provided on the HarperCollins The Wednesday Post page, I knew they would only respond to my submission if they wanted to see more. I didn't realise it at the time, as I had no prior exposure to publishers or publisher habits, but their promise to make contact within four weeks, if contact was to be made at all, rendered them a particularly considerate publisher.

Many publishers can make you wait for six or more months before they contact you. Together with the suggestion that you only ever contact one publisher at a time, that can make the road to publication a very long one indeed!

As it turned out, I didn't even have to wait four weeks. Just two days after submitting I received an email from The Wednesday Post. I saw the email come through on my phone, which was lodged in one of those mobile-phone holders you stick to the inside of your car windscreen. I was nearing the end of an almost two-hour drive to Toowoomba to see my mother on her birthday, when I heard the little ping. Obviously I was concentrating on highway driving, but a ping-following glance in the phone's direction quickly revealed The Wednesday Post had just sent me an email.

I could not believe my eyes. This was beyond incredible. This was insane. As little knowledge as I then had about publishing, I knew that getting a book published was no small feat. I knew that HarperCollins was a really big publisher and they were emailing me. Two days after I submitted to them. Two days! But then, as quickly as my almost peeing-my-pants excitement began, it was replaced by an inner voice telling me this email was probably nothing more than an automated 'thank you for the submission' response.

Without endangering my life, I was able to see with another glance phonewards that the email started with the words, 'Thank you so much …' My mind whirred with possibilities, but what seemed clear was that this wasn't automated. Automated responses don't include things like 'so much'. An automated response would stop at 'thank you'. So much. *So* much. They must like it. They would not be saying 'so much' if they didn't like it. That was it. *This* was it. I could not possibly wait the extra fifteen or so minutes' drive it was going to take to reach my destination. I pulled over on the side of the highway so I could read this wonderful thank-you-so-much email:

'Thank you so much for submitting your chapters from 'Bea-wildered' to The Wednesday Post. I have really enjoyed reading them and it's extremely impressive that it only took you a few weeks! I love the light-hearted voice, the satirical but believable dialogue, the warmth of Maria and her various neuroses … There's no doubt you have a flair for fiction writing and should keep going to see where it leads. Unfortunately, there's not much we can do without a full manuscript, so I am writing to ask to have a look again once you've been able to finish it. Looking forward to hearing about your progress.'

The 'dot-dot-dots' contained advice about some overused puns and the possibility of changing the title, but who the hell cared about that? HarperCollins was talking to me. They were talking to me like these three chapters could conceivably become a book! The submissions editor, Kate Steinweg, was interested. I believe that, once again, fate played a large part in all of this, as Kate was not only someone who enjoyed my sense of humour, she also shared the name of one of my main characters. Even more fortuitously, perhaps, she happened to be a huge fan of netball. The fact that *Up and In* revolved around a group of mothers who were thrust together due to their daughters all attending the same exclusive school, and also on the netball sidelines each Saturday, certainly helped to get her attention.

So, back to the side of the road – I was literally screaming for joy. Restrained in my seatbelt on the shoulder of the highway, jumping wasn't an option. After a few moments of self-congratulatory squealing, I called my husband. Much to my surprise, he didn't start squealing with me. He, in fact, took on a rather cautionary tone and advised that I shouldn't go telling everyone about it. He pointed out that writing a whole book was still an enormous task that lay ahead, and he suggested I should wait until that was done before I started letting people know. In retrospect, I know he was just being protective, but at the time, I wished I hadn't called him at all. What a killjoy! So, I continued my journey up the hill to Toowoomba, and sat through my mother's birthday lunch with my sister and brother-in-law without saying a word to any of them. Kill-joy or not, I decided to take my husband's advice. Even though a little voice told me this was the start of something gargantuan in my life, this bit of encouragement from HarperCollins was still a *long* way from a publishing deal. Almost a whole book away, in fact.

In the months that followed, I set about writing the rest of the book. By the time the summer school holidays rolled around, I had written about ten chapters. Kate had continued to take an interest. I would submit a few more chapters to her at a time, and she provided feedback to keep me going. That was important for me, not only for the content of the feedback, but – possibly even more so – for the reassurance that this big publisher was still very keen on my book.

During the summer, my flow was interrupted. The children were home, and there was other *paid* writing work to be done. My manuscript had to be shelved – temporarily anyway.

I started writing *Up and In* again the following February. I set myself a deadline because I knew myself well enough to realise that this could easily fritter into nothingness if I didn't make myself finish by a certain date. The date I set was my 44th birthday, May 5. As is so often the case with deadlines and me, I was still finishing the manuscript on that date. I submitted it at 11.40 a.m. that morning. I remember that because it occurred to me later that I was born at 11.40 a.m., and there I was exactly forty-four years later, submitting a whole book I had written.

Kate responded within the hour, saying she was really snowed under and wouldn't get to look at it for a while, but would come back to me as soon as she could. Given my own slack pace with *reading* whole books, I genuinely expected it would be at least a few months before I heard any more. Once again, it was a happy surprise when she contacted me just four days later to say she thought *Up and In* was wonderful, and she was taking it to the HarperCollins acquisitions meeting the following Tuesday. I hadn't really understood at the time just how much power is wielded by the sales department at the acquisitions meeting, and how easily that meeting could have been the end of it, but Kate had faith, and so I had faith.

Kate reported back the next week that HarperCollins would be publishing my book. You might think this would be a timely place to conclude my story. However, there was a rather large 'but' that came with that email. The 'but' was that it would be published digitally:

I pitched your title to my colleagues on Tuesday, and everyone agreed that you are an exciting and wonderfully amusing new voice, and that we would love you to consider publishing your work as an eBook with us!

It would be an eBook. EEEEEE-book? I didn't want my brilliant foray into the published world to be an eBook. They were for sixteen-page how-to guides, weren't they? eBooks were contained in annoying little ads that popped up in the corner of my PC screen offering me the inside info on 'How to get rich quick in 4 short steps'. This wasn't what I had had in mind at all when I had been tippety-tapping away in all the months leading to this eye-popping moment.

Conversations with Kate ensued. At no time, not for even one second, did I ever consider taking my book to another publisher. Kate had been with me from *Up and In*'s embryonic first days, had guided me and been utterly available to me all along. Despite my paltry knowledge of the publishing industry, I was always fairly certain that very few first-time, completely unknown authors have a publisher, let alone a big-five publisher, instilling confidence in them every step of the way. So if HarperCollins, with full knowledge of my complete lack of social media skills, presence or even *interest*, was prepared to take me on, even as only an eBook author initially, then that was what I would agree to. That and going on Facebook.

A contract was forwarded to me on my best friend's birthday. I read it and read it, and read it again. I signed it and sent it back two days later. On my sister's birthday. The fact that all of these significant events kept happening on significant birthdays was truly bizarre.

After getting my head around the whole eBook idea (helped along by a visit to the iBooks site, which, prior to this, I hadn't even known existed), there were a couple of other bumps in my publishing road. Firstly, I had a little meltdown when I decided *Up and In* should be written in present tense instead of past tense. I believed that my main character Maria's state of bewilderment would have more authenticity if it was unravelling in present tense. Given the manuscript was completed, this was an enormous decision to make. I re-wrote a sample chapter. However, Kate believed past tense was better. I sent the sample to a friend and she thought present tense was better, like me. Ultimately, after days of wrangling with the issue, I decided to stick with past tense, and I am so glad I did.

My second meltdown within the space of a couple of weeks happened when I was reading a *Mamamia* article about different 'categories' of school mothers. I was mainly interested in the comments, and how the article was being received. One comment referred to a novel about school mothers. I located the book and read a sample of it online. *Holy crap*. Not only was the premise similar to mine, the book's protagonist had the same name as my antagonist – Bea. I decided I had to let HarperCollins know what I'd found, even though I realised my publishing dream was probably about to come crashing down. Thank God my husband had told me not to tell people, I thought. I resigned myself to it being over. On my morning walk I thought to myself, well, on the upside, I have a helpful contact at a big publishing house. All those months of writing weren't *completely* for nothing.

I spoke to Kate. I told her about the other book. She didn't seem particularly concerned, but she went away and looked at it, and came back to me later and said not to worry. She assured me there were heaps of books out there with characters who shared names with my characters. It was impossible for there not to be. There were other school gate stories, too. This was not the first. It wouldn't be the last. She was exactly the voice of calm and reason I needed. What was important to her, what was important to HarperCollins, was that my writing 'voice' was fresh. That was what they were after. That was what made them want me to come on board and develop my writing career with them.

So it was all back on. My book was still going to be published. In the coming months, I was lucky enough to meet with Kate at the HarperCollins offices in Sydney, during a scheduled stopover on our way back from holidays in New Zealand. She was working on the structural edit and it was a great opportunity to get together and go through her notes over a cup of tea. While we were chatting, Kate mentioned there were lots of women in the office who had read parts of my book and thought it was hilarious. They were big fans, she said. I could hardly believe it. When I had reached the HarperCollins office that morning and stood admiring the sensational views over Sydney, it seemed like a world away from the little Catholic primary school I had attended in Toowoomba. A school so small it had to have composite classes as there weren't enough kids to run the usual seven separate grades. I was already pinching myself enough about the fact I was even there, about to be a published author, but now I had *fans* as well. Kate then trotted out four of these 'fans' who, she said, wanted to meet me. As they stood there, looking at me expectantly, I felt enormous pressure to say something funny. But I had nothing. Nothing but polite smiles and concerted attempts to remember their names. I am sure they wandered back to their respective desks in disappointment. *She's really not that funny in person.* They had to be thinking that.

And then Kate brought out someone else to meet me. Her name was Shona Martyn. Shona seemed lovely, but I didn't have anything funny to offer her either. Other than when she told me they were excited to have me on board: 'Not as excited as I am!' I goofed out. She laughed, but I was pretty sure it was more *at* me than with me. It wasn't until I was googling several weeks later I realised that 'lovely Shona' is the publishing director at HarperCollins. I didn't even stand up when I met her.

My second face-to-face meeting with Kate came shortly after, at the inaugural HarperCollins Author Day. What an event that was. There were informative sessions on subjects like social media and cover design, and presentations from the CEO about present trends in publishing. It was a bombardment of information for someone like me who was coming from a place of zip when it came to publishing industry knowledge. But it was a welcome bombardment. I was fascinated. I was hooked. If there had been any doubt previously (there hadn't) there was certainly no doubt now this was exactly the career I wanted to pursue.

Even after all of this, though, it seemed I hadn't yet passed all of the bumps in the road to publication. The Monday following Author Day, I received a call from Kate. 'I have some bad news,' she started off. I immediately suspected the worst. It was over! They'd changed their minds. They didn't want my book after all. Thank God again my husband told me not to tell anyone. 'I will be leaving in a couple of weeks and I won't be able to finish your copyedit with you.' My audible sigh of relief must have been confusing and a little insulting. It wasn't that I didn't value the work she had done with me, or that I didn't think she was by far the best person for the job of seeing *Up and In* through to its fully edited conclusion. Far from it. It was just that all I could think was, *at least they are still going to publish it!*

I was fortunate to have Maddy James help me finish the edit. She brought a new perspective and I am sure there were jokes and sayings Kate and I assumed worked as *we* both found them funny, but with fresh eyes, Maddy pointed out some things that readers may have missed and I was then able to clarify them in amusing ways. Maddy was the silver-lining in my Kate-loss cloud.

Before Kate left, there was one last job she wanted to see through and that was the cover art for *Up and In*. When she sent through the first round of concepts, I could not have been more thrilled. It was: 'Pencils down, designers, we have a winner!' Having that cover really made it seem real, and it made me brave enough to tell everyone about it. Everyone. Everyone I could think of.

This brings me to my final little bump in my road to publication – but it was a life-learning bump and one that in a way I am grateful for: not everyone was happy for me. Not everyone was spraying congratulations in my direction. Some people, in fact, altogether ignored that this was happening. Not only did they *not* say anything like 'That's great!', 'How exciting!' or 'Good for you!' … they didn't say anything to me about it *at all*. My experience of writing a book became a bit of a no-go zone with them. For a while I felt hurt and confused by this. It wasn't just one person, either, it was a number of people – including a family member and someone whom I had previously considered one of my closest friends. What this bump taught me, though, is that when someone is genuinely happy for your happiness, that, *that* right there is a friend. I am lucky – truly lucky – to have quite a few of those friends in my life, and their love and support is something that I have come to value even more through this whole publishing experience.

I acknowledged some of the many people who helped me along the road to publication at the end of *Up and In*, but there are a few more people whom I should mention, and I wish I had indulged myself in writing an extra page at the back of the book to do it there. My older sister, Sharon, taught me to read before I went to school, so from the very beginning she was giving me a leg up. (She's my only sister, but she looks younger than me, so I have to stress 'older'). Sharon also opened doors for me with the magazine editor who first published an article for me, and the advertising agency where I cut my creative teeth on a bus tour brochure. As sisters, we have certainly had our ups and downs (and it was a definite down the Christmas lunch just a few weeks after *Up and In*'s publication when her name wasn't in the acknowledgements!) but I thank her for helping to carve me into the person I am today.

There is also my almost-lifelong friend, Susie, the one who told me to submit to a publisher. Without her, there is every chance *Up and In* wouldn't even have been written, let alone submitted for publication, so I will always be grateful for the confidence she instilled in me to send it off. And my gorgeous friend, Di, who has counselled me through all the bumps, and loves me through all of my neuroses – I am not entirely sure where I would be sitting on my road to publication right now without her, either. I also wish I had mentioned Kate Steinweg by name. There is every chance my book would not ever have been finished if she hadn't been the one wading through that slush pile. If it had been a humourless submissions editor who had read my first three chapters, or one not so keen on my particular 'voice', then a four-week period of hearing nothing back from HarperCollins may have ensued, and been enough of a confidence-crusher to stop it all right there. But Kate was with me from the beginning, cheering me on from the sidelines, coaching me through my missteps and applauding my goals with great vigour. I will never forget her.

Finally, Liane Moriarty, for writing the great, funny books that my friend could tell me about. I thank her for having had something to do with HarperCollins at some point – or as a minimum for having her name in the same space as theirs in a Google search. I thank her for becoming my inspiration and my role model –even though she is fairly clueless that I exist.

Road bumps and all, my publishing experience has been a dream, and I know that when one dream is fulfilled, other dreams quickly follow. I still dream of my first book, and subsequent books, being published in print. And when that happens, I'll start dreaming of translation rights and movie deals. Writing is a career built on dreams, but more than that, for anyone whose true love is writing, and who writes well, it is a dream of a career.

FIVE TIPS FROM DEBORAH DISNEY

1. Don't be too rigid with your storyline – always leave room for the magic to happen.
2. Character credibility is important – make an identikit of each character's key traits and refer to it often.
3. Your imagination can be a distraction. Make quick notes of any great ideas that interrupt your flow so you can go back to them later.
4. Proofread. Proofread. Proofread. The less time your copyeditor spends changing it's to its, the more time they have to help you with the big stuff.
5. Keep your eye on the prize. Writing a book rarely leads to significant income. Focus on saying something significant instead.

And finally, good luck! X

The Landscape of Writing

by Sara Foster

ON those glorious occasions where I am 'in the zone' as a storyteller, I am in some other place where nothing and no one can touch me. Lost in a world I can contemplate and manipulate according to my will. Even then, my stories do not present themselves whole – they reveal themselves in tantalising pieces, a breadcrumb trail that I'm compelled to follow. I converse endlessly with characters, asking them questions, teasing out their secrets. I plot on paper, reworking as I go along. I study pace, timing and language as I go, trying to tease out the best possible descriptions of a person, a moment, a feeling. All these elements of novel writing are immeasurably satisfying, and the excitement of those eureka moments when it all comes together is irreplaceable.

In addition to this, there are certain aspects of your writing that become your trademarks, sometimes without you even realising it. In my case, I have developed a special affinity for setting, something that is repeatedly remarked upon by readers. For me, location is far more than just a backdrop to my stories.

My settings are living, breathing foundations for my novels, weaving through each character, inseparable from plot, adding their own individual, vital ingredients to every aspect of my stories.

I see a lot more discussion and advice about plotting and characterisation in novel writing than I do on setting, and yet location is an integral part of every story. Those books that enter the public lexicon – from *Room* by Emma Donoghue to *The Hunger Games* by Suzanne Collins – each have vividly imagined, unique settings that, once glimpsed, are forever identifiable to the reader.

A choice of setting will determine the freedoms and limitations with which characters can talk or act, the choices they can make, the kinds of lives they can lead. A setting may be imagined as something separate to character, but the best settings also permeate character – altering mood and language, while heightening the atmosphere around them. Even the most mundane of settings can be transformed depending on how the character interacts with it. A home bathroom is a pretty boring, functional place, but not if your character shrinks to the size of an ant, or the taps suddenly start running with blood.

Sometimes the settings for my stories come to me at the same time as my first ideas about characters and plot. For my third book, *Shallow*

Breath, the very first image I had was of a woman looking out towards the ocean in grief and desperation. However, for my fourth novel, *All That is Lost Between Us*, my original idea was of a teenager with a dark secret – which meant I could choose from numerous settings. I went for one that had been waiting in the wings – the Lake District in the UK. It felt like a natural progression from writing my second novel, *Beneath the Shadows*, which is set among the stark, empty landscape of the North Yorkshire moors, perfectly mirroring my main character's emptiness and desolation as she searches in vain for her missing husband.

That novel taught me a lot, in particular to approach setting like a detective hunting for clues, examining all the small details, searching for those elements of the surroundings that might contribute another layer to the story, or bring it further to life.

Beneath the Shadows is about Grace's struggle not only to learn the truth of what happened to her husband, but to keep faith in her beliefs when everything around her causes her to doubt her own mind. The Yorkshire moors were the perfect place to play with the dark, gothic feel of the novel. I wanted this empty landscape of contrasts – this hauntingly beautiful place – to echo and underscore Grace's state of mind as she travels through the murky, uneven terrain of her doubts and fears; to offer her promise, and to threaten her with devastation. So the driving wind seems to push and pull the characters while they walk, sending their hair in stinging slaps across their faces like some mischievous sprite. The darkness of winter is so absolute that Grace cannot see her fingers just in front of her face, and wonders in the dead of night if she still exists at all. And the cold is raw, and numbing, like the grief Grace tries to hold at bay. Finally, just as the secrets begin to unravel, the moors turn white with snow, trapping Grace physically and emotionally, casting one final, persistent shroud over the truth.

And so the North Yorkshire moors became the silent character in my novel, just as forbidding and unfathomable as some of the others you meet in the small village of Roseby.

I didn't have to look too far for symbolic resonance either – the moorland is rich with folk tales and superstitions, and the hardest part was leaving so much great material out. What I also loved was that many of the symbols of the moors seemed to have ambiguous origins and multiple explanations, so you could never quite get to the truth of them, which perfectly mirrored the difficulties faced by my characters.

My desire to learn about anything and everything comes into its own when I begin to study settings. On every occasion I have found the same maxim to be true: the more you look, the more you will find. Ideally, that means visiting a place I have in mind for a story – if working with a real location, that is. There's nothing better than talking to locals, poring over obscure books rather than Wikipedia, and tramping the ground so that when I come back to describing the place I have a complete sensory picture of what it is like.

Without this approach for *Beneath the Shadows*, I wouldn't have discovered the legend of the black Barghest, an ephemeral black dog that, if seen, is said to signify the coming death of a local. Nor would I have found the huge stone way markers that appear over the moorside like giants' tombstones, with various explanations as to their origins – from ancient signposts, to places where you might leave pennies for poor travellers. This approach has been important for all my books so far. I came up with the finale for my third novel, *Shallow Breath*, while standing on a hotel roof in a small fishing town in Japan. My fourth novel, *All That is Lost Between Us*, wouldn't be the same without the teenager who competes in the relatively unknown sport of fell-running, or the winding track called the Spirit Road, which is connected by both ancient and modern stories of the dead.

Where does this passion for setting come from? Possibly the wild landscapes of the Brontes, or the vivid scenes in and around Manderley in Daphne du Maurier's *Rebecca*. I loved all these classics as a teenager. I adored Nancy Cato's *All the Rivers Run*, and one of my ambitions as a backpacking twenty-something was to stand at the helm of the paddle steamer *Philadelphia* and pretend I was on the Murray River with Brenton a hundred years earlier. It was on that same trip, visiting so many wondrous, untouched natural places, I began to feel a deeper connection with my surroundings and to notice the impact different locations had on me.

In the subsequent years, before I began submitting my own work for publication, I worked as a book editor. While helping other published authors to polish their work, I was also learning from all of them. Therefore, when I finally had a finished book to send out, I had a good idea of what publishers were looking for, and a fair idea about what to expect during the publishing process. That didn't make it any easier for me to endure the long waits for answers to submissions, and it didn't entirely lessen the challenges of the editing process, but it did mean that I understood that an editor is only critiquing your work because they want to bring out the best in your book.

---

*Some authors are very open to the editing process,
whereas others find it difficult to let go of their work and
open up to constructive critique, and when this happens
the whole process becomes difficult on both sides.*

I had a dream experience of publishing my debut novel, *Come Back to Me*, when it managed to get on the *Sydney Morning Herald* top ten bestsellers list. *Beneath the Shadows* followed a year later and sold even more copies. However, between this and my third publication, *Shallow Breath*, the Australian book industry took a beating when Angus & Robertson and Borders closed their doors. Suddenly there were only half as many places to sell a novel. Unsurprisingly, *Shallow Breath* – published in a very competitive Christmas period, and a difficult book to market because of its subject matter – didn't do as well in terms of sales, even though it had the best critical reception of the three.

That was disappointing, but I was still so proud of the novel I had written that I didn't let it bother me too much at the time. What I hadn't anticipated was publisher reaction when we went out with my fourth novel, *All That is Lost Between Us*. Quite a few of the rejections mentioned this dip in sales, and for a short time I worried that perhaps my career had flat-lined without me noticing it. It was the most difficult time of my published career so far, but what sustained me was going back to all the things I loved about writing, which had nothing to do with publishing. My intrigue and love of learning about places, and creating characters and storylines that interweave with these spaces, was at the top of that list. So even while I was waiting to see what happened to my completed novel, I was busy writing descriptive passages about London in winter for the next book.

Thankfully, Simon & Schuster got behind my book, so my Lake District story has now made its way into the world. However, as with any experience, there were lessons to be learned in that turbulent period – ones it's still good to remind myself of today. The main one being that publishing is a business, but my writing – and your writing – only becomes a product once it is linked to that business.

I have no problem with my novels being products. As a professional author, I get the opportunity to create for a living, and explore the different landscapes I'm drawn to as part of my work, which is wonderful. However, this is the end result. The foundation of my writing begins with my passion to explore, interpret and find meaning in my life, experiences and surroundings, and this provides a constant, exciting purpose to my life that is completely independent to the vagaries of the industry I work in. Following my heart may not always be of direct benefit to my career, but it is vital for my creative soul. That's what authors mean when they say, 'Write for yourself, first of all'. If you follow your own passions, find your own voice and purpose in your writing, then it becomes a lot easier to remain calm in the turbulence of an ever-changing, consumer-driven world.

I'm well aware that authors can grow stale, so for every book I write I like to issue myself a new challenge. Often this is to do with structure or narrative style, but a forthcoming challenge of mine will be to work with a purely imagined setting – one that I can't visit or research. This time I will have to not only paint a vivid backdrop, but I will also be responsible for imagining the symbolism and history of this landscape, as well as every tiny material detail of the place. It's a daunting task, but an exciting one, and only time – and my imagination – will tell us where it leads.

FIVE TIPS FROM SARA FOSTER

1.   Use everything in the landscape and surroundings of your story to add tension. If you want comfortable, the sun is enjoyable. If you want tension, the sun will burn.
2.   Be unpredictable. Don't always go for your first idea when you're thinking about plotting; ask yourself what you can do to make it better or add more of a twist.
3.   If you get stuck, spend some time analysing your story structure. It may help you figure out what's holding you back.
4.   If you set word counts as targets, be kind to yourself. If you fall behind, readjust your schedule rather than thinking you won't achieve your goals.
5.   Don't wait for the perfect circumstances to write. Write whenever you can – you can reread and edit later. I've never heard of anyone writing a perfect first draft.

Ultimate Dreaming

by Monique Hall

IT'S a fairly safe assumption that publication is a dream for most writers; a bestseller to their name, the ultimate dream. But it's something that doesn't always come easy. Sometimes all we have are daydreams. Initially, it can be hard to fall asleep and then there are bouts of insomnia or nightmares to contend with. When we wake, we don't always remember our dreams – and understanding or making meaning from them is even more challenging. If we do manage to achieve what we set out to do, there are always more pleasant dreams we could be having.

So it is with a writer's dreams.

DAYDREAMING: WANTING TO BE A WRITER

As a little girl, I dreamt of being a writer. I had a great love of books, and from an early age I wanted to see my name on a front cover one day. I remember being about twelve years old and sitting down to my family's new computer with my best friend to write the world's next masterpiece. She wanted to write horror – I, on the other hand, was scared of my own shadow. But I indulged her. We wrote our way into the second chapter, saved our document, she went home, and that was the end of that.

DIFFICULTY GETTING TO SLEEP: STARING AT A BLANK PAGE

My early daydreams didn't do much to help send me to the land of nod. I knew I wanted to write, but I didn't know what – I just knew it wasn't going to be horror. The older I got, the more my dream of becoming a writer became just that – a dream. Sadly, it seemed unattainable. I felt I just didn't have the imagination to write something that people would want to read. I didn't even have the confidence to write something that was just for me. When I was sixteen and working for a casual hourly rate, I invested my hard-earned money by enrolling in a correspondence writing course. I can't remember if I even completed the first lesson, but I continued sending off my monthly payment of thirty-five dollars. I wanted desperately to start working at achieving my dream but my head was stopping me from even giving it a shot.

DRIFTING OFF: WRITING THAT FIRST SENTENCE

Upon entering adulthood, I had practically given up on the idea of being a writer, though I continued to be an avid reader. After having children, I found myself devouring anything in the romance genre.

Romances were easy to read and entertaining for those times I just wanted to relax from the daily grind. I read a lot of amazing books and discovered some much-loved authors, but also came across some poorly written cringe-worthy titles as well – we all know they're out there! But this got me thinking that maybe I could give this a shot.

All I needed was an idea.

In October 2013, I visited a small town called Nannup in Western Australia's South West – and I fell in love. Everything about the town seemed idyllic to me, from the buildings, to the people, to the trees and the scenery. I thought it would make a wonderful setting for a romance novel. And, I swear, it was like a little cupid-esque writing fairy shot me with her arrow of inspiration. I suddenly knew that *I* would be the one to write a romance novel set in a town inspired by beautiful Nannup. The town had become my muse. I was drifting off – one giant step closer to achieving my dream.

INSOMNIA AND NIGHTMARES: WRITER'S BLOCK

Never having done any kind of creative writing before, I began jotting down a few notes and then started writing. The words flowed; I got excited – I was writing a novel. I wrote my way through my bullet points and ended up at around 30,000 words – not *quite* the length of a novel – but I had no idea what was supposed to come next.

Monique, meet Writer's Block.

At that point, I lost confidence and stopped writing. Staring at the computer screen with no idea how to proceed was depressing. I told myself I'd put it aside and come back to it again one day, when deep down a little voice was saying, *you have no idea what you're doing, you may as well give up.*

And I did.

For at least six months, I barely gave my writing a second's thought, until a link popped up in my social media feed: HarperCollins' The Wednesday Post. They were inviting unsolicited manuscripts from aspiring authors.

Hey, that's me! I thought.

Oh, how naïve.

I opened my manuscript document and started to read. It was cringe-worthy to say the least. But all I needed was a kick up the backside to open the document again. Re-reading gave me a focus and, having distanced myself from the work, I was able to see where I had gone wrong. I re-wrote parts and when I came to the place where I'd left off, I was able to form a clear idea of where I needed to take the story. I was off and racing once more, my fingers flying across the keyboard.

REMEMBERING YOUR DREAMS: TAKING YOUR WRITING SERIOUSLY

At this stage, I was working part-time as a teacher, so the summer holidays gave me the perfect opportunity to put my nose to the grindstone. The end was in sight – I'd mapped out the final quarter of the book and I knew where I needed to get to and how I was going to get there.

My confidence grew and I started to feel the need to seek out a writing community. I scoured the internet for writing groups and came across the Romance Writers of Australia (RWA). Almost immediately after I'd joined, I started reaping the benefits – I attended a marketing workshop and learnt about author branding, I received invaluable advice from fellow members, I entered competitions and got constructive feedback and, most importantly, I became part of a supportive community of like-minded writers.

Joining RWA gave me the confidence to start thinking of myself as a writer and not just any writer – a *romance* writer. I was proud of what I was doing. I still wasn't ready to declare myself to friends and family, but I knew that one day I would be ready. I just wanted to get that manuscript ready to submit first!

MAKING MEANING FROM YOUR DREAMS: SEEKING FEEDBACK

Luckily, surrounding myself with a community of writers taught me enough to complete the first draft – and rewrite most of it! But up until this point, not even my husband had been allowed to read a word of what I'd written. I kept my manuscript from view in the same way a vampire would shy away from the sun. Whenever someone would walk into the room, there would be a lot of hissing and flailing of arms attempting to protect the work in its infancy.

There came a time though, when I knew I needed fresh eyes on it. I knew the book wasn't perfect – far from it. But I was at my wits' end figuring out how to make it so and, quite frankly, I was sick of looking at it.

Handing my work over to beta readers was not as daunting as I expected. I'll admit, the first time I hit 'send' there were a few deep breaths and a bit of nail biting, but then it was a matter of sitting back and waiting for the comments to roll in.

If you're a writer seeking feedback from beta readers for the first time, you may find the idea of handing your work over to another writer incredibly daunting. Start simply – ask family and friends, but choose wisely. It's important to seek feedback from people you feel will be honest and not just tell you it's fabulous because they're afraid of hurting your feelings. Eventually though, you'll have to hand your work over to another writer – someone who knows the craft and can give you the technical, structural tips you need.

Another tip would be to choose people from a variety of backgrounds. My beta readers all bring a wealth of experience, which helps with different aspects of my manuscript. Consider their professions, reading preferences, and lifestyles. I sought out one of my beta readers because she lives in a small rural town and my novel is set in such a town. Never having experienced rural living, I wanted feedback on the authenticity of this aspect of my story; I needed to know if it was believable.

I would also suggest preparing questions for your beta readers. Think of areas where you are struggling, or where you want clarification that you're on the right track, and jot down some questions you would like them to consider. This will not only give them some guidance if they've never done this kind of thing before, but you'll get feedback that is useful to you. Also, ask for positive, as well as constructive, feedback. Although it's important to know where you're going wrong and need to improve, it's equally important to know what you're doing right and where you've impressed readers. Those positive comments will give you the motivation to keep going and help steer you in the right direction with the areas that don't work.

Once I started receiving feedback, I found it helpful to categorise it. Remember that it is only one reader's opinion and you don't need to take everything as gospel. However, if every reader mentions that the scene in which the cat manages to overpower the flesh-eating zombie is totally unbelievable and utter crap then you may need to take notice.

I categorise the feedback I receive by my reaction to it:
- *Yes! That's the answer I was looking for!* when the reader gives me a clear idea of how to address areas I've been struggling with.
- *Bloody good idea!* I love this kind of feedback because the suggestion can improve the story in a way I had never considered.

- *Nah, that won't work.* Sometimes a beta reader will mention something that I know just won't work or readers won't be interested in. This is where you need to remember one reader's opinion doesn't always mean you need to make changes.
- *Haha! You have no idea what you're talking about!* Occasionally a beta reader's background or experience will influence their feedback. For example, one of my male beta readers was confused by a certain physical reaction my heroine experienced when confronted with her hero. Obviously, never having experienced this, it was no wonder he'd been confused!

With a few drafts under my belt, I felt ready to pitch my manuscript to editors at the upcoming RWA conference I was planning to attend. I had a social media presence by this time, but felt it was time to give a boost to the number of my followers. What better way to do this than to come out of the writing closet! I made an announcement on my personal Facebook page, letting my friends and family know that I was a writer and that I'd written a book I planned to pitch to publishers in less than a month. My author Facebook page received more than five hundred likes in less than two days, but even more exciting for me were the messages of support and encouragement from the people I cared about. It gave me the strength I needed to walk into that pitching room, that's for sure!

The experience of that first conference was incredible – I had expected to have a good time, learn loads and meet a great bunch of people, but what I got out of it was so much more – and that's pretty impressive for someone who finds crowds and meeting new people exhausting. The RWA did an amazing job in preparing and supporting new conference attendees.

At the conference Gala Awards Dinner, I was seated with a wonderful group of fellow newbies. We got on so well, we decided to form our own critique/support group. Despite being from all over Australia (and one inspiring individual living overseas), we use a Facebook group page to keep in touch and support each other through writing highs and lows. It's so valuable to be connected with people who understand the creative challenges you face.

I had a few pitch appointments scheduled during the conference and preparing for these helped me to get a clear idea of what my story was about. The appointments themselves were interesting – a group of about eight writers arrived at the pitching room, had their name checked off a list and the location of their designated editor clearly explained, before waiting nervously for their chance to pitch. They watched as other writers emerged from the pitching room looking victorious or overwhelmed, or as if a great weight had been lifted from their shoulders. Then, after a short break, the next group was herded into the room for an adrenaline-filled five minutes to 'wow' their chosen editor.

My two pitch appointments were both successful. This meant that I could send my manuscript direct to the editors and avoid the 'slush pile'. Post-conference, however, I started to panic – I had learned so much during the workshops that I felt overwhelmed. How on earth was I going to incorporate it all into my manuscript in a suitable time frame without the editors losing interest?

I'm ashamed to say I didn't do justice to my newfound knowledge. I gave my baby one last polish and sent it out into the world. I couldn't stand to look at it any more – unable to formulate any kind of plan with everything running through my head, I felt I couldn't improve the manuscript any further without help. Perhaps I should have sought the advice of a freelance editor, but still, I didn't want to waste the opportunities the pitches provided.

Now all that was left to do was watch my inbox constantly for reply emails.

SWEET DREAMS: PUBLICATION!

There was no point twiddling my thumbs though. After staring at the same manuscript for two years, I took the opportunity to submit to Serenity Press's 2015 *Rocky Romance* anthology. The call was for romantic stories set in Rockingham, Western Australia, a seaside city close to where I live, so I was again inspired by setting – the beautiful landscape that is Rockingham foreshore. Writing a new story about new characters in a new setting was exhilarating, and it was clear to me how much my writing had improved. The experience did wonders for my confidence, particularly when my submission of *A Healing Hand* was accepted for the anthology and there were plans for it to eventually be released as a single title.

Publication was a surreal experience. I had thought I would be most excited to see my name in print, but it turns out that seeing my words on the page, the story *I* had created, was more exhilarating than I had ever imagined. There was also the knowledge that people were going to be reading my work. Many people I knew were purchasing their copies of *Rocky Romance* and telling me how much they had enjoyed *A Healing Hand*, but I also saw the book in the hands of complete strangers. That was a bizarre feeling! To know that people I had never met were going to be reading my work – now I *really* felt like an author!

THE ULTIMATE DREAM: MY NAME, MY NOVEL

A while after submitting my manuscript to the two editors I pitched to at the conference, I received every writer's rite of passage – my first rejections. Both editors, however, gave good feedback; one in particular was very constructive, for which I was incredibly grateful. It gave me some specific things to work on and I am told not every rejecting editor will take the time to provide feedback in this way. I had received a 'positive rejection'.

You will recall from my daydreaming years, that what I've always really wanted was my name on the front cover of a book. So, although I've experienced the sweet dreams of publication, I'm still hoping to achieve my ultimate dream.

It's back to the drawing board. What am I going to do with that manuscript, I hear you ask? Well, I plan on enrolling in some courses that will help me learn the craft and the skills involved in editing. I recently attended the 'Plotting and Deep POV Masterclass' run by Natasha Lester and Lisa Chaplin. It was fabulous – I have already found a plot hole in my story!

As a former teacher, I understand the importance of taking responsibility for one's own learning and that's what I plan on doing. Nobody else can make my dreams come true, and I intend to work hard to make them a reality.

FIVE TIPS FROM MONIQUE HALL

1.   **Join a writing community:** Nobody knows the creative challenges you face like other writers.
2.   **Ask for feedback – and be specific:** Focus on those aspects of the manuscript you are struggling with.
3.   **Learn to take criticism:** You will need thick skin if you're going to make it as a writer.
4.   **Take responsibility for your own learning:** Be pro-active: take courses, attend workshops, ask questions.
5.   **Commit yourself:** Self-doubt, confusion and frustration will be your constant companions, but if being a writer is your dream, set your sights and work hard to make it your reality.

Writing Historical Fiction

by Anna Jacobs

THIS book is about 'writing the dream' and yes, you do need a dream (and a really compelling one, too) in order to become a writer. But you also have to realise that it takes time to learn to write books good enough to get published. You not only have to learn your craft, and writing novels is a very complex one, but you have to develop a practical and business-like approach to writing and understand how the industry functions.

Let's face it, you need an enormous amount of passion, patience and persistence to do all this!

There's a lot of hard work goes into publication, but storytelling itself is fascinating, so most people enjoy the journey. Be warned – it's addictive. Nearly two thousand years ago, the Roman poet Juvenal (active in the late first and early second centuries) called it 'the insatiable itch of writing' – note, not 'itch to write'! I feel that's as true for writers today as it was then.

I have more than seventy novels published, and I've written and been published in several genres: historical, romance, modern, fantasy, science fiction. But I've written more historical stories than anything else and when I started out, that was all I was aiming to write. I'm therefore concentrating on historical fiction in this article.

I believe historical stories run the whole gamut from serious historical novels to what I call 'costume drama', where very modern sounding characters run around wearing old-fashioned clothes and behaving in a thoroughly modern manner. The historical detail in costume drama can be rather minimal, but such stories can be gripping reads if done well.

At the other end of the spectrum are dry-as-dust historical stories loaded with far too much information. Most of these don't keep the reader well enough entertained, even if the facts are deeply and thoroughly researched.

So how do you go about creating a story that is true to the history and the people of a particular era, but so engrossing that readers can't put it down? Ah, there's the challenge. Good luck in your search for your own path.

If you're looking for a series of rules, you'll have to look elsewhere. There's only one as far as I'm concerned: produce a wonderful story with vivid characters.

Here are a few random thoughts which may help you along the way.

CHOOSE YOUR PERIOD IN HISTORY CAREFULLY

I think the first thing is to decide which period interests you most. You can't cover the whole of history if you're going to research it properly, and since readers have favourite periods, they look for authors who write in that era, not authors who zip around the whole historical spectrum.

I, for instance, won't read novels set in the French Revolution. Why not? Because I studied it interminably at both school and university, and didn't find it interesting in the first place. Nor do I enjoy reading about heads being chopped off. That's just a personal quirk, of course. Other readers love the era and don't mind wading through piles of heads.

When I decided I wanted to write historical novels, I found a suitable part-time history unit at the University of Western Australia. The year's course covered English History from 1750 to 1950 approximately. I took that single unit 'not for degree purposes' (I already had a Master's Degree in other subjects) but because I wanted the knowledge it offered.

The lecturer was excellent and the course gave me a solid foundation for my future career, and with it, training in doing research 'properly'. Both necessities, as far as I'm concerned.

I've written novels set from 1730 to the present day, and for each one I've had to do extra research into the relevant details, but that course gave me a solid foundation to build on. I have no interest in delving into other eras. Those years are eventful enough to give me plots for three lifetimes!

How did I choose which historical period to use? Partly my own love of the era and partly for business reasons such as what readers prefer and what sells most books. I am unashamedly commercially-minded. One needs to earn money to live on.

I was reading widely anyway, as I'm an avid reader with a three novel a week 'habit'. But as well as enjoying most of the stories I read, I began to analyse what eras and historical topics other novelists have focused on. Similar plots came up again and again, so I decided to avoid that type of story and setting.

Why was I so certain this was the right thing to do? Because a senior Australian editor once told me that every time she saw a manuscript with a heroine transported to Australia in the convict era after being wrongly accused of a crime, she felt like throwing up. In other words, it had been done to death.

So I looked for fresh 'corners of history' and I found most of them in the research books I read. Some of the books made gripping reading, while others were tedious but full of information I valued. I did whatever I had to.

I took careful notes each time I found what might be a new idea. Some of them I kept in an ideas file for more than twenty years before writing about them. My ideas file is still growing.

As an example of applying this approach to a series I was planning, I took a preliminary look at the history of the music hall. The two areas of England where music halls were most popular when they were just starting up were Lancashire and London. I specialise in books set in Lancashire, where I grew up, and I hadn't seen any novels about the early days of music halls there, so this topic seemed worth looking into more carefully.

But the scenario that a poor heroine makes her fortune by her beautiful voice has been used so many times I was determined not to go there, even for minor characters.

In the very early days of the music hall, there were no fancy theatres, just singing rooms attached to pubs. And my heroine couldn't sing a note in tune. She was working in the catering side of the music room, because the law at that time said you could only have music in a pub if you were serving food.

The first book in this series was her story mainly. To my great delight *Pride of Lancashire* won an award, the Australian Romantic Book of the Year.

In the end I wrote four books set against the early music hall background. Another heroine ran an animal act because her voice wasn't strong enough to be a singer in the days before electricity and microphones.

---

*You see what I mean? Find a new twist, don't follow
the same old plot trail.*

ORGANISE YOUR RESEARCH NOTES FOR EASY RETRIEVAL

Information has to be gathered to write historical stories. Once you've researched a specific topic, such as early photography, World War I, suffragettes, or whatever, you should keep your notes carefully. Well, you should if you intend to write for many years.

I know you can find all sorts of information online, but how much easier is it to gather it all in a folder the first time (whether on your computer or on paper) and have the whole topic ready if needed again?

Indeed, you should beware of too much easy dependence on the Internet. First you have to make sure your site and its authority on historical matters are good, and that the site owner knows what they are talking about. And even when you find good information, some sites change their content over the years and remove topics completely. Then you'd have to start finding the information all over again.

So it's no use just bookmarking a site. You need to grab useful information and keep it safe.

MAKE SURE YOUR HISTORY IS AN INTEGRAL PART OF YOUR STORY

If you create characters who fit into the period and you choose a story/plot which could only have taken place in that period, you can give your readers a rich experience that will bring history to life for them. People love to find out about daily life in the past and often relate it to their grandmothers or to family stories and legends.

Your characters can't always have a modern, politically correct attitude to life if you do this properly. However, if you read biographies and autobiographies from your period, you'll see what exceptional men and women did in the past to push the envelope of their world – far more than you'd think. So you've a fair amount of freedom.

Just after World War I, for instance, was a fascinating period where women had come out of the kitchen and were not always willing to be pushed back into it when the men returned from war. And it was the period where women got the vote – at last! I wrote *Tomorrow's Promises* and *Yesterday's Girl* about women of that time who refused to be sent back to the kitchen.

Really, the historical background is like another character in your story. Your particular plot simply could not have happened in any other era. Otherwise why is it a historical novel at all?

AVOID INFO-DUMPING

Do not stuff your story so full of historical facts it reads like a lesson in school. Embed historical 'titbits' in the action, one here, another there. But don't shove whole 'meals' into the story and make your readers' eyes glaze over with boredom.

Mention something casually in passing, choosing only relevant or interesting historical information and occasional details about daily life. Otherwise your characters will fade into the background and your story will lose pace. Good pace is vital if you're to keep your reader interested.

Find some favourite authors and see how they've managed to colour in the historical backdrop to their stories. It's not just a matter of long skirts for the ladies and riding around in carriages!

COLLECT INFORMATION FROM THE ERA

I believe you can learn more accurately about what life was really like in the past by looking at old items and listening to people from that era. These people were there, living it. Historians weren't. Wonderful as they are, historians inevitably filter the information before you get it.

Don't wait till you need material – always keep an eye open for potential sources. I've picked up a lot of useful books in second-hand shops and markets, or from online retailers. And though I've paid a lot for some rather special books, I've mostly bought at bargain prices. I've also picked up interesting booklets in tourist bureaux or village shops in the UK and Australia.

I enjoy reading biographies and autobiographies, but the best and most useful ones for my purposes have been self-published by amateurs. Some of them are stapled booklets with limp coloured card covers. Badly typed and photocopied pages can be so crammed with words and old photos that you have trouble finding your way through them. But oh my, they can be a rich and wonderful source of real-life information! And I bless the writers and compilers many times as I use the information.

Auntie Mabel's War: An Account of Her Part in the Hostilities of 1914-18, for instance, is based on material and diaries compiled by Mabel herself, who went overseas as a nurse in World War I and didn't much fancy returning to the restrictions of her family life afterwards. Her family kept the material for decades till chance got a publisher interested.

What do your characters wear? History of fashion research books do just that: show you what was high fashion at the time. In their everyday lives people do not wear high fashion. Well, do you? I certainly don't.

When I first started writing in the 1980s, I had trouble finding out about working class women's clothing in the early 19th century because historians seemed to have avoided focusing on women's history. I had to hunt high and low for relevant material.

I could go on, but I have stories to write. I hope these thoughts of mine will be of help to those wishing to write historical fiction. Off to join my heroine …

FIVE TIPS FROM ANNA JACOBS

1. Above all, if you're unpublished, realise that for most people it takes more than one novel written to reach a professional standard, preferably three or four. My best advice ever to writers is to complete a book, polish it and then set it aside and write another story. When you've set No 2 aside, come back to No 1 and read it again. Trust me, you'll see so much you can improve on with your extra skills as a writer. Do this again and again if necessary until publication results. I'd not advise anyone to self-publish their first book before they've written several.

2. Work out where your chosen era sits on the historical fiction landscape and what style of books are expected by readers (and therefore editors) who love that area, especially look at word count and plot complexity. It's a simple equation: the longer the book, the more complex the plot needs to be.

3. Go to the nearest large bookshop and study recent historical novels and check out as many authors as you can at your local library. Find what topics have been done to death. Only you can do this research so that you can work out how and where to make a niche for yourself.

4. Realise that your first completed version of a story will only be a 'dirty draft'. It will need a lot of work and polishing before it's really finished and ready to submit. Hopefully the more writing you do, the less polishing you'll need. But you'll always need to do some. You're competing with other writers for an editor who will give your book the nod out of the hundreds submitted. You need your manuscript to sparkle.

5. People learn to write by writing. It's an activity. Sure, you'll find it helpful to attend a few courses and workshops, but they won't teach you to write your own stories because there are no magic tricks to be learned. A swimmer reaches Olympic standards by untold hours of practice. It's the same for writers. You reach publication standard by writing, writing, and then writing some more.

The Accidental

Writer

by Kylie Kaden

UNTIL my first book was sold to Random House, writing was my secret: a file on my laptop, something I did for me in between the morning rush and afternoon hum of raising my sticky brood of boys. I didn't think much of it at first. Writing started out as a housework-avoidance strategy; a sanity preserver as the only female in a house of males. It's cheap, quiet, and can be done anywhere in yoghurt-stained pyjamas. You can do it breastfeeding, on the bench at swimming lessons – you can even do it in your head while burning risotto. I enjoyed every minute.

I never thought anyone would *read* the damn stuff.

It's true; I didn't set out to write a book. I'd never done a workshop or read a how-to-guide. In fact, on maternity leave with my third son, I was flat out finding the time to read a book, let alone write one. But calm coursed through me when I wrote. Time raced by when I was with my imaginary friends. It was liberating: they asked nothing of me, and gave so much in return.

So I'd write in the left overs of my life. The gaps. The twenty minutes here or there when no-one noticed me escape the real world. The scribbled idea on the back of a receipt whilst jostling for a seat on the train. That hour of think-time in the morning before the whinge-fest commenced over *who ate whose toast*, and 'Where's your library book?'

The process lacked any continuity and planning (I'd cut a paragraph, defer 'World War III', and return to find I'd forgotten where I was pasting it). But it's the piece of the day I owned. The 'peace' that was only for me.

After a few months, my secret file grew. When no-one was watching, I would skulk away to my laptop (sometimes in the laundry so I couldn't be found), and purge out the product of the day's fermented thoughts.

Eventually I came clean, and told my husband my dirty secret (to explain the dirty house). He was not surprised; writing novels about quirky, flawed characters combined two great interests of mine – psychology and fiction. I realised then that my love of words was nothing new; life had just gotten in the way of our relationship.

It's fair to say that growing up, I was an *indoor* girl. I couldn't draw, or paint or dance or sing, but I breezed through English and always had a sense that I could find the right words in any situation. I was the girl who'd ride her bike to the library on a Saturday morning to return home with the wicker basket brimming with books; the one asked to stop writing during journal time after 'little lunch'. As a kid I wrote a diary, as a teen I devoured books. At university I considered journalism, but my fascination with human motivation and emotion – my drive to understand relationships and the role we play in them – led to an honours degree in psychology (oblivious to the fact that it would become a great foundation for creating flawed characters).

Yet I was still fascinated by the power of language, how word selection influenced people's perceptions and emotions. Words are powerful.

My mum always said I'd write a book (and when I did, I dedicated it to her for believing I could). When I was a teenager, she took me to see my favourite author. As I slid my dog-eared copy of *Watermelon* across the table for signing, I squeaked out: 'I'd love to write a book, but don't think I have a clue where to begin'. In her guttural Irish accent, Marian Keyes looked up and said: 'Don't think; just start.'

And so twenty years, two degrees, and three children later – with only a vague premise in my mind and a clunky keyboard at my fingers – I did just that.

I can't say I had any light bulb moments in terms of plot – it evolved on the page. I was clueless. I didn't even know what 'genre' it was, for a while. Did I have to put it in a box? Good books are as multifaceted as people. You just know you like them, whatever they're called. But apparently a clear genre helps readers find it in stores (but I figured- if it's good enough they'd find it easily with the bestsellers).

I had the vague intention of having two equally important story arcs – the second chance at love for Frankie and Jack, and the unpacking of the mystery of what happened to their friend Kate (who disappeared thirteen years earlier on a beach during schoolies – an Australian tradition where high-school graduates have week-long breaks after their final exams). Structurally, it was a brain-bender – many whiteboard markers and Post-It notes were sacrificed as I interwove scenes from two parallel stories, linking the action from when Kate went missing to the residual emotional baggage the characters carried, and unpacked together as adults. This sounds very intentional, but most of this was discovered in hindsight. I was winging it most of the time. E. L. Doctorow once said words to the effect that writing a novel is like driving at night – 'You can see only as far as your headlights, but you can make the whole trip that way.' That was very much my experience.

I taught myself. I'd write in scenes (and completely out of order). I purged whatever inspired me at the time (figuring – if I'm not feeling it, neither will readers). I started with a point – to create a red-herring, to invoke sympathy for a character – and imagined the best scenario to demonstrate it. I'd make sure each beat of the story changed the protagonist's mental state in some way, and the overall conflict raised a question that is resolved in a later scene. These concepts became my litmus tests.

I've since read endless articles and blogs on writing (subconsciously hoping they'd provide a 'magic button' that I only need press to reveal the secret way to get published) and found a lot of prescriptive rules and endless high-brow talk on character arcs, turning points and sub-themes.

It sounded so procedural for something fundamentally creative (and a lot of it was just hoity-toity words for things I'd picked up intuitively anyway). But as a clueless-wannabe-writer with a good smattering of self-doubt, I clung to advice like life-rafts, only to find much of the well-meaning suggestions drowned me. My plot became formulaic. I forced scenes to subscribe to some deeper theme (a good writer has a point, right?). Characters lost their quirks to fit into carefully constructed profiles.

The so-called 'rules' sapped the originality from the page.

It was about then that I realised, while I had very little knowledge on the technical points of writing fiction, I was an experienced *reader*. One of the greatest joys of my life was finding characters that wormed their way into my head. Books that refused to let me put them down. For me, characters I care about always trump plot. So that (and not the frightful technicalities) became my bar; create characters you worry about, and a story that compels you to stay. To keep readers reading. To place those pesky words in that magical order to make people turn the pages, and keep turning them.

It took a while, but I gradually discovered why some bits sucked, and others didn't – and put it down to a few basics: 'Show it, don't say it', using active language, chopping unnecessary words and being mindful of the all-important cadence – the rhythm of each phrase, the pattern in each paragraph.

It was about six months after I started writing, when I spent more free time with imaginary friends than real ones, that I realised I needed to justify it somehow. My ego started to crave a signal, some form of validation that 'someone with cred' (outside my gene pool) thought I could write. So I did what any clueless person with no connections does: I googled.

I had just devoured *The Light Between Oceans* by M.L. Stedman — a Random House bestseller. I figured, being the biggest publisher in the world, they'd be more inclined to take a risk (on a no-name mum from the 'burbs) than a boutique printer, and figured that was a great place to begin.

I'd start at the top, and reject my way down.

I had no agent, but was surprised to find most publishers accept unsolicited manuscripts directly. I just had to go through the 'slush pile'. I'd read the horror stories that less than one per cent of unknown authors are published, and that you need an agent to even be read (they don't call it 'slush' for nothing). I'd meet experienced, talented writers on their fifth book, still without a contract or representation. Why would I be any different?

My expectations couldn't have been lower.

It was about then — with the help of the Queensland Writers Centre website — that I realised I was in need of a strange beast called a 'query letter'. The guide advised to include all previous publication success (squat), writing awards (diddly) and connections I had to assist marketing strategies (my mum wants two copies, at least!).

This was going to be a rather short letter.

On a mission to rectify this (to find *someone* who thought *something* I wrote was worth the ink), I madly bashed together a few rants about the realities (and mayhem) of parenting, and became *My Child Magazine*'s new columnist. My confidence grew. I was overwhelmed when readers took time out of their day to write about how my articles made them feel less alone in the daily grind.

On a roll, I threw my hat in the ring for the Romance Writers of Australia's (RWA) selling synopsis competition. It was written in first person to mimic the voice of the book and I was oblivious to how unorthodox that was, that you *just don't do that*. Well I did. And I was a finalist.

Perhaps I was up for this after all. *What did I have to lose?* While I've never much been one for silly rules, I knew some things weren't negotiable. It had to adhere to submission guidelines. It had to be polished. It had to be my best: you only get one crack at a first impression. So I read my manuscript countless times; editing, restructuring, cutting and polishing so much that I could recite the damn thing verbatim. I was so 'bored' (having figured out what happened to the missing girl many, many renditions ago …). I started to prefer the newer sections (not because they were any less sucky, but because I had only read them twelve times, not twenty-six), before I realised I was reading from cached memory – recalling the words, not seeing them. I'd lost all perspective.

It was time to come out of the closet. I subjected my inner circle to the drafts. Through the RWA's critique partner scheme, I paired up with the wonderful Lily Malone and took on her feedback. I gave it the 'drawer treatment', allowed things to ferment and made some final adjustments with the fresh eye that only distance provides. At last, it felt done. At least, that's what I tell people. (*Is it ever 'done', or are we just done with it?*)

So I sent off fifty pages. My query letter. My rebellious first-person synopsis.

Submission guidelines indicated a response time of six to nine months (yes – you can make a human in the same time). Nevertheless, my heart still fluttered with every 'ping' from my phone, every envelope icon on my taskbar. I tried to forget my little story … out in the world on its own … smothered under a mountain of unopened slush … wondering if I should have … oh, to heck with it.

I started on my next work in progress.

A fortnight later I had a contract. A few days after submitting, Random House requested the full manuscript, before the (jaw-dropping/face-hurt-from-smiling-so-hard) moment an offer to publish arrived, of all places, in the *junk mail*.

I was gobsmacked (not only by the offer, but how close I came to trashing it). My eyes raced through the unbelievable words: *'impressed this is your first novel'* … *'beautifully crafted characters'* … *'palpable romantic tension'* … *'to be sold in stores across the country'*.

I wondered if it was all just an elaborate practical joke. I was plagued by the sense that I wasn't entitled; that I hadn't paid my dues – that they'd change their mind.

But they didn't.

Other than a new title (and the removal of a few hundred commas that I needlessly sent to their deaths), very little changed (plot-wise, at least) from manuscript to 'first pages'. Like some famous person, I was allocated a dedicated publicist, editor, copy-editor, proof-reader and marketing team. Radio and magazine interviews, writers' conferences and blog tours were strategically scheduled for the April release. I was fascinated by the process, and grateful for the chance to be part of it.

After submitting in July 2013, my first novel, *Losing Kate*, was published ten months later (right in time for Mother's Day – a huge sales period for women's fiction). I soon learnt that *Losing Kate* was the first manuscript plucked from the slush-pile in Beverly Cousins' twenty-five-year career as a leading publisher.

They say launching a book feels a little like when your children leave home; you did your best and hope you brought them up right – even though you know they won't get on with everyone. April 1 arrived. My debut reached number one in contemporary fiction on the iBooks bestseller list (almost entirely due to some limelight as one of April's books of the month – having eyeballs at a point-of-sale does wonders). I took a screen shot of it, of course – adamant it would drop into the nether within seconds.

Reviews were overwhelmingly positive. I was stoked.

Translation rights were also snapped up by another major publisher, Ullstein Buchverlage (based in Berlin) at the Frankfurt Book Fair the same year, and I went on to become a finalist in both the Australian Romance Readers Association and AusRom Today Reader's Best New Author awards. It seemed readers did want to discover *what really happened to Kate*.

I recommend to anyone who publishes a book to celebrate the moment (even if you feel 'big-notey', even if you feel like a fraud – you're not). I still feel like I'm impersonating a real author even after countless author talks and book signings. You'd be surprised how many authors feel the same.

A book launch also feels like a farewell, a last hurrah to the characters that have stowed away in your brain for the last year. An exorcism, of sorts, as they make way for a new bunch of imaginary friends.

Now my 'secret' leads a simple life, sitting pretty on my bookshelf with only a thin, glossy-jacket to keep her 12-point-Bembo-font warm. It was amazing to imagine my little story was out in the world, keeping people up at night, and I will be forever grateful to Random's Lex and Bev, and my wonderful readers who breathed life into Frankie and Jack's story. I'm also indebted to my supportive husband, who never once doubted my story would become a 'proper book' (and forgave the messy house …), along with my parents for instilling both a love for words and belief in myself. But I've often wondered what was it about me, about my writing, that made it rise to the top of that pile. There's as much luck on the road to publication as there is talent and determination. But if I had to pick one thing I believe you need to stand out, it's got something to do with voice.

Finding a writer's voice sounds hard. Like a windswept voyage one must take involving a hip-flask and walking stick. I travelled no such arduous journey, suffice to say finding my voice was a short and fluky ride. For me, writing is an unconscious, gut instinct most of the time. The all-important 'voice' is the relationship you have with your reader. What makes the work distinct. So how can that be anything but raw, essentially you? Hone your craft, consider structure and pace, research your setting. But voice? It's within you. It's organic. It's the one thing most susceptible to being 'lost in translation' – kind of like *soul*. Like the core of the onion after all the layers are stripped away (layers like the way someone said you *should* write, the word that *sounds* cleverest …).

Be brave. Say the things people want to know but are too scared to ask. Don't try to emulate anyone else or please everyone – readers yearn for honesty: a different spin on the well-trodden plot; the quirky turn of phrase; the off-beat observation; the slightly-insane interpretation of a common scene. I believe these little nuances make fiction shine. If it's not working, you may just be trying too hard.

Not all writers are published, and even fewer make a living from it. But what the coveted writer's life lacks in terms of bank balance, it makes up for in life balance. We've all got families and day jobs and chores – those pebbles in the glass jar of life – but even if your essentials are boulders, they all have curves and crevices that grains of sand can meander through – if you let them. (C'mon, reality television should be easy to ditch – you could just about write a book in the ad breaks alone!) But jars, as with life, are not infinite.

I'm no Wonder Woman. My children's drawers have been replaced by a perpetual pile of unfolded washing. My house often looks like it's just been burgled. The wheels fall off on a daily basis, so it can be hard to keep that lid on. And sometimes, it just doesn't seem like there's anything left to give. But without that sand, that little something for yourself, that glass jar of life can seem like a bunch of rocks weighing you down, and leave you feeling empty. If you feel off balance, if you just don't feel like *you* if you haven't written, then you know you are a writer.

So writers, keep finding the time to do what you love, and don't give up. The least you'll end up with is time well spent, and a more balanced life.

I write in the corners of my life, but I enjoy every minute of it, and thank all of my supporters for making it possible for me to keep writing, and to keep mustering those precious stolen moments and use them up on something I love.

FIVE TIPS FROM KYLIE KADEN

1. **Persevere:** You know the one thing all published books have in common? They were finished.
2. **Find your pack:** When instincts fail, craft takes over. That's when you need support.
3. **Read:** Read *lots*. Even dissecting the bad books helps, as you (a) notice (and feel clever) and (b) feel better about your own work.
4. **Treat advice like a smorgasbord:** Taste it all, but only revisit the bits you like.
5. **Readers aren't idiots:** The best way to make them invest is to leave a gap to fill. The hardest (but most valuable) thing to learn is subtlety.

From Freelance to Fiction

by Rebecca Laffar-Smith

IT'S strange, the journey of a lifetime. We start as dreamers, imagining a distant future in the world of today, unable to see the world of tomorrow. Life takes its turns and, through it all, we wonder if we're set on the right course. Will we get there? Will it be worth it when we do? I could never have imagined the path of my life; I just knew I was always meant to tell great stories. I knew there was nothing else that filled me up like creating wonder from words.

I was six years old when I knew I wanted to be a writer. Aspiring to be a princess, or a doctor, or a mermaid was far too normal as far as hopes and dreams go for a child. Instead, I wanted to spend my life making up stories and immersing myself in language. I'm not sure how conscious a thought it was. I'm not sure if my six-year-old self knew what it was to be a writer, but I put words on paper with passion. My first poem was two simple lines. I remember them to this day and still feel a strange connection to the couplet:

*'Little whispering flower, stand tall and make a shout,
let everything around you, know that you're about.'*

Even at six, I knew that words were a powerful way to leave a lasting mark on the world. A writer has a gift that can transform lives. They create characters who linger in readers' hearts. They imagine worlds that entice readers into their wonder. They shape stories that alter the way readers see reality. I knew, for me, words were the way I could connect with people. I spent a lot of my childhood in a world of my own. I wrote words that no one saw but would someday shape the life I wanted to lead.

As years passed, I grew brave in the fearless way of a creative child. Children have a youthful exuberance. They have the freedom of knowing so little that they don't know the mistakes they are making. Such innocence allows them to take chances and to run heedless into the next adventure. When we reward effort and foster passion, early exploration can lead to masterful things. I had the thankful joy of a supportive mother. I was also emboldened by the positive reinforcement of an early primary teacher. With the encouragement of both, I submitted poetry to anthologies and competitions. By the time I was twelve I'd become an internationally published, award-winning poet.

Poetry is another gateway; like fiction, it has the power to transform. Poetry can shape the minds and hearts of readers. It does so in crystal fragments of exotic literary art. Poetry requires an economy of words. Through poetry, I discovered that every word is unique. There is a fundamental and core difference between 'glisten' and 'shine'. The thesaurus lies; there are no synonyms. But I also learned that language has rhythm and cadence. It dances on the tongue, and in the mind, of the reader.

Alas, as I grew older, I learnt that poets don't tend to make a living writing poetry. There are competitions to enter; anthologies requesting submissions; and, in rare cases, collections published. There are wonderful circles of talented poets who write for the love of language and the beauty of words. As I looked ahead to an independent future I wanted more than that. I didn't want to work a 'day job' forever. I wanted words to be my bread and butter.

Thankfully, a love of language can allow significant breadth. Words exist beyond poetry. I played at story, and wrote 'novels' with abandon, but there seemed to be so much more I hadn't tried. So began an exploration into the many facets of a written world.

Professional writers work in many fields. We often think of writers as book authors. What we don't think about is that video games, movies, and television have writers, too. Magazines publish feature articles, but they also publish tips and filler. Corporations publish white papers. Students and researchers publish academic papers. Businesses need writers for advertising and promotional media. Newspapers and radio have press writers and journalists. And, in an age where the Internet was coming into every home, I discovered the 'net was a void waiting for words. I discovered the busy world of copywriting, and life transformed again.

I was eighteen when I earned my first dime from words that I had put on a page for pay. It was just a single dime; ten American cents. The value of that coin was worth even less because of exchange rates and taxes, but I felt on top of the world. To me, that first dime meant something significant. I was a paid, professional writer.

There is a transitionary mindset when you change from writing as a hobby to writing as a professional. There are dangers, but also joy and significant power in owning the 'professional' title. It becomes more than an identity of the heart; it becomes something you can proclaim.

For many writers, particularly those of us who write books, it can be hard to make that mindset shift. It can be difficult to transition from identifying as a 'writer' to being an 'author'. Sometimes, we even struggle to own the 'writer' title in public. A dangerous, limiting psychology can hold us back from declaring ourselves. A phenomenal empowerment comes from moving away from insecurity and owning your passion. When I felt that shift, I wanted to cling to it.

Unfortunately, other people can have a poisoning effect on our confidence and security. When I told my partner I had earned income as a writer, he asked, 'How much?' He was, unsurprisingly, underwhelmed. For me, I knew that dime was a launching point. I earned per page view and I knew those dimes would accumulate. Still, his reaction tainted the experience. For a long time, I retreated, not wanting to share my bliss with the people I cared about.

Fortunately, there is a wonderful community of writers online. My heart bounced back as I surrounded myself with friends who understood what it was to be a writer. Over the years, my life as a writer has continued to transition. I move on from some circles and find new tribes. Through the support, encouragement, and advice of my writing community I continue to grow. The writing community gave me the courage to keep writing.

That first article was the beginning of an adventure in freelance writing. Freelancing is a marvellous way of gaining a great deal of experience in paid fields of writing. A freelancer is an independent contractor who takes on jobs for clients. You get to pick and choose the work you do, you set your own rate, and you work your own hours, but it's not all bliss.

For the next twelve years, I experienced the hills and valleys of an uncertain income. I faced the insecurity of an economy prone to recession. Some jobs pay better than others. Some need more hours than imagined. In the end, I found I did less and less creative writing as I strove to keep food on the table. The pay was better in editing, and better still in web design. The skills required for both were more specialised, and professional competition more limited. It was a time when I published a lot of words that never wore my name. I edited a lot of words written by other people. I created business foundations and brands for corporations that were next to faceless.

There were wonderful experiences over those years, too. Some of my most memorable jobs include:

- Writing a memorial poem for a retiring school teacher, much loved by her pupils.

- Helping an English as a Second Language (ESL) student pass his British university studies. (I helped him use correct English conventions in his academic work. The research and material were all his own. It was fascinating to learn from the wonderful academic essays and reports he wrote.)

- Editing a poetry anthology full of poems themed around empowering women.
- Designing websites that helped friends and fellow writers launch their careers or businesses. (This includes a website that helped a young mother with an ill, premature infant. We raised funds needed to afford accommodation near her son's life-saving hospital.)

There were rewarding days, and a lot of hard work, but the uncertain income was hard on our family. More and more I was taking jobs for the money they paid rather than the value they held in my heart. The hours I worked to keep food on the table were too demanding. I felt disheartened and exhausted. Bouts of depression, related to Bipolar disorder, were taking a toll in my unbalanced life. I rarely worked the jobs I loved because I was so desperate just to make it day-by-day. I yearned to write fiction, but lacked enough hours in the day to give myself that gift. Freelancing had become soul-destroying and I had no means of refilling my creative cup.

Through those years, I had become a single mother. My youngest child struggled with emotional and academic challenges related to undiagnosed disabilities. Not only did I need to look after myself, I knew I had to give up something so I could be there for my son. After months of struggle, I conceded defeat. I needed to give up on my dream of being a professional writer so I could be the mother my children needed me to be.

Thus began two years when I exchanged freelancing for full-time online study. I dedicated time to my family and secretly stole spare minutes to write fiction.

Over the course of that first year, I spent more time with my son. The challenges my son faced inspired interest in early childhood education. Those interests led me to switch from a Bachelor of Arts to a Bachelor of Education. Again, my life transformed.

Through my studies, I could see the challenges my son faced. I knew that, despite the 'specialists' insisting he would be fine, he wasn't. There was something more they were missing. From Kindergarten through Year Two, we had battled tearful meltdowns every school day. His teachers assured me he calmed when I left, but I lingered to hear him cry for twenty minutes after I'd 'gone'. It felt wrong, but I trusted that his teachers knew what they were talking about. Then, his cries turned silent, and that was worse than the anger and noise.

It felt like a ghost had replaced my son. He walked through the world but did not see it. He shut down. As I learned more about the human brain through my university studies, I recognised that he had given up. It was heartbreaking to see the defeat in him. I did not know the extent of his hopelessness then, but I could feel the wrongness in what had happened. Things needed to change. His experience of the world needed to transform. I needed to get my son back.

Through Early Childhood Education, I learnt that his stress was not conducive to learning. I also developed confidence that *I* could give him the one-on-one attention he needed. So, we made the next big leap in the structure of our family life. I stepped back from my university studies and committed to home-schooling my son.

One might imagine home-schooling would demand more time and energy than anything else. The opposite was true.

My daughter had good friends and loved school, so our school routine stayed much the same. But, from the day I announced that my son would not be returning to school, a weight lifted from his shoulders. The light in him began to shine again. Over the following year, we bonded more than ever before. Having his stress removed, lifted my own to a significant degree, and we found a rhythm in life.

We experienced fewer meltdowns and shutdowns. I started to recognise his thresholds. I learnt how to guide his learning and development. I began to see and understand him in a way I had never done before. What I saw was eye-opening. My son was Autistic. I couldn't understand why his teachers, psychologists, doctors, and therapists had not discovered it. I became his champion and I fought for his rights. I fought to be heard. When specialists told me I didn't know what I was talking about I challenged them to prove it, and I won.

Our home-school journey was the beginning of a transformational experience in publishing. One of my son's greatest challenges has always been with language. Dyslexia coupled with Autism led to his being primarily non-verbal and illiterate. The negative reinforcement he faced in school gave him a hatred of anything bookish. And he wasn't wrong to hate the books. For the most part, the early readers he had experienced were dull, dry, boring, and laborious to read. There is no joy in that kind of literature. Until a child experiences true joy in literature they have no investment in wanting to learn. It is difficult to convince a struggling reader to invest effort in learning to read and write. The difficulties my son faced in his early attempts had left him with no confidence to try. He did, however, have a fascination with penguins, and a mother passionate about words.

In the two years I studied at university, I'd made a hobby of writing. I'd become an advocate within my local writing community. In November 2012, I wrote 70,000 words of the book that would become my debut novel. I took on the role of Municipal Liaison for National

Novel Writing Month and felt like I needed to lead by example. During that first year of home-schooling, I finished my novel and began exploring self-publishing. I worked hard to polish up *The Flight of Torque*, which I then self-published in paperback using Amazon CreateSpace's print-on-demand services. I also published eBooks with Kindle Direct Publishing, Kobo Writing Life, and Apple iBooks.

Self-publishing a book is an adventure. While I had experience in writing and editing, there was more I had to learn to understand publishing. I continue to learn more every single day. The industry changes with rapid succession. There are core aspects I learnt by making mistakes and having small successes.

For example, the first edition of *The Flight of Torque* struggled because of its cover. Sometimes, a great-looking cover is not enough. Book covers have genre tone and it is more important to have a cover true to your genre than true to your book. The first edition of *The Flight of Torque* failed to have a cover that matched its genre.

I also learnt the value of professional editing. After twelve years as a professional editor, I felt confident I had a well-edited book. The trouble is, a writer tends to be blind to the words on the page. I knew my story so well it was impossible to focus on the words I had written, rather than the story I intended to write. A writer needs distance from their work. Even with distance, it is impossible to catch everything.

That's why investing in a professional, impartial editor is worth every penny. To them, the work is fresh and they see the faults like the creator never could.

There were hurdles, but I learnt and grew. The debut is imperfect, but I love that it's a badge honouring the courage I had in getting the work out there. It's proof that, although secreted away in stolen hours, I had the courage to take it somewhere. It's proof that the 'little whispering flower' within me could shout. It was a step toward the next book I could never have made if I hadn't pushed that first fledgling creation out into the world.

With a 'real' book and a significant crash course in self-publishing, I had confidence. I knew creating something was the best way to foster a passion for it. With this in mind, I incorporated storytelling into our home-school curriculum. Together, my children and I wrote *P.I. Penguin and the Case of the Missing Bottle*. I invested in a professional artist to create fabulous full-colour illustrations. I implemented techniques in layout, text, and design for easy reading by dyslexics. This all came together to make an 800-word picture book. I wanted this book to be something my son could hold in his hands and feel a pride of ownership. I hoped that by creating a dyslexia-friendly book, he would want to read it, over and over again.

The day he held that book for the first time he was beaming, I was proud, and we both felt accomplished. Then he said, 'I hope the kids who buy it from the shop enjoy reading it. We should make more books for kids like me.'

The simple words of a unique child can create mind-blowing transformations in thinking. As a child, I'd dreamt of being an author. I'd pictured my name on the spines of books on the shelves of bookstores. The dream had tarnished over time, but I'd fostered it in the hidden parts of my heart. I was making headway in the time I stole for myself. Never before had I considered becoming a children's book author. Never before had I considered publishing children's fiction. In that simple sentence, I heard a yearning need in little boys like my son.

He was right, we should make more books for kids like him. There was a market for books written for children with language and literacy difficulties. And so, Aulexic publishing house was born. Since January 2015, we've gone on to write more P.I. Penguin books. We invested in professional offset printing as opposed to print-on-demand. We're finding distributors and developing a business we hope will launch the careers of fellow writers and illustrators.

The adventure has been amazing. I finally feel like I've found my calling. The balance happens because we love what we do. We share it all as a family, with my son and daughter both helping to write and create the P.I. Penguin books. My daughter shares my passion for writing and we are collaborating on a young adult novel together. She writes a lot of her own fiction, too. In those stolen moments, I keep working on my own adult fiction. Before 2015 ended, I released two Regency romance novels under a pen name. In 2016, I'm set to release two new supernatural thrillers, and another romance or two. As a family, we're busy, but we love it. There is a balance and rightness in it all that brings us closer together every day.

The thing about being a writer and publisher in today's age is that you wear all the hats. It's an immersive experience playing with all parts of the writing and publishing wheel. In some moments, I'm a marketing manager, others I'm immersed in layout and design. Every day I write new words, but I'm also an editor, a sales executive, and administrator. I hire outsourced help by bringing on board freelance designers, editors, and artists. We hope to bring in more authors and are looking ahead to how the publishing house can grow and flourish. Ultimately, writing is a business and I'm thankful for my early foundations in freelancing.

I'm also excited about where this is heading in the years to come. In today's age we experience an extravagant freedom to follow our passions in life. When you find your passion, and can feel the change those passions create in the world, you can set a path. You can let the adventure of walking that path inspire you. And, you can be heard, because, at heart, I listen to my six-year-old self who begged me, and now begs you:

'Little whispering flower, stand tall and make a shout,
let everything around you, know that you're about.'

FIVE TIPS FROM REBECCA LAFFAR-SMITH

1. **Hone Your Tools:** Words are our medium, our tools. Understand and care for them.
2. **Explore Every Facet:** Consider all the ways your words can exist. Try your hand in other facets; you may discover several that excite and inspire you.
3. **Build A Community:** A positive writing community helps fuel your fire and gives you a safe place to be yourself.
4. **Follow Your Passion:** Trust your heart to find what you're destined to do.
5. **Be Heard:** You have a unique and powerful voice. Don't let fear stop you. Let everything around you 'know that you're about'.

Thrill of the Ride

by T.W. Lawless

WHAT made me want to become a thriller writer? I've had to think hard about where the impetus came from. I mean, what makes anyone want to write about crime? What is it that impels a writer to dive into that murky, fathomless sea of evil and make best friends of characters who'd send any sane person running a mile?

I'm told that romance novels sell more (and, let's face it, far less research is generally required), but I'm just not that kind of writer. Call me warped, but I associate a heaving bosom with an impending death-rattle. To me, a gruesome murder is infinitely more exciting than a tale about the unlikely pairing of Lord Ponsonby-Wiffington with his groom's beautiful and headstrong-but-impoverished daughter. The fantasy genre may knock thrillers for six, but that just doesn't do it for me either.

I have no qualifications from the military and I was never a government agent. I'd love to claim that I've been a mercenary in a war-ravaged African country, or that I'm a former hard-bitten police detective who chose to knock out a crime novel rather than burn out on the job, but that simply wouldn't be true. Besides, you don't have to have an adventurous background to qualify as a thriller author. James Patterson, for example, was an advertising executive and Stephen King was a teacher. It may have been the mundane that drove them into that inner-sanctum of vice and gore that is the thriller-writer's domain.

I don't remember ever picking up a book or attending a seminar on 'How to Be a Best Selling Thriller Author'. So then, did my experiences and the books I read ultimately make me a thriller writer? Could writing thrillers be my tribute to an unorthodox life?

I'd had at least six near-death experiences in forty-five years (more about that later). I guess one brush with death every seven or so years from infancy into middle-age isn't too bad and, having beaten the odds, I'm glad to say I'm still here. Was it the tenuousness of my own existence that propelled me towards thriller-writing?

My knowledge of forensics was, until fairly recently, restricted to my twenty-five-years-plus as a registered nurse. For any writer, that is a great place to start. I've seen blood by the litre, suppurating wounds, and traumas and injuries of all types. Oh, and I've seen death. Death: natural and unnatural, an agonising struggle, or as gentle as a summer breeze. I've soothed patients, watched them, patched them, and listened to them. I know a lot about the human body, but I suspect that's not what really qualifies me as a thriller writer. It's probably more due to my understanding of the human condition and my fertile – if dark – imagination. I certainly have experienced events and influences that have ultimately steered me towards writing thrillers.

I think it all began when I was a child. I've already hinted at an unconventional upbringing: I spent my first ten years on a cattle station. It was one of four owned by my family and ours was ninety miles from the nearest town. It was an idyllic life for a child (most of the time). No school, no shoes. At times it was scary and it was often dangerous, but I loved it. The bush was a mysterious, welcoming place and abundant fodder for the imagination. Look into the bush and you could imagine fairies living in there, or that's what I did anyway. I soon learnt that if you didn't respect and listen to the bush, you would be dead very quickly.

Imagine a child of the bush, if you will. Imagine a skinny, scabby, shoeless wild-child taking off as soon as his parents turned their backs. That was me. Normally I wouldn't wander too far from the homestead, but once I disappeared for a whole day. I was only about two or three at the time. Now, the North Queensland bush isn't particularly benign, especially not for a toddler about the size of a light lunch, and it wasn't that long before I got myself into strife. I must have wandered a fair way by then and, as the shadows began to grow longer, a rustle in the undergrowth signalled impending doom. Suddenly, a feral pig charged out of the gloom, tusks and all. I would have been dead, except that two of our cattle dogs had decided to take the journey with me, and they saved my life. They fought off the pig.

It's always made me think about how life and death can be so closely interlinked, how an event can take you to the very edge, but someone or something pulls you back. I guess it's like the twist in a thriller novel.

The bush is still a backdrop for my some of my novels and I recently developed a number of books around it. It's my Outback Noir series.

My first great story-telling influence was my father. He was a fantastic raconteur and he would regale us with stories of the bush every day of his life. He had a way of transporting the listener, of turning the bush into a predator, and the screech of a bird into a screaming woman. His ancestry may have been part Irish, part Scottish and part Mediterranean, but he was entirely a *seanchaí*: a master of tales. As a child, my particular favourite was the one when he was nearly eaten by a crocodile while crossing the river one night. Infinitely more sinister was the one he told of a young Indigenous girl, murdered by members of her tribe at one of our family's stations during the early days of settlement.

When the family finally sold up the stations, my parents moved into a country town, but I was never comfortable living there. Our stations combined were the size of one of the smaller European countries – all horizons but no borders. In town, I always felt I had been locked up; no room to roam, no freedom, and I had to go to a school (out bush I was taught by correspondence with the help of a governess). I had never had to fit in with other children before. It was daunting and I retreated.

I've been back to that country town over the years. It's a nice place. I never saw racism when I was a kid on the cattle station. My parents treated everyone equally. It was only when we moved into town that I saw it and I didn't like it. Country towns can be insular, judgmental and racist. Indigenous people had always been good to me and now I saw them living in hovels on the outskirts of town, only allowed to drink at one pub, trying to survive in a hostile world.

Displacement and discomfort fuelled my imagination. When I wasn't playing with mates around abandoned gold mines, I was reading. I liked to read. I devoured general knowledge books and magazines. My parents bought me a set of encyclopaedias and dictionaries when I was eleven. Those books more than anything else gave me a world view, not just one confined to a remote country town in Australia. The dictionaries opened up a treasure trove of words. I read Robert Louis Stevenson, and Enid Blyton's Famous Five books. I created an imaginary world to cope with my oppressive environment. It was a world of possibility and adventure. When my real world wasn't happy, Jim Hawkins came to the rescue.

My parents never got over having to leave their beloved bush. It hadn't been their decision. A family member who ran the family company decided their fate and imposed it on them. To add insult to injury, the same family member embezzled the company, thereby ensuring that my parents would never receive their fair share of the proceeds. My dad was reduced from station owner to working as a truckie. My parents' hearts had been broken. It was too much for me and all I wanted to do was escape.

Thank God for books and the imagination they fuelled.

Then there was the school I attended for nine long years; a punitive, all-boys college that dished out corporal punishment like lollies, all under the guise of religion. Bullying was State-sanctioned and the Brothers ruled with an iron fist. I once saw a poor kid flogged until he was black and blue. I can still remember him screaming for mercy. There was a large library I could escape to, although the books I sought out were getting darker; ghost tales and war histories were high on my reading list. The required reading books for school were to me just children's books. *Blue Fin* by Colin Thiele simply didn't cut it with me.

The world, as I saw it, was inhumane, violent and inequitable – and I wasn't even fourteen. I wanted to take charge of my life; revenge fantasies ran through my mind on a loop. I considered life on the open sea. Were there any jobs for pirates? I longed to be totally free again. Around this time, two seminal events helped mould me into the author I would become.

A man lived within spitting distance from our house who, these days, would have been diagnosed with schizophrenia. Back then, if he'd been wealthy, he'd have been called eccentric. He wasn't, so we all called him crazy. He rode around on a bicycle yelling obscenities at everyone and he was generally regarded as harmless. He had built a mud brick house and cut out a running track around it. The crazy man would run around his track for hours, yelling out his delusions for the world to hear. Of course, everyone in the neighbourhood steered clear of him.

One Christmas Eve, in the nearby city, an unfortunate man was murdered. The victim had been walking home and he'd been shot on the footpath. The police were baffled. It was a random attack with no motive attached. Those things didn't happen often in Australia in 1974.

After Christmas, the crazy man walked into our yard. I was doing my chores – watering plants in the garden at the time. I froze when he approached me. I don't know why, but it flashed through my mind that he might kill me. I still remember his eyes, lifeless like a snake's. Emotionless. Dead. My voice stammered as I called out for Dad. Dad sauntered up and took his measure. The crazy man asked him for a hacksaw, but Dad bluntly told him he didn't have one. The crazy man left. The next day police swamped the area. The crazy man had been arrested for the random murder. He had wanted a hacksaw so he could cut up and dispose of the rifle he had used. For a long time afterwards, I thought anyone in the neighbourhood could have been the victim. Someone living and another person dying could be as random as that.

The following year, I was in a car with an older cousin and her boyfriend, driving down the main street one Saturday night when we saw a commotion outside the pub where the Indigenous population liked to drink. The ambulance officers were putting a lifeless body into the back of the ambulance. Although it was covered, it was the first dead body I'd seen. Once again, there had been a murder. The publican had shot dead one of the Indigenous patrons because the patron was fighting in the bar. The publican only received an eighteen-month sentence, which served to reinforce what I already thought of the world. It was inhumane and inequitable. I'm sure that if the patron had been white, the outcome would have been different.

I started writing that year – graphic tales of violence that would probably have had me assessed by a psychologist these days. I was also learning to play the guitar. Rock music was my new escape (I recently rediscovered lyrics I'd scribbled on a notepad back then – they were disturbingly dark). I also discovered the novels of Leon Uris. This all fed my gloomy view of the world.

Whether through rock music or literature, I wanted to make sense of the world and my place in it. I wanted to tell the world it was screwed up and I yearned to be paid lots of money for the privilege. Unfortunately, it was going to take a long time to achieve that.

By the end of school, I decided that the best avenue to express myself creatively would be as a journalist, so I enrolled at university, majoring in journalism and media studies. I studied journalism and film-making for a while, but I had no confidence to pursue a career in either. For a while, the creative bulb in my head grew slowly dimmer while the bitterness grew brighter.

I did occasionally write during this time. I took courses on writing. I did a screenwriting course because I thought I'd like to see my name in lights. I wrote a thriller novel in longhand, although the title now eludes me. I think it was set in a country town during World War II. I had it typed up, and sent it to a publisher, who promptly rejected it. I never gave up, but I also didn't step up. I was on the treadmill and the light was nearly out.

When I look back on those years now, I regard them as my research years. Certain situations, locations, characters, and even dialogue have ended up in my books. So the years weren't wasted, for the desire to create was always in the back of my mind.

The light snapped back on when I met my wife. We shared the same passion for writing and the same frustrations. My wife had even wanted to be a journalist. We started to collaborate on screen writing. We wrote three comedies and one thriller. We came close to having one comedy about a spoilt rich girl picked up by a major television producer in America. I wasn't writing thrillers, it's true, but I believed any writing was good practice. Writing outside my comfort zone proved a challenge, but it was a good way to add another dimension to my writing.

The television producer looked at our script a second time and then she asked for a hard copy. We were excited, but that presented us with a small problem. When you write for the American market, you have to write in American English. No problem. You also have to use American paper sizes. We were living in Queensland at the time and tracking down American paper was nearly impossible, but we eventually found a shop that stocked it. The script then must be attached by copper brads. We hunted high and low and found steel brads, but no copper ones. In the end, the film wasn't made. I blame the lack of copper brads.

Disappointed, we kept creating. My wife hurt her back and while awaiting surgery and in severe pain, she wrote a book that was accepted by a publisher. It's called *The Lornsleigh Legacy* and is a brilliant book about a dynastic grazing family. She said it was her only way of diverting herself from the pain. Then I developed health problems which eventually turned out to be thyroid cancer. Like my wife, I thought writing a book was the only way to escape a world that seemed to be throwing a lot of misfortune our way. I chose to write a book rather than a screenplay because a book offered more room to move with regard to plot development and characterisation. It was also a good legacy to leave behind. I established investigative journalist, Peter Clancy as the main character because I wanted someone who bucked the system, who stood up for the defenceless and who was complex and flawed.

I wrote my first book, *Homecountry*, feeling like death warmed up and looking as thin as a whippet. Writing was a great diversion. I debated at the time whether I should try to get a publisher or do it myself. In the end I decided to self-publish because I wanted artistic control. I still do. After surgery and treatment, my health improved. *Homecountry* has become an Amazon bestseller and I've kept writing since then.

So far, I've written two further Peter Clancy books back to back, with another one due in 2016. One of those (*Thornydevils*) was also an Amazon bestseller. My first Outback Noir novel is also due out in 2016. I'll just keep writing because I have a lot to say, and I'll continue to do so until my hands can't operate a keyboard. Then I'll dictate. Or I'll make a movie.

FIVE TIPS FROM T.W. LAWLESS

1. Don't overwrite. Keep it succinct. Concentrate particularly on dialogue. Make it realistic. Make it appropriate to the character. Read the dialogue aloud to someone.
2. Don't have one dimensional characters. Macho ex-special forces types don't cut it with me.
3. Make it hard for the main character. Obstacles and twists will drive the plot.
4. Rewrite, rewrite, rewrite. Then get it professionally edited.
5. Writing is tough; getting published is tougher and selling is toughest of all. If you think you have a great story to tell, don't give up.

Journey to publication

by Natasha Lester

I THOUGHT I'd share with you the story of how *A Kiss From Mr Fitzgerald* came into being from a place of despair and disaster, and turned into a beautiful triumph. I hope you find this story inspiring, and it reminds you that even when it seems impossible, continuing to work and dream and learn from failure can lead to wonderful rewards.

MY DISASTROUS ATTEMPT AT A THIRD BOOK

When I finished *If I Should Lose You*, my second book, I had an idea for a story that I thought would be my next book. It was another work of contemporary women's fiction, in a similar vein to my first two books. I sat down to write it but found it to be incredibly hard work.

I told myself it was normal, that I'd always found writing hard and that some days I didn't love it, that I just had to push through it. But I couldn't shake the niggling feeling that this was different. That I almost hated this book. That I had no joy in its creation.

But I don't like giving up on things. So I made myself finish the damn book. Then I sat down to read it and thought, *there is something wrong with this book but I don't know what it is.*

WHAT WENT WRONG

There were a few problems. The first was that I was writing yet another book like my first two books. It was safe ground. Not all that challenging. Another first person narrative about motherhood and all its myriad glories and difficulties. Which is a great topic to write about. Except I'd already done it. Twice.

I was also having a crisis of confidence. My second book hadn't sold as well as my first book. I'd thought a second book was sure to sell more because there was an existing pool of readers to draw from. But I kept running into people who would say, *I really wanted to read your book, but I've heard what it's about and I thought it might be too sad.*

I had written a sad book. It had its happy moments, too, but I hadn't realised how averse people were to reading about very emotionally difficult situations involving mothers and their children. And I completely understand now, in hindsight, why some people would have been hesitant about reading it.

The publishing industry was also going through a major shake up at the time, which didn't help my crisis of confidence. It seemed that contracts were getting shelved everywhere I looked, that books weren't selling in the quantities they used to, that everyone was being careful. For an author who wanted to move to a bigger publisher, who had no contract for their next book, careful wasn't the kind of industry it would be easy to pitch to.

I knew I needed to go out with a strong book, a book I loved. And the book I'd written just wasn't it.

CHANGING AGENTS

At the same time, I came to believe that my agent wasn't perhaps the right agent for me. She is a great agent, highly respected and with an impressive list of authors. But I needed someone I could get more feedback from about my book-in-progress, especially in the face of the contracting publishing industry, and my crisis of confidence, and I needed more advice about my writing career. Even though I'd published two books, my confidence was low and I needed a sounding board.

BEGINNING *A KISS FROM MR FITZGERALD*

So, there I was with a manuscript I hated, a feeling that I needed a different agent, at a complete low in terms of my confidence in myself as an author, and with very little idea how to get what I wanted, which was a publishing contract with one of the big publishers.

So what did I do? I threw my manuscript away. 70,000 wasted words. Except that they weren't wasted. Because I learnt so much in the writing of them. That I was trying too hard, in some ways, to write a book that would be more commercial and less literary than my previous books. But that I also wasn't trying hard enough. I was writing on ground that was too safe, too much the same, and I was being too serious.

What I wanted was to write something fun. Something that would make people smile. Something that would also make them think and feel and cry perhaps too, but that would ultimately bring them joy.

I thought about all of my favourite books. That one of the things I loved about those books was their love stories. And I thought, *why don't I write the book I would love to read?* The book that would sweep me away in the pleasure of it all.

Another thing that many of my favourite books had in common was that they were historical novels. And so the germ of an idea began to grow. I could write a beautiful love story. I could set it in one of my favourite cities, New York. I could set it in one of my favourite eras, the 1920s. I could see where this crazy idea took me.

THE BEST WRITING EXPERIENCE I'VE EVER HAD

It took me into one of the best writing experiences I've ever had. Sitting down to write this book every day was joyful. I loved it. I looked forward to it. I wanted to do it more than anything else. The first draft poured out of me in about four months. I felt like it was good. I felt like I might be onto something.

So I redrafted. I re-wrote. I did massive amounts of research. And the whole time there was a little voice inside my head saying, *What if this book never gets published? What if you never publish another book again for the rest of your life? What will you do then? What will you be if you can't be a writer?*

I hated that voice. Some days it got to me but most days I just ignored it. I was lucky to be so swept away by the book I was writing that I was able to forget almost anything. It was too devastating to dwell on. I had to believe in myself and my book more than I believed in that negative inner voice. I had to write on, regardless.

BUILDING MY PROFILE

And at the same time, I was rebuilding my website, blogging every week, building up my Facebook page, doing everything I could on social media to make sure I had a good solid platform that a publisher would like. And thank goodness I did. Because that was how I was able to find a new agent, one who believed in me and my book, who worked with me on my book, who has been a wonderful support and instrumental in helping me get the publishing contract I'd been dreaming about for years.

EVERYTHING HAD TO BE PERFECT

So there I was writing my book, which was a really joyful experience. But I also knew this was my one chance. I wanted to move to a bigger publisher and I had to do it with this book. There was no room to make a mistake with anything: the book, my pitch, the approach to publishers and so on – everything had to be perfect.

I had an agent, but my agent was very much on the literary fiction side of the equation, which suited my previous books. The book I was writing this time was much more commercial and I didn't think it would be a good fit for her. I felt like I must be mad to even be thinking of moving away from her. It was a big risk and I worried over this for months. Luckily, I had some lovely writing friends who were able to give me advice and they convinced me to go with my gut. And my gut was telling me that, crazy as it sounded to give up a great agent, that's what I wanted to do.

And yes, I could have decided to give up on agents entirely and pitch to publishers myself. But I knew that if I had a good agent, I would get a better deal because agents know their stuff and are worth every cent. I also knew that the right agent would work with me on the manuscript and I wanted that extra help to make the book as good as it could possibly be.

AN EMAIL FROM AN AGENT

And then came the email that changed everything. It was an email sent through the contact form on my website from an agent I'd heard of, asking me if I'd ever considered working with a literary agent. After I'd picked myself up from the floor from the shock of an agent approaching me, rather than the other way around, I promptly checked out this agent's website and the authors she represented. What I saw there sounded great.

So I emailed back saying I was soon to finish a manuscript and that I would send it through to her when I was ready. When the manuscript was finally finished, I carefully pulled together my pitch. I wrote a strong synopsis, I detailed my social media platform, and I summarised my book in the most enticing way that I could. Then I sent it to her and sat back to wait.

YOU NEED TO BE SOOOOO PATIENT

And here's the thing. Pitching out to agents and publishers takes more patience than you would ever think it's possible to possess. Because agents mostly read pitches from new authors on their weekends, on their time off. The rest of their week is taken up with doing work they are paid for, for their authors who already have deals with publishers. And that's as it should be. I do my paid work before I do my unpaid work, just like they do.

So, from the time I first sent my pitch off to my now agent, to the time I signed my publishing contract was eighteen months. Yes, that's a long time. But that's how long things take. You have to be prepared for that.

I sent my pitch to this agent in October 2013, with my first three chapters. She responded in mid-November, asking to see the whole manuscript, which was very exciting! In mid-February 2014, she let me know that she hadn't had a chance to get to it as she was so busy with her other authors and that she would get back to me by the end of March 2014. She also told me I was free to send it out to other agents, but I didn't. I was pretty sure she was the agent I wanted.

True to her word, she got back to me at the end of March with an email that made me celebrate. She wanted to take me on! I was super excited, as you can imagine. But that was just the start of the hard work.

REWRITING, REWRITING AND MORE REWRITING

Because it had been a few months, I'd had some ideas about how I could redraft the manuscript to make it stronger. I knew it was important to go out with the strongest possible manuscript and my agent agreed. So I sat down to redraft, which took a couple of months. Then I sent it back to her and again, because she has lots of other work to do for authors who were actually making her money, unlike me at this stage, it took her a couple of months to read it.

She came back to me suggesting another quite comprehensive redraft. It wasn't exactly the news I wanted. I wanted the book to be ready, of course! But the more I read her email, the more I knew she was right. I could ignore everything she was saying and ruin my chance, or I could take it all on board and sit down and rewrite the damn book again. And this was what I'd wanted. I'd wanted an agent who would give me great editorial feedback. It would be silly of me to reject that feedback. So I redrafted again, which meant another couple of months passed by.

I sent it back to her in October 2014 and crossed every finger and toe that I had. I didn't know if I would be able to rewrite it again. Luckily I didn't have to. She said it was ready to go! I had never been more relieved in my life!

And that was the start of yet more waiting. My agent sent the manuscript out to publishers in November 2014. But I only signed my publishing contract in March 2015. Why did it take so long? And how did that whole process work? And how did it feel to get offers from, not just one or two publishers, but three publishers?

THE PITCH TO PUBLISHERS

My agent sent the pitch and the manuscript off to eight publishers in mid-November, with a pre-Christmas deadline to respond. The manuscript went out to:

- HarperCollins
- Penguin
- Allen & Unwin
- Pan Macmillan
- Random House
- Harlequin
- Simon & Schuster
- Hachette

Once she'd sent it out, I basically tried to put it out of my mind because there was no longer anything I could do. But I did regularly find myself thinking unhelpful thoughts along the lines of: *What if they all reject it, what will I do then?* I think this is normal, but it's also completely terrifying because, as optimistic as you try to be, of course it is a possibility. Supportive husbands are wonderful at this point because they say things like: *Of course somebody will take it. They'd be mad not to.* And you try to believe them.

THE FIRST ROUND OF RESPONSES

The first response we had was on December 3, from a publisher who I would have been completely ecstatic to be published by. They said they wanted to take it to their acquisitions meeting, but they wouldn't be able to organise an acquisitions meeting before Christmas and could they have more time. Several other requests for more time filtered in as well and so my agent agreed to give them until January 22, which I absolutely concurred with.

This was the first point at which I began to have hope. Because someone actually wanted to take the manuscript to acquisitions! It was such an exciting day and I found myself re-reading their lovely email over and over again to keep my confidence up. Their email said, among other things: 'I absolutely love this book and would love to take it to acquisitions to discuss with everyone. I was reminded of three of my other favourite New York novels, *Fever* by Mary Beth Keane, Colm Toibin's *Brooklyn* and Caleb Carr's *The Alienist*.'

So, you can see why I was excited. But it was only December 3 and I had to wait until January 22. Again, I tried not to think about it. Even when we received one pre-Christmas rejection from a publisher who already had a thematically similar novel in her stable, and who, in her rejection, said: '*Thanks so much for sending me this delightful novel. It's beautifully written and raises some compelling issues about the treatment of women,*' I kept being hopeful because that rejection made me feel as if the novel had some merit and it was just a matter of finding it the right home.

When Christmas came, I knew we had one rejection, one publisher wanting to take it to acquisitions and six more publishers whose responses were as yet unknown.

THE MOST AMAZING TWO WEEKS OF MY LIFE

January 22 arrived and I think I checked my email a hundred times before breakfast. Luckily my agent knew I'd be doing that and her email arrived in my inbox at 6.25 a.m. She said she'd spoken to two publishers who she was hopeful of receiving offers from by the end of the week, including the one we knew was taking it to acquisitions.

My heart leapt at this news. But we also received rejections – once again, lovely rejections – from two other publishers. So we were down to five left, with two possibly interested, but no offers on the table. Gin and tonic for breakfast seemed very appealing at this point! Other publishers had asked for more time so the new deadline my agent gave them was February 6. Two more weeks of agony!

January 23 arrived and with it some fabulous news. We had an offer! And not just an offer, but a great offer from a wonderful publisher. I was ready to crack the champagne and say, *To hell with all this stress, let's take it,* but my agent, being far more sensible and having much stronger nerves than me (this is why you should have an agent!) said she hoped this would flush out the other offers.

And of course she was right. Another publisher called and said they were poised to make an offer and could we wait until the middle of the following week. At this point I just about fell off my chair. Two offers! I was delighted with one. The prospect of two, which, let's face it, is something we all dream about, was not something I'd ever thought would really happen to me. Another weekend of anxious waiting passed by.

The middle of the following week rolled around and we received our second offer, which was amazing. Then another publisher told us she was taking it to her acquisitions meeting, too. But of course that was going to be the following week so there was yet another weekend to get through! Yes, I drank a lot of gin in January!

So, at the end of those two weeks, we had two firm offers, plus one other publisher taking it to acquisitions, and four rejections. We hadn't yet heard from the final publisher and of course, being pessimistic me, I decided that was because they didn't like it and they weren't interested. Turns out I was wrong.

THE UNEXPECTED ELEVENTH HOUR OFFER

The next week began. The publisher who was taking it to acquisitions didn't get it through the meeting. I don't know why but these things happen. I still had my two publishing contract offers and I was utterly delighted with those. I was preparing to make a choice when, at the eleventh hour, we heard from the final publisher on the list.

This is where timing turned out to be everything. The publisher in question was Hachette. Their new fiction publisher had just arrived in Australia that week from her previous position as publisher at Little Brown in London where she was known as the wunderkind of commercial fiction, with an eye for spotting great manuscripts. My manuscript was the first thing she'd read in her first three days on the job and she was emailing to say that she loved it.

Understandably though, she needed more time. It was her first week on the job here in Australia! She had to finish reading the manuscript and then pitch it to the team at Hachette. So, of course, we gave her more time.

Yes, another weekend passed! More gin! And of course I spent the entire weekend worrying that the other publishers would withdraw their offers because it was taking too long, even though everyone told me that would never happen. But I had to freak out about something!

Then on Monday, I had what I never thought was possible: three publishing contract offers from three amazing publishers, any of whom I would have been happy to go with.

THE BIG DECISION

So how do you choose? There were pros for each choice and very few cons. I had several long chats with my agent. I swam a lot of laps in the pool to help me think.

---

*I talked about it incessantly to my poor husband. And
I listened to my gut.*

In the end I went with Hachette, due to their amazing successes with books of late, but also because of their new publisher. She was so persuasive and so lovely and her track record is incredible. She published Nicholas Sparks. Need I say more? I know I'll never be selling the number of books that he does but she clearly knows what sells. And she wanted me and my little book. And I was pretty damn thrilled about that.

So I signed with Hachette, which was a process that took another five weeks.

REPRESENTATION BY A US AGENT

Given that my book received offers from three publishers, my agent felt it was worthwhile getting in touch with the literary agency she has connections with in the US. She sent the manuscript off and rang me a couple of days later with some very exciting news. The agent had stayed up all night reading my book and loved it! And she wants to take it out to US publishers!

I'd never thought of anything other than an Australian publisher. I'd never imagined someone in the US would like my book. I was completely stunned and then so excited that I'm pretty sure I did a little dance around my office. The agency taking my book on is called Inkwell Management, and they represent authors like Markus Zusak and Lionel Shriver so I don't think I could be in better hands.

The book has recently gone out to the US market but we haven't had any bites yet. And while I know it's a long shot, that being submitted to US publishers and actually getting a contract with a US publisher are two very different things, I'm just thrilled that my book is being given a chance to be read in the wider world.

SIGNING THE CONTRACT

So all that was going on in the background while I was signing a publishing contract with Hachette, which took around six weeks from an email agreement to a completed contract. Why does it take so long?

It's because a book contract contains so many different rights. And again, this is where an agent is invaluable. They know all this stuff so that you don't have to know the tiny details. For instance, you can sign away world rights or Australia/New Zealand rights only. This was why we had to find out about the US agent first, to know which rights we wanted to keep and which ones we were happy to sign over.

There are eBook rights, serial rights, extract rights and many, many more. There are also audio rights, which could have been signed over to Hachette, or to one of the audio book producers, such as Audible. Given the success of the manuscript, my agent felt we could reasonably talk to Audible to see what they could offer.

And they came back with a fantastic offer, including an extra advance, which was wonderful. If I hadn't had an agent, I wouldn't have a contact at Audible, nor known how to approach them, and I would have missed this great opportunity. Once again, I would have just been looking at the obvious, at what I had right in front of me, rather than knowing to look beyond that to other opportunities. *A Kiss From Mr Fitzgerald* has since been published as an audio book, which is something I've not experienced before.

It's been a huge learning curve for me and an amazing ride.

(Reprinted and edited from natashalester.com.au with permission)

FIVE TIPS FROM NATASHA LESTER

1. Write anyway. No matter how tired you are, how busy you are, how sick you feel, how terrible you think your work is, how much you don't feel like it, just write anyway.
2. Go to writers' festivals, author talks, writing conferences, writing courses. Soak up the world of writing, learn everything you can, let it inspire you.
3. Support the Australian publishing industry by buying books written by Australian authors, at local bookstores. If we don't support the local publishing industry, it may not be around when we want it to publish us.
4. Read.
5. Be prepared to re-write everything more times than you think possible.

Keeping the Dream Alive

by Juliet Marillier

MY writing journey started as soon as I was old enough to sit on my mother's knee and look at a picture book while she read aloud to me. My parents loved and valued reading: my mother because she had grown up in a book-rich household; my father because, having left school at twelve to be the breadwinner for his family, he wanted his daughters to have the opportunities the Great Depression had denied him. He'd have loved us both to become doctors, for like many of his generation he had a deep respect for the medical profession. But my sister became a librarian and I became a teacher. I wish Dad had lived long enough to see me have a second career as a successful published novelist. And to see my daughter become a doctor.

At first I was a little slow at school. Then someone realised I was severely short-sighted. I got my first pair of glasses at age six and soon made up for lost time. My home town – Dunedin, New Zealand – at that time had a magnificent children's library, housed in its own two-storey Victorian building, with a great collection and a fearsomely intelligent head librarian. Over the years of my schooling I worked my way through many, many books, from Alison Uttley's Little Grey Rabbit series with its delicate, beautifully framed illustrations, to Tove Jansson's Moomin books, full of quirky humour and Nordic angst, and probably my first real fantasy reading. Then there was C.S. Lewis's Narnia series, and authors like Noel Streatfeild (*Ballet Shoes*), Antonia Forest and Rosemary Sutcliff. But running through all of this was my passion for folklore, fairy tale, and mythology. There was something about those traditional stories that struck a deep chord with me, and I've retained a special love for them all my life.

The sense of wonder, the feeling of a deep inner truth,
and the way they transport the reader into a world that
is both familiar and utterly different made a special
kind of magic.

I was a promising writer when young, starting off in primary school with sagas about killer robots, prehistoric life discovered in a remote corner of New Zealand, mountain climbers lost in the Alps and so on – clearly I was not a believer in 'write what you know'. I filled many an exercise book, writing late into the night. My school friends loved to read these epics. At high school I wrote a play in French which we performed, as well as a lot of poetry. Set the topic 'At the Beach' in class, I chose to write a poem about soldiers at Dunkirk watching their mates die around them and waiting for the little boats to come in (I wonder if I still have that somewhere?). I did seem destined for a writing future. But I had another love, music, and that was what I chose to major in at university and pursue as a career. After leaving school, I didn't write fiction again for around twenty-five years.

I often wonder what might have happened if I'd written my first novel at the age of twenty-something rather than at forty-something. Would I have twice as many books in print as I do now? Would I be a better writer? I suspect the answer is no. I believe that long fallow period formed an important part of my development as a writer.

During those years of not writing fiction I did a lot of other things. I raised my children, worked at various jobs and moved house numerous times, sometimes happily, sometimes unhappily. I wrote business reports and teaching materials. I wrote and arranged music. I had some successes and some bad reversals in both my personal and professional lives. I learnt about the world, about human relationships, and about myself. In short, I grew up. Reading continued to be a source of great comfort to me. But towards the end of that period I was worn down, disillusioned and just plain tired. I didn't have a scrap of creative energy. Write a novel? Hah! In your dreams. That child who had so loved fairy tales and had written her own stories with such dedication was gone. Or so it seemed.

But the human spirit is pretty resilient. I decided to make a huge and difficult change in my personal life. After a couple of years' recovery time, I started writing again. Not for publication. Not for sharing even with trusted friends and family. Just for me, because there was a story I really, really wanted to write my own version of, a story I had loved passionately since childhood. A story with a brave, stoical young woman as its protagonist and a family of siblings who have to endure a life-shattering event. I wondered how facing that awful challenge would change each of them. Who would become strong in adversity? Who would fall apart? Would they remain loyal to one another? From that came my first novel, *Daughter of the Forest*, loosely based on the fairy tale *The Six Swans*. It took me three years to write. At the time I was a single parent and had a demanding full-time day job. I didn't know there was a genre called fantasy. I had only the most basic knowledge of the publishing process and no ties in the local writing community. This was before the age of social media.

Daughter of the Forest eventually found its way onto the slush pile at Pan Macmillan Australia, where they just happened to be looking for a new fantasy writer. I had sent in the opening chapters and outline of a sequel along with the manuscript, and a one-paragraph description of a third instalment, and they offered me a three-book contract. *Daughter of the Forest* was published in 1998. I now have nineteen novels and a collection of short fiction in print. My work is published in the USA as well as Australia, and also appears in a number of translations. I've made a good enough career out of writing to free myself from the need for a day job.

I have some lessons to share from this part of my story.

Inspiration comes from life experience. Be observant. Store up what you see, what you experience, what you learn. The bad stuff as well as the good. It's all raw material for your writing. It doesn't matter if you are writing contemporary fiction, a Regency romance or a space opera – some elements of storytelling are universal.

Fallow (unproductive) periods are not necessarily a bad thing. My long period of not writing fiction allowed me to write in a more mature way when I finally had the emotional space to get started again. Being responsible for a family and for a team in a workplace taught me patience and developed my organisational skills – invaluable for a working writer.

Write the story you feel passionate about. Don't write for the purpose of being published or being successful. Don't try to tailor your work to the market. Write because you want to and need to. That first novel of mine almost wrote itself – it was as much personal therapy as anything. It remains one of my most popular works.

Reading, and reading widely, is the best preparation for being a writer. My years as an avid reader taught me how language works. I learnt how to tell a story effectively. Reading is the most painless way to learn the tools of the trade. Note, I was lucky enough to be educated in an excellent system at a time when primary school children got a thorough grounding in grammar, and high school English included Shakespeare and classic novels. That solid grounding certainly helped.

It's never too late to start. I began writing what became my first published novel at the age of forty-seven. I got the call from Pan Macmillan offering me a publishing contract on my fiftieth birthday. Others have started even later.

Don't write off your chances because you are of mature years. All that life experience can only make your novel better.

Of course, it wasn't all plain sailing for me from the day I got my first contract. I faced a steep learning curve and I made plenty of stupid errors along the way, though my Australian publisher was (and still is) very supportive. I was thrown in the deep end with panel appearances at the World Science Fiction Convention when I was so new to the whole thing I had never heard of most of my (world famous) fellow panellists. On another occasion I had to front up as guest of honour at a scarily upmarket dinner in London with my UK editor and a bunch of booksellers, and respond to questions I barely understood. I'm quite an introverted person, happiest at home with my dogs, and I've never forgotten the excruciating awkwardness of that experience. It's only now, after establishing myself as a published author, that I can respond with confidence and good humour to most questions that come my way. Or tell people straight out if I think they're talking bollocks.

A couple of things would really have helped me in those newbie days. The first was an agent. I didn't sign with an agent until I already had five books in print and several foreign contracts as well as my Australian ones. As a result, I made some ill-advised business decisions out of pure ignorance. A good agent is worth his or her weight in gold. The other thing I could have benefited from earlier in my career was a peer group/support group of fellow writers. I felt on the outer for years, partly because I had never been heavily into science fiction and fantasy as a reader – I read mostly outside the genre, with an emphasis on historical fiction. So I was not part of that geek group, the fans who religiously attend every convention and can quote from any number of cult science fiction novels, television series and movies. Many of the local writers of speculative fiction had grown up in that culture. When I did meet them I thought they were a little weird and I felt invisible to them.

Eventually I started offering my services to give workshops at the writers' centres, putting my name up to present panels at conventions and so on. Slowly but surely I became accepted into the loose local and national network of speculative fiction writers and publishers. I now see their weirdness as a good thing! I've also been in two critique groups, one all romance writers, one cross-genre. What do we learn from this part of the story?

Don't try to do it all on your own. If you don't have much experience with contracts or with the publishing business in general – most of us don't – educate yourself before you dive in. The Australian Society of Authors (ASA) offers various seminars including some that deal with the business side of writing. Talk to other writers. Find out what agents do and how to go about approaching them. There may be a professional association specifically for your genre, such as Romance Writers of Australia.

Find your peer group. Look for opportunities to link up with other writers either face-to-face or online. Critique groups are useful – you can learn a lot by analysing and giving feedback on other writers' work. Having your own work critiqued, though sometimes painful, is a valuable part of learning to write better. Even more precious is the support and understanding you can receive from fellow writers. With your peers you can talk about things nobody else would understand. You can share news of opportunities, commiserate over reversals, provide practical advice and rejoice in successes, large or small. Social media supplies useful ways to do this, but nothing beats a face-to-face meet-up, whether it's just to chat or to write together.

Now for the third and last part of the story (in keeping with the three dwarves, three bears, three wishes tradition of folk tales). Fittingly, this part starts with druids. My novels are historical fantasy, and some include druid characters. I had to research the history of druidry – not easy as the ancient druids never wrote anything down. They memorised vast bodies of lore and sometimes used Ogham, a cryptic sign language that could be scratched on a stone or tree trunk or indicated by the positions of the fingers. During that research I discovered that there are modern druids and became fascinated by their beliefs, which chimed very strongly with my own. Fast forward a few years and I was a member of a druid order, the Order of Bards, Ovates and Druids (OBOD). My spiritual path has a significant impact on the way I write, and I'm not only talking about historical research.

Druids love traditional storytelling – the same fairy tales and folklore I felt so close to as a child. We recognise the value of those old stories in teaching life lessons and in healing emotional wounds. That has been so since the days of the early druids. When the druid characters in my books tell stories relevant to the dilemmas of their audience, they're doing what their counterparts would have done centuries ago – providing life guidance. And when I receive emails and letters from readers, telling me one or other of my novels helped them through particularly difficult or dark times in their own lives, I feel as if I'm carrying on a very old tradition. There's a strong thread of folklore and fairy tale in my novels.

Another of the central beliefs of druidry is that the divine (god, goddess, spirit) is not an entity set above us, but a force that exists in every part of nature, ourselves included. It's like a flame inside us, keeping us strong and good. Sometimes it burns strong and bright. Sometimes it flickers and weakens. Sometimes we forget that it's there. But it links all of us, and all of nature, in one shared life and one shared responsibility. Druids are environmentally aware, conservation-minded, and can often be found mucking about with compost or making Save Our Wetlands protest banners.

At the time when I was thinking of starting writing fiction again, I'd had years of feeling beaten down emotionally. My self-belief was at an all-time low. That philosophy about the divine existing in and linking all living things was a revelation to me, as it meant I could no longer hate myself or be disappointed by my own efforts. Instead, I worked on living the life I had as bravely and well as I possibly could. It also meant recognising the essential goodness – the spark of the divine – in other people, even those who were not especially easy to like.

So what is the relevance to writing?

Just as the idea of the divine within allows us to love ourselves and our fellow human beings, it also allows us, as writers, to feel compassion and understanding toward our characters, even the darkest villains. Remember that every character, however flawed or misguided, however unlovable, is the hero of his/her own story. To that character, her own actions make perfect sense. She believes in what she is doing. Whether she is the protagonist, antagonist or a secondary character, she has a full set of aspirations, prejudices, hopes and fears, like anyone else. When you write a character, write in the knowledge of that and they will become real on the page.

Know your characters and learn to love them. That's it in a nutshell. See every character as a real person. Note: it helps to engage with a wide range of people in the real world. Insight into character is not something you can learn from books.

Above all, don't let go of your dreams, writers. You know how it goes in fairy tales. The gormless youngest son or the overlooked third daughter often becomes the hero of the story. They are the ones who take risks, use their brains, or extend the hand of friendship to those who are shunned by other folk. And they are the ones who, against the odds, end up achieving the quest. Good luck with your writing. Put mind, heart and soul into it, and make it real.

FIVE WRITING TIPS FROM JULIET MARILLIER

1. Inspiration comes from life experience.
2. Write the story you feel passionate about.
3. Reading is the best preparation for being a writer.
4. Don't try to do it all on your own – find your peer group.
5. Know your characters and learn to love them.

Explore. Dream.

Discover

by Jenn J McLeod

'Twenty years from now, you will be more disappointed by the things that you didn't do than by the ones you did do. So throw off the bowlines. Sail away from the safe harbor. Catch the trade winds in your sails.
Explore. Dream. Discover.'
Mark Twain

WRITING is all about dreaming: we imagine page-turning plots, wish for bestseller status, and fantasize about million-dollar bidding wars, movie deals, extravagant book launches and Hollywood premieres.

That's *the dream* – right?

Until that day a writer is hunched over a keyboard in a kind of self-imposed solitary confinement and developing addictions to coffee and chocolate. We infuriate our family and we lose contact with the real world because our heads are already full to overflowing with fictional friends. We also all share the same dream – to see those characters come to life for others as they read the pages you've slaved over for years.

Ten years ago I remember wanting *the dream* so much I told people I'd write for nothing. I even said: *'I'd pay a publisher to turn my story into a real book'*. (Little did I know back then there was a thing called vanity press publishing – companies eager to give you *the dream* in exchange for your hard-earnt cash.)

TIP #1: MONEY ALWAYS FLOWS TO THE AUTHOR. NOT FROM THE AUTHOR

Remember this advice as temptation knocks – and it will knock, somewhere around rejection number ten when despair also sneaks up on you and it seems more and more people are popping out books left, right and centre.

Your first instinct will be to panic. I did, and those dreams of writing soon turned into nightmares about the world running out of trees (paper), or publishers no longer contracting books written by people with the name *Jenn*. Oh, and then there's the nightmare about the rarest mosquito in the world that wakes from a one-thousand-year hibernation to find me and strike me down with an incurable strain of writer's block.

Some writers (with less vivid imaginations, perhaps) convince themselves they've left their run too late (the ship has sailed and they didn't get on board) or those evil things called eBooks are systematically destroying the traditional publishing business to make print books extinct. I could even picture the thousand mournful eulogies hitting Facebook from wannabe writers who, like me, weren't quick enough.

TIP #2: TRY CHANNELING THAT VIVID IMAGINATION SO IT BECOMES YOUR FRIEND, RATHER THAN YOUR ENEMY

I could at least justify my anxiety. I was preparing to submit my completed and highly polished debut novel when the publishing industry began teetering on supposed collapse, with the Australian book chains of Borders, Angus & Robertson and the Whitcoulls chain of newsagencies in New Zealand all placed into voluntary administration only a day after the Borders company in the US also collapsed.

There I was, poised to submit *House for all Seasons* and the publishing and book selling world was ending – my dreams shattered. No sense even trying to jump on board to throw off those bowlines, only to bob around aimlessly in the ocean. Nope! I'd well and truly missed the boat – or so I thought at the time.

Fast-forward to 2016. With four books now published (and I hope more on the way), I guess you could say the tide did turn in my favour. But the journey hasn't been all smooth sailing, which is why, when asked to write a piece for this anthology about writing dreams, I thought about the many ups and downs of my journey. Do I keep the subject matter positive and feed your writing dreams with fairy dust, or do I give the warts-and-all version? As a rule, I'm pretty open and genuine when aspiring authors approach me after an author event.

The first thing I explain is this: the dream is very different from the reality.

I'm not saying it's a *bad* different – more an *unexpected* different, which brings me to Tip #3 …

#TIP 3: EXPECT THE UNEXPECTED

So, what do I tell you about writing the dream when I'm no publishing expert? Gosh, I'm not even a book expert. I hold no creative writing degree and, to be honest, study and research has never been my strong point, mostly because learning to dissect something I love, simply to understand why I love it, makes me not love it so much any more – too many rules, too much control. Structure and discipline is one thing, but to control is to limit the imagination (in my opinion). Okay, so maybe I should have listened a little closer to my high school English teacher; I might see a lot less red pen on my edits. But not knowing how to do something should not stop you from trying, no matter where you are in life.

I'm proof that you're never too old to learn, and dreams can come true if, to borrow from Mark Twain again, you have the courage to throw off the bowlines, sail away from the safe harbor, and let the trade winds catch your sails: Explore. Dream. Discover.

That image of a sleek sailing ship slicing through a gentle swell sounds very romantic, when the truth is, there's a lot of time in those early days spent floundering and feeling insignificant, like a cork bobbing on an ocean crowded with wannabe writers. I knew I'd never get noticed if I stayed with the crowd. I needed to break out. I needed a lifeboat. I found a writing organisation and suddenly I wasn't on the journey alone.

Solo circumnavigator Paul Lutus once said: 'You can't steer a boat that isn't moving. Just like life.' I made my own wind (hmm, that doesn't sound too good) and the rest is history. Suddenly (yes, it seemed sudden to me even after years of trying) I'd landed a four-book deal with Simon & Schuster Australia and I was a LinkedIn, blogging, tweeting, Facebooking fifty-something charting my way through new territory at an age when a book like *Fifty Shades of Grey* by E.L. James made me think of my hair rather than my love life.

In contrast to grey, and four books and many more years on, my message for those charting their own course for publication is very black and white:

- It doesn't have to be fiction. Anything is possible.

- Extraordinary things do happen to ordinary people.
- It's never too late to follow your dreams.

The greatest challenge to following your writing dream is overcoming self-doubt. While our mainsails are filled with possibilities, it only takes a small shift in wind, or an uncharted reef, to take us off course. In the beginning, I relied on family and friends to keep me buoyant, but I soon discovered something about family and friends.

They might love us to bits, but love doesn't always equate to understanding. People's perception of the publishing/writing business can make those who love you worry to the point of discouraging you. While as writers we can happily lose ourselves to the dream, our family and friends can fret about the disappointment we'll face. They worry about us 'wasting our lives sitting at that computer all day'. Others can be pessimists and killjoys. Some even expect us to fail – not because they want us to, but because they simply don't *get* the dream. This is especially true for those people whose only reference for 'being an author' is their favourite bestselling novelist, or the likes of J.K. Rowling.

The notion that a friend of theirs – an ordinary, everyday person like them – might become a published author fails to compute.

For a self-confessed self-doubter like me, maintaining my own belief in the dream was a major challenge, especially with comments like: 'You're only setting yourself up for disappointment' and 'Why are you wasting your time?' Or my personal favourite: 'You're too old.'

I'd dabbled and daydreamed for decades waiting for that magical *right time* to start submitting my work. But as Dianne Blacklock says in her novel *The Right Time*: *'There's never a perfect time for life-changing decisions. There's just the right time.'* And pursuing publication is life changing.

I was forty-seven years old when I decided to focus on my dream. I set a few small goals and a do-or-die date. Should I fail, by my fiftieth birthday, to nudge a little closer to the dream with something tangible, I would accept the fact that I *had* left it too late, that ordinary people like me *don't* get published. I would stop wasting my time, avoid disappointment and be content to write for myself.

Instead I learnt this: Just when you think it's time to give up, something amazing happens.

TIP #4: BELIEVE IN DREAMS

One of the writing world's biggest believers became author of the best-selling book series in history and while J.K. Rowling conjured up amazing stories, dazzling us with wizards and magic wands, the writer's reality (her journey to publication) was far from magical. Every step was the result of hard work and determination. The dream doesn't come easily to everyone, much like the main characters in the *Harry Potter* series who each had to put in varying levels of work to achieve the same result in class. For example:

- The bumbling Ron Weasley was born into a family of wizards. He hardly had to try (or be too smart about it). Magic came naturally.

- As a Muggle, Hermione worked hard, not so much at the magic, but at fitting in, always proving to others she was capable.

- Harry had the magic, but he didn't believe. Raised by an ordinary family, he saw himself as an ordinary boy. He had to be convinced about the magic.

Believing is a message woven through the Harry Potter stories, and mirrored in J.K. Rowling's own success story. For anyone who has been living under a rock, I'll explain …

J.K. Rowling was a single mother facing depression and at the lowest point in her life when she started writing. At the time she saw herself as *'the biggest failure she knew'*. Her marriage had failed and she was jobless with a dependent child, but she described her failure as liberating. At the Harvard commencement address in 2008, she said:

'Failure meant a stripping away of the inessential. I stopped pretending to myself that I was anything other than what I was, and began to direct all my energy to finishing the only work that mattered to me. Had I

> *really succeeded at anything else, I might never have found the determination to succeed in the one area where I truly belonged. I was set free because my greatest fear had been realized, and I was still alive, and I still had a daughter whom I adored, and I had an old typewriter, and a big idea. And so rock bottom became a solid foundation on which I rebuilt my life.'*

She not only believed in the dream, she didn't stop believing. She made it happen. Imagine if Harry had missed the Hogwarts Express that day because he didn't have enough belief in himself, or in the magic, to reach the elusive Platform 9¾! All Harry saw on the train station that day was a brick wall. Luckily there were people around who did believe in the magic – and in him.

There's also no magic for a writer faced by the impenetrable publishing brick wall. You just have to be courageous. Like Harry, surrounding yourself with people who believe, and engaging with an encouraging community of like-minded people (writers online or face-to-face) can help you break through any personal barriers and self-doubt.

No one was more surprised than me when, in 2012, the publisher from Simon & Schuster telephoned to offer me a book deal. How lucky did I feel? My sails were full and there was land in my sights.

> *The real differences from writing for pleasure to writing for publication are the demands on your time, and the deadlines.*

There are copyright issues and contracts with interesting clauses – some of which can lock an author into a specific genre or word count, etc. My publisher stipulated that I produce four contemporary small-town novels, each of 120,000-plus words. This is not a bad thing for an author. If I had an urge to write (probably under another name) about flesh-eating zombie fish growing legs and lungs and challenging the local sheriff to pistols at dawn, I could do so without fear of breaching my existing author agreement. Out of professional courtesy (and loyalty) my publisher would get first right of refusal, but I'm fairly certain Simon & Schuster would not muddy the marketing waters with a novel that doesn't meet its existing readership expectations. This kind of contractual query might be something an agent would handle.

Speaking of agents … In my experience, a good agent is a writer's best friend. How do you identify a good agent from a bad one? Go to the novels you like and check out the acknowledgements and dedications. When I found Monica McInerney and Bronwyn Parry both shared the same agent, that was enough for me.

Some authors may disagree about having an agent, but I've seen that a good one will pay for themselves by negotiating contract clauses that favour the writer. Agents are not hard to secure if you have a good product. (That means a great manuscript, polished and professionally presented.) An author brand and online presence can also help. Agents maintain positive and open lines of communication between the author and their publisher and really earn their keep during those tricky times in the publishing process. For example, when there are issues with the cover art or a deadline. Their job is to also keep abreast of industry changes and to manage certain administrative tasks so you can keep writing.

Record your journey. Keep a log of not only the highlights, but all the rollercoaster emotions. Believe me, those detailed feelings will come in very handy the next time one of your characters needs to portray emotions such as happy, sad, desperate, crazy, etc. By the time your journey is over you will have stopped off in every one of those ports – some several times over!

When you dream about writing, if you're anything like me, it's during that first hour after lights-out that you stare wide-eyed at the ceiling, your imagination in overdrive. You will have had a great writing day at the computer and you feel closer to getting The Call with each chapter you edit. Anything's possible, right? You lie back in bed and imagine the ultimate dream – when a publisher on the end of the line tells you how much they *love* your story. You picture your official author photo shoot. You see readers queued to have their copy signed. There are the radio interviews and five-star reviews, awards to accept and, oh, don't forget lunch with Reese Witherspoon and Nicole Kidman to discuss your book becoming an HBO mini series. (Such dreams can become a reality. Just ask Liane Moriaty about HBO.)

While a newly published author is encouraged to keep writing and avoid the dreaded Second Book Syndrome, I paused and I breathed and I realised how lucky I was to have achieved my dream. I had, hadn't I? I mean … *House for all Seasons* made #5 top-selling debut novel in 2013.

What was once the ultimate dream (a book on a shelf) was suddenly one of many. I was no longer content with having my books in bookshops.

My writing dream shifted, reshaped itself and emerged from a deep I hadn't even dared imagine. There's yet another unexpected side to being published.

I was there. I believed anything was possible, and the more you put into your writing career, the more reward you reap. So I started mentoring a local writer, Shannon Garner – a mother of two wanting to tell a non-fiction story about her choice to become a surrogate to a gay male couple (and the emotional journey that entailed). Suddenly my wide-eyed staring at the ceiling at night had changed. I dreamt of getting that manuscript up to submission standard so I could introduce it to my publisher. I was imagining *her* launch, picturing Shannon's author signature on a book, wishing her bestseller status. Shannon's book, titled *Labour of Love: A Story of Generosity, Hope & Surrogacy*, hit the shelves mid-2016.

No matter where you sit on the aspiring, emerging, established, bestseller scale, every manuscript is a labour of love. Some will say the process is as fraught with emotion as delivering a real baby, with any pain forgotten as soon as you have that baby in your hands.

Writing for pleasure is one of many creative hobbies. It can be fun, especially when you print, bind and wrap up those stories for every member of the family at Christmas. (Yeah, I did that too!) Writing for publication is arduous, overwhelming and frustrating. It might not always make us rich in money terms, but it sure does *en*rich our lives, especially those prepared to pay the dream forward.

I consider myself lucky enough already, but if I'm due any more, and one day I hit the jackpot of dreams – my name a household one and with a raft of screenwriting credits added to my achievements – I know I won't want to be so famous that I stop (or worse – delegate) the all-important connection with readers, because they are, after all, the reason I tell my stories.

For now, I am happy to be spinning tales from the country, connecting on Facebook and sharing inspirational stories on my blog. A couple of years ago I traded in my fictional sailing ship for a real-life caravan. I sold everything I owned, downsized into a twenty-four-foot fifth-wheeler, and I plan on living the gypsy life for as long as my writing allows me. I'm exploring, dreaming, and I'm definitely discovering small towns and quintessential Aussie characters to inspire more stories.

TIP #5: HELP FAMILY AND FRIENDS UNDERSTAND THE DREAM BY INVOLVING THEM IN YOUR JOURNEY FROM THE START

Any journey, be it writing or packing up the caravan, is a lot more fun if you share the experience, whereas solo journeys are fraught with challenges.

Find a trusted friend or writing buddy to join you. Finding a mentor isn't as easy and there is no best way of finding one. My advice would be to join a writers' group or your State's writing centre. Many have mentoring programs you can pay for, or apply for, or maybe win. Do enter writing contests and grow a thick skin to absorb the feedback that is sometimes hard to see as constructive.

If you think you can jump on Facebook and message your favourite author for advice, keep in mind they probably get at least one request a day to mentor, promote, or *LIKE* a Facebook page. (Tip: Before you ask an author to *LIKE* your author page it is always a good idea to *LIKE* theirs first. And don't be offended if they don't accept your offer of a manuscript to read.) There are many reasons why an established author will reject an invitation to any number of things and that reason is usually something to do with them having to actually write their book. Remember what I said about deadlines, demands, contracts and clauses?

And about that luck thing … I do tend to agree with J.K. There is definitely a case for *right place, right time*, and in the publishing business luck does play a hand if you also have the right story with the right publisher at the right time. But I believe luck happens when preparedness and opportunity meet, and we control both these to some degree. We can make opportunities by connecting with other writers online, and we can prepare by learning our craft and writing the best story possible. It's a big world and opportunities for writers are growing, not declining. No need to panic. By all means take your time, but remember, you won't sell a story that sits on a hard drive. I procrastinated for months – polishing and perfecting. I read and re-read *House for all Seasons* so many times I began to question everything. I kept cutting and polishing for extra shine to make sure my manuscript stood out from that slush pile. Faultless – or so I thought.

Lucky for me, my publisher's decision was not based on my *faultless submission* and she was willing to see beyond the typos and poor grammar. (I died a thousand excruciating deaths when my first round of edits arrived and I saw the errors I'd missed.)

At the start of this piece I compared that desperate state of an aspiring author to a cork bobbing on an ocean – a sea of arm-waving wannabe writers all crying out, 'Pick me! Pick me!' while treading water, waiting for *HMAS Publisher* to rescue them and welcome them on board with warm, comforting blankets. (Kind of like Harry Potter's invisibility cloak, only this is more a *come-on-board-you-brilliant-writer* blankie.)

The reality of being a first-time published author is not all warm blankets, book signings and Sunday brunches. (Sad, but true!) So, what's really changed for me since I was published? I'm still hunched over a keyboard in a kind of self-imposed solitary confinement and developing addictions to coffee and chocolate, only now I've developed new addictions to Amazon rankings, Goodreads star ratings, and sales figures. Oh, and then there's balancing the need to write with the need to self-promote so you attract new readers, because unless you are an A-lister, your publisher's marketing budget will last only a specified time. Your assigned publicist will have moved on to their next scheduled book release and you will need to pick up the promotion if you want to keep your name out there.

You probably think that having the ultimate affirmation – a published novel – would make a writer feel six feet tall and want to brag. No! I actually *am* six feet tall and the thought of spruiking about myself and my work is still daunting.

Most writers would be familiar with Charles Dickens's *The Tale of Two Cities*. The opening lines sum up the highs and lows — the groundswell that builds as your book hits the shelves.

'It was the best of times, it was the worst of times, it was the age of wisdom, it was the age of foolishness, it was the epoch of belief, it was the epoch of incredulity, it was the season of Light, it was the season of Darkness, it was the spring of hope, it was the winter of despair…'

Hope and despair fight for centre stage when those reviews start coming in and the writer starts to feel the most vulnerable. One minute your boat is swept up in a tsunami of promotion: guest blogs, bookshop signings, Twitter storms (I wish). Life is but a dream, and you're riding so high until that wave of expectations — reader, publisher, family, friends, *your own* — becomes the dumping kind that turns you in every direction, flips your stomach inside out, and leaves you gasping for breath.

Book four and I'm still trying to hold my head above the water: trying to breathe, desperate to know if I'm meeting everyone's expectations — reader, publisher, *mine!* The reviews are great, but are they as great as Author B's or Author C's reviews? Why did that newspaper not review *my* book? Are my sales good enough? Is the publisher happy? Will there be another book contract? Will they …?

Shhh! Breathe, Jenn.

Close your eyes, take a deep breath and dream a little.

FIVE TIPS FROM JENN J MCLEOD

1. Money always flows *to* the author. Not from the author.
2. Try channeling that vivid imagination so it becomes your friend rather than your enemy.
3. Expect the unexpected.
4. Believe in dreams.
5. Help family and friends understand the dream by involving them in your journey from the start.

The Best Training Ground

by Monique Mulligan

WRITING THE DREAM

'Did your mum or dad sign this?'

My Year Two teacher, Mr Barton, peered at me over the top of his glasses. His smile was kind as he perused the slip of paper that confirmed – the signature 'M-U-M' spelt out in green crayon and big childlike letters – that I had read a book for homework.

I wavered. The crayon was a giveaway. I knew it; he knew it.

'My sister did.' I crossed my fingers behind my back and hoped he wouldn't remember that my sister was four years old and unable to write.

'I see.' He nodded and sent me on my way.

Relief was a warm rush that swept away the pang of guilt for the white lie; of course, it was I, not my sister, who had signed the form. I'd convinced him and that's all that mattered.

I LOOK back on this innocent memory with a mixture of embarrassment and sadness. Of course, I hadn't convinced my teacher and over the years I've reflected on my fib with more than a little guilt. So, why did I concoct the 'my sister did it' story? My memory is hazy, but I remember that Mum and Dad had other things on their mind than signing my note; their marriage was struggling and I hadn't wanted to ask. Mr Barton, aware of my love for reading even at that early age, would have believed me if I'd simply said I'd read a book, without giving him the note, but in my desperate desire to please, I hadn't wanted to disappoint him by not producing it. That desire to please follows me today in the guise of Self Doubt.

Whether deliberate or not, reading became a form of escape early in my life. Words and stories fascinated me; I was bored only if I had no book to read (or paper to draw on, if I had no book).

Although I enjoyed writing, and proved good at it during my school years and beyond, books were my constant companion, the 'friends' I could not live without.

My childhood is filled with memories of being a reader. Sitting on a hard chair at my grandfather's house sifting through old Reader's Digest issues for the funny bits. Being given a merit award for being 'a walking encyclopaedia'. Hiding in the corner of the school library on my once-a-year and much anticipated library duty day, pretending I couldn't hear the librarian calling. Reading the hymns (and mentally high fiving when I found one I recognised) instead of listening to the pastor in church. Using a half-nibbled carrot as a bookmark (I know, it's shameful) when Mum called me to do a job for her. Walking into a pole because I was reading instead of looking (this happened more than once, which either proves that I was a slow learner in a spatial sense, or that some books were too good to wait for). Not minding Sunday drives because it meant uninterrupted reading time. Disappearing to my bedroom as a teenager with a book and a bowl of popcorn. Friday afternoon library trips during which I always checked out the maximum number of books. Enduring a muttered 'That book is disgusting' from a well-meaning librarian who thought I was too young, at sixteen, to read *Puberty Blues*. Hiding said book from my Mum, and secretly being appalled by the things the thirteen-year-old girls got up to in panel vans (although I would have died before admitting this to that librarian).

For some, books are one of the forgotten relics of childhood, left to gather dust alongside balding teddy bears (and posters of once spunky rock stars who these days invite the 'What were you thinking?' question), dolls, marbles, fragranced eraser collections and well-thumbed comic books. While I've never been a hoarder (moving around a lot as an adult put paid to that), reading has remained a constant means of relaxation. Surrounded by candles in the bath (I've only ever dropped a book once). Curled up under a bed with a torch and book while playing hide and seek with my three-year-old half-sister. Driving straight to the library post-university exams every semester to indulge my need for comfort, not academic, books. Listening to *The War of the Worlds* while crossing the Nullarbor (does that count?). Reading to the babes in my belly. Donning fingerless gloves in winter (full gloves don't work) but still having to turn pages as fast as possible before shoving my hands under the blanket for a precious warm minute. And although I've never again used a carrot as a bookmark, I still experience that fleeting irritation when my nose is in a book and I'm interrupted.

When people ask, 'What books do you like best?' I'm stumped. At eight, I discovered the Narnia series and immersed myself in C.S. Lewis's fantastical world of anthropomorphic animals, dryads, naiads, fauns, witches, goblins and magical wardrobes. By the time I was ten, I'd devoured the Nancy Drew, Trixie Belden, Naughtiest Girl and Famous Five series. My liking for Enid Blyton won me no respect from Mrs Bounds, the librarian of the foghorn voice, who did not rein in her disappointment at finding I'd chosen a Famous Five box set as one of my

Year Five Pupil of the Year book prizes. I stuck my nose in the air. What did she know?

By twelve, I was racing to the library along with all the other Year Seven girls to be the first to get the new Sweet Dreams or Sweet Valley High book. And then I discovered *Anne of Green Gables* in a cardboard box set aside for the op shop. Oozing that old-book smell, it had long lost its dust cover and had a simple yellow hardcover. Is it possible to fall in love with reading all over again? I read that book over and over, followed by the rest of the Anne books. How I wanted Anne-with-an-e to be *my* kindred spirit (I tried talking like her for a while but my overtures about being in the 'depths of despair' when Mum said I was too young to go to the shops with my friends went unheard). I wish I'd kept that copy; it's long gone – a victim to those multiple relocations.

In my late teens I added Stephen King, Jackie Collins, Colleen McCullough, Danielle Steel, Robin Cook and John Saul to my reading list; in my twenties I was hooked on James Patterson, Jonathon Kellerman, Patricia Cornwall, and other psychological and crime fiction writers. In my thirties, I set such books aside for less psychologically disturbing reads, which I'd found were a little close to home during a difficult period in my life; I still have trouble with books that wobble my psychological balance. So, you now have a picture of a reader who resists putting one genre on a pedestal, but has more insight as to what is good for her soul.

If reading is a constant in my life, equally so is writing.

My career has involved a series of jobs – unrelated at first glance – that have had writing as their base connector: a trainer in two Australian Government departments before I was twenty-three; a children's curricula writer for a Christian publisher; an editor and staff writer for a short-lived but inspired magazine called *South Culture*; a journalist and newspaper editor; a publicity consultant; a freelance writer with a book about local industry under her belt. Aside from the children's curricula, which included what we'd now call flash fiction, rhymes and a couple of plays, most of this writing was non-fiction. Writing this way came easily to me; its legacy is the ability to write in diverse styles. I learnt to write fast, to be concise, and to adapt quickly to different writing situations.

Creatively, though, this type of writing did little for me, apart from deliver regular pay cheques. Living creatively is like food for my soul – it's a hunger that demands to be fed. Ignoring it starves what makes me, me. Photography, drawing mandalas, cooking, scribbling down the occasional poem, and making things like candles – all of these feed my urge to create. And yet, creative writing scared me, even though my efforts at university were commended. It scared me because I wanted to do it well *so* much, that it crippled my attempts to try. So, I put off creative writing for the elusive One Day, burying the stories I knew were waiting for life.

*I allowed Self Doubt, Perfectionism and One Day to
drown my quiet dreams. Mostly.*

Inspired by writing the children's curricula and boosted by my sons' appreciation of my sense of humour (sadly, I am now heckled as a tired mum-joker), I penned a picture book: *Alexandra Rose and Her Icy Cold Toes*. Based on my uncle's tales of a little me (Alexandra is my middle name) who plonked her cold feet on his tummy, I could visualise Alexandra Rose waking her household with her icy toes. When I say visualise, I knew what I wanted the illustrations to look like. I researched publishers and submission guidelines, and submitted my precious text to Scholastic ... and I was devastated when I got a letter saying their list was full for now. My first rejection.

Looking back, it's sad how easily I let Self Doubt turn that into my last for many years; you can't be rejected if you don't put yourself out there. Alexandra Rose still sits in my writing drawer, along with *Fergus the Farting Dragon*, an unfinished chapter book. My boys loved the excerpts I read to them, but instead of giving Fergus a chance, he's in the drawer, warming Alexandra Rose's icy toes. Another picture book manuscript resided in this drawer for some time – it was then called *My Mum is the Silliest Mum in the World* (the 'silly' was an amalgamation of my own mother and myself). More on that later.

Fast forward a few difficult years which burned my creative spark nearly to ashes; these were years in which autopilot was my guide. My only respite was reading in the bath. It was all I could handle. I tried keeping a journal, but it felt fake and shallow; I wanted my thoughts to be profound, but something stopped me from sharing the real me, even on the pages of a notebook not meant for other eyes. Reading over this paragraph reminds me how much my dimmed creative spirit reflected the mask I put on for others at this time; in hindsight, I recognise that period was necessary, prompting life changes that led to where I am now.

One of these changes was leaving my job as a newspaper journalist and editor. After months of suffering chronic occupational overuse syndrome, tendinitis and anxiety as a result of workplace stress and fatigue, I resigned from what I'd thought, as a teenager, was the job of my dreams. Over time, that sorted the physical and emotional issues – and I found the part-time job I'm still in today – but I had to look elsewhere to address the whispers that hinted at a more creative life. A life I sensed I had to make happen, rather than wait for the right time.

I started with a blog called Each Day a Gift, a spin-off of columns I'd been writing for the newspaper. My focus was on positivity, looking on the bright side and humour; looking back, that blog was more for *me* than any readers who happened to stumble upon it. At the same time, I thought, why not start a book review blog? It seemed like a no-brainer; the perfect way to combine reading and writing ... and get free books. It paid off. Within months I was receiving advance copies of new releases from Australia's major publishers (I'm on first-name basis with the staff at my post office), sometimes nine or ten a week! Those weeks, my husband would give me 'the look' which, as all good wives do, I ignored. My profile as a reviewer slowly grew and soon, I was receiving pitches from authors and lesser-known publishers who wanted me to review their books.

Having thirty books on a to-review shelf is not all it's cracked up to be. The pressure to keep up, despite choosing not to adhere to a strict schedule, drained me sometimes. I felt a strong sense of obligation, even responsibility, to review *all* of the books. It all comes back to that desire to please that lurks deep down. I'd spend an hour at least on each review – that's many hours of unpaid writing each week. It took a long time to say no to some of the publishers and authors, to allow myself the choice of not reviewing every book on my shelf, and to stop worrying about what people think. On the last point, I have a long way to go.

When people asked me if I was a writer, I would say yes. Book reviews counted, didn't they? What people meant (and invariably followed up the first question with) was, 'What have you had published?' and 'Would I have read your work?' They weren't referring to book reviews. Or newspaper articles. This unfairness irked me and Self Doubt once again took advantage, reminding me that I was too busy to write what I was increasingly realising I wanted to write: fiction. And even if I could make the time, it probably wouldn't be very good. Not like Amanda Curtin, whose *Elemental* astonished me with the tale and its telling.

---

*And yet, Self Doubt couldn't extinguish the word
'story' that was now branded on my creative soul.*

It wasn't until mid-2015, while reviewing Fiona McIntosh's *How to Write Your Blockbuster*, that I had my now-or-never moment. *Now* was the time to write, to put into practice all I'd learnt from reading, to tell *my* stories. I had to get up earlier, cut back on reviewing, and take back some time for my own writing. I had to shake free of my insecurities and doubts and seize the gift of words with every ounce of my being. I had to act like I was already an author. Creativity had emerged from its box stronger and more demanding than ever, and this time, it had free rein.

Although I'd never visualised myself as a romance writer, I took up the challenge of writing a short romance for the *Rocky Romance* anthology published by Serenity Press. Imagine my surprise when my story, "The Point of Love", was accepted into the anthology. Imagine my excitement upon holding a copy of the book in my shaking hands a few months later. At the same time, I wrote a piece for the City of Rockingham Short Fiction Awards: 'Valiant Return' is a contemporary short story about a mother and son reconnecting after a tragic loss. That story was highly commended in the competition; just the affirmation my praise-hungry self needed. I also submitted *My Mum is the Silliest Mum in the World* to Serenity Press and to my joy it was accepted for publication and released in May 2016 under the shorter, simpler name *My Silly Mum*.

And then, after a couple of false starts, I started writing a full-length contemporary novel about a couple who move to a small town for a fresh start following a tragedy. *Wherever You Go* (working title) is now 70,000 words in. Interestingly, I've learnt that while I can churn out newspaper stories, I'm a slow writer when it comes to fiction. People say: write, write, write – just get it on paper. That approach doesn't work for me – I've tried. This cooking simile explains how I work: creative writing is like cooking a meal for loved ones. It's choosing the best possible produce, mixing ingredients, adding seasoning to taste and a dash of love, and plating it up with flair. It's like alchemy for words.

I've set my bar high. After reading *Elemental* and Stephanie Bishop's *The Other Side of The World* I thought, 'I want to write like this': evocative landscape descriptions, powerful imagery, emotive narratives that tear at a reader's heart. Aware of these lofty ideals, Self Doubt is quick to slip in with the debilitating words: you can't. It has taken me a long time to understand and accept that instead of emulating other writers, I need to write like Monique.

When asked 'What advice would you give to a novice writer?', bestselling author Stephen King says: 'If you want to be a writer, you must do two things above all others: read a lot and write a lot.' He also says: 'If you don't have time to read, you don't have the time (or the tools) to write. Simple as that.' Other authors echo this wisdom – it's the predictable, but common sense response. Reading widely provides inspiration, knowledge, language awareness, vocabulary, and genre appreciation. It's the best training ground for becoming a great writer – not just someone who knows how and when to put an apostrophe in its place.

My eclectic reading history forms an intensive research base which influences what and how I write. But here's the thing I've noticed: the more I write, the more my approach to reading is changing. It's no longer only about the story, about sinking into the couch and transporting myself to another world, another life (although that is still part of the experience). Narrative techniques and plot structure were assessed informally as part of my reviewing role, but now that evaluation has stepped up a notch. When I read, I'm observing technique, dialogue, structure, point of view and language from an even more analytical aspect. How well did the writer do this or that? Did this narrative style work? How would I have done this differently? I'm reading as a student of words, not simply an absorber of words.

Does this affect my reading experience? No, because there are still moments when I'm swept away by something beautiful, clever or laugh-out loud funny. My reading experience is enriched because beneath every story I read, there is something wonderful for me to put into practise as a writer.

FIVE TIPS FROM MONIQUE MULLIGAN

1. Read widely, read well and think about what you're reading. Use your reading time to enjoy the words but also to study writing techniques and styles.
2. Write what you love to read.
3. Become part of the writing community in your area. You will be encouraged, inspired and challenged.
4. Keep a notebook with you for unexpected ideas. I also have a box under my desk for ideas, articles and scenes related to other stories I'm not working on the time.
5. Make time to write. Schedule it in. You do that for appointments, so why not writing?

Anatomy of a Fetish

by Michele Nugent

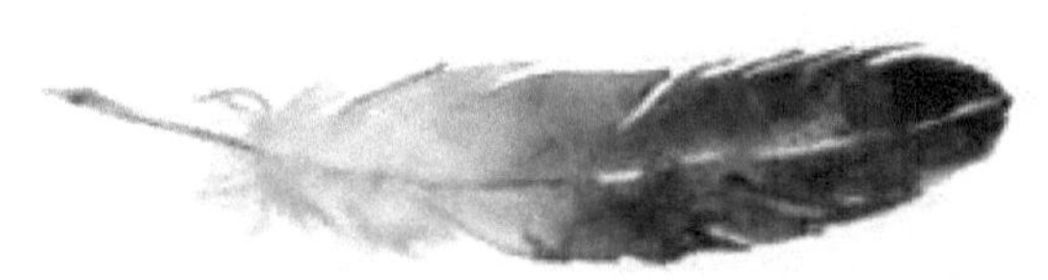

IT began in Year Two. My stomach-souring dread of maths.

I don't remember completing anything to do with numbers in Year One – it was such a whimsical school year, spent building topple-y towers from what felt like about a hundred tiny wooden cubes. I was in love with Mrs Power of the pastel lips and silky black Agent 99 bob. She knew just how to bewitch her impressionable students – with storybook reading every afternoon.

In Year Two, I was introduced to anxiety. Even lining-up was terrifying. 'Miss Cummings is coming!' we would all surreptitiously whisper, as she headed our way, her blazing red curls bouncing, denim A-line skirt flapping, depositing her snappy impatience for we of the numerically challenged grey matter.

That year I do remember doing maths – just another subject our teacher (I use that term loosely) appeared to dislike teaching. And while addition and subtraction seemed logical, division – or finding out 'how many groups of' four apples there were in a basket of sixteen – dumped me deaf, dumb and blind on a whole other planet.

Progressively, my 'mathsmare' worsened. Adding and taking away was so easy, but predictably, these 'problems' disappeared from our maths lessons.

By Year Six my maths phobia was so bad – Mr Dunne, take a bow – I could barely function in class because I was so scared of fractions, percentages, isosceles triangles and something called pi. Not that I'd ever been a big fan of pi, even with the addition of tomato sauce.

Imagine my horror in Year Eight when I was required to compute 'how many hours, minutes and seconds it took a jet passing over the International Date Line to fly 30,000 kilometres at an altitude of 20,000 feet at a median speed of 880 kilometres per hour'. (I don't care).

Even the word itself – maths – continues to have a sweat-inducing effect on me. This clumsy, ugly, awkward-sounding arrangement of letters is derived from the word mathematics which comes from the Greek *manthanein*, meaning 'to learn'. I maintain that is the problem – I never learnt it because it wasn't taught to me properly.

Apparently it is the foundation of all life. Now why wouldn't a curious, questioning girl like me be interested in that impressive claim? I still wonder if, one day, it will finally click. Now that we have arrived in the Federal Government sanctioned age of STEM – Science, Technology, Engineering and Maths (eerrkkk) – what will become of other digital dummies? Are literature and the humanities so passé that future employment will rarely require these skills?

My complete hatred and misunderstanding of digits, numerals and numbers is a bit puzzling because for the longest time, I clearly remember my favourite childhood picture book was about a top-hat wearing worm called Eddie, who, like the Count from *Sesame Street*, loved to count.

Eddie's Numbers told the adventurous tale of how Eddie managed to usher other small defenceless creatures – who he counted along the way – safely aboard his leaf as it rushed down a raging river swollen by worsening torrential rain.

I read it over and over, again and again. But it wasn't the counting that had me hypnotised. Not only was this very grown up book mine alone – I fiercely but unsuccessfully protected it from the destructive fingers of little brothers – it told a fantastic story of how a squishy, uninspiring invertebrate courageously saved other misunderstood creepy crawlies from certain death, delivering them safely from an almost biblical flood.

It was a nature-themed adventure with an unassuming hero and a happy ending. And I could read it all day long, all by myself. Forty-odd years later, this book sits sentimentally in my bookcase, old-fashioned stitched spine rent asunder from its thick A3 pages full of bright illustrations.

This bookish Christmas gift shunted my love affair with stories into top gear; I continue to ride that sticky clutch every day in myriad ways.

I read stories, I hear them, I see them, I recognise them, I learn from them, I enthuse over them, I wonder at them, I am humbled by them, I share them, I collect them, I celebrate them. But what I love most, is to write them.

My very-able literary brain has always overcompensated for my dis-abled maths brain

And it has taken me on some fascinating journeys. And some bland ones, let's be honest ... reporting on electors' meetings is rarely entertaining.

While long division, longitude and latitude and how steel boats loaded with still more steel stay afloat will forever remain a mystery to me, words – and by extension, writing, reading and speaking them – have sustained me. And my family. Financially, emotionally and cerebrally.

My top tips for writers, derived from personal experience, may be cliché, but they are authentic, and I include them below, for your selective edification.

IDENTIFY YOUR STRENGTHS, THEN LOVINGLY NURTURE THEM

Half way through Year Ten, it dawned that adulthood was breathing down my neck. This realisation was heralded by subject choices, looming Year Twelve exams, the stultifying threat of university study, and the pressure to get my driver's licence. I had no desire to be in charge of what I felt was a weapon of mass destruction! And that was just the university study ...

It was time for my inaugural trip into the room of mirrors.

What was I good at? Writing! What did I want to avoid for the rest of my life? Maths! It was a no-brainer.

I would have to give up my high ideals of becoming an archaeologist, so I could dig up old stuff, or a marine biologist, so I could ride on the backs of killer whales, to be a journalist, so I could write ripping yarns.

It sounded slightly unrealistic, a little bit glamorous (it wasn't), self-indulgent, and possibly a good money earner (it certainly wasn't – we women bruised our brain stems batting against the ceiling of a glass elevator stuck two-thirds of the way up).

Mimicking *Sesame Street's* Bert and Ernie's 'it's so crazy, it just might work' mantra, I set about honing my writing skills and working out where and how I could become a journalist while living in the small, isolated mining town my family called home.

In Year Ten, I got off to a great start by offending my English teacher with some of the opinion pieces I wrote, to such a degree that she marked me down for writing about pro-abortionists, land rights and capital punishment. The situation got so dire that my mother met with her, ultimately deciding that my teacher's Christian views were clouding her objectivity. It was typical of Mum's support of me, but it was important that I continue to get good English marks if I wanted to get into university to study journalism.

In Year Eleven, I decided I was good enough to give English Literature a go. I couldn't have been more wrong. It was so convoluted and mercurial, and the aged male teacher so sexist, dragging his young buxom wife and baby into the middle of nowhere to chase his career goals. Bolshy, moi? Perpetuating stereotypes? Maybe a bit.

We clashed on the fundamental meanings of everyone from Robert Frost to Sylvia Plath to e.e. cummings. For him, everything related back to sex. I went from a B to a D in three terms and ran back into the open arms of general TEE (now ATAR) English. It was that or score an F in my school report.

With my ego bruised and my self-confidence shattered, I felt directionless and close to failing at life.

Until, encouraged by my parents, I applied to do some work experience at the town's weekly community newspaper.

A fantastic, loud, energetic woman editor, a professional acquaintance of my mother, gave me some basic articles to follow up, and I eagerly completed them. And she dutifully printed them, including the photos I took on the office camera.

I was hooked. I was writing! And I was doing something that was interesting and potentially useful to someone other than myself. All my buttons were pushed right in!

I blame a couple of early influencers – Trixie Belden, a bold young self-appointed detective in a series I read hungrily and religiously, and Sarah Jane Smith, the feisty companion of Doctor Who in the early-mid 1970s – a curious, nosy, determined reporter who may have provided my first vocational inspiration.

If you like writing about maths, finances and accounting, or if you're more of a fashion blogger, own your voice and write it loud.

ACCEPT HELP AND ADVICE – ESPECIALLY IF IT KILLS YOU

Probably the thing that should be said in preface to this point is, we are never too good to accept help and advice, simultaneously if necessary.

If you don't feel you are confident enough to 'just say yes' to this concept, you especially need to do so. It will make you confident in your own abilities, and sharpen your professional writing direction.

I firmly believe that not only do strong people accept help and advice, they go in search of it. Of course, I learnt this as an adult, but if I had realised the value of this behaviour as a young woman, who knows where I'd be now.

I may have found myself an awesome mentor, had my mind expanded by unearthly horizons, conquered mountains or even become a member of Australia's pathetic percentage of women in leadership roles in Australian media. But I digress.

Search for opportunities for improvement, open yourself up to them, be available, never say no to opportunity and do all of this before you begin to absent-mindedly think about babies. Because that is likely to happen. Investing in your professional growth and raising your children each need your undivided attention, if you are to be satisfied and effective.

Accepting help and advice should be a life-long commitment – it's a form of learning after all.

Then, you can confidently share your skills with others, especially with those a little too shy to speak up and ask for help.

Know your writing will benefit and just go with it.

BE PERSISTENT

Got a goal? Tried to achieve it once? Twice? Didn't get anywhere, so gave up? Never give up!

If there's one thing I learnt the value of early, it was that being persistent – even to the point of feeling like you are an actual pain in the arse – pays dividends. Fortunately, this skill was endlessly handy in my journo life as I embarked on the daily hunt for news and stories to research and write.

After having several articles printed in my local newspaper, I was starting to build a portfolio that I added to my resume – along with my casual jobs as an announcer at the local radio station and at the town's sole supermarket weighing fruit and veg.

My folks egged me on, and I can probably attribute much of my bravado to teenage naïvety, plain and simple. What could people say? Yes, or no. Those were the two choices, I was already aware of both outcomes, so no unexpected surprises there. I wrote to the group editor of the newspaper company that owned my local rag, and told him how wonderful I was, and how much I'd like a cadetship when I finished high school.

I even guilelessly rang him up on our family dial phone to say hi and reiterate that message. After a year of letters and phone calls, every time I had a new article printed locally, the poor man finally gave in. He had been telling me for the longest time no openings were available. But Mum and Dad urged me to keep reminding him I was still there and still interested. And so I did, even as it pushed me beyond my comfortable limits of confidence.

But the day did arrive when John Brown (deceased) called to offer me a cadetship if I could get to Perth in the next week, to begin the MS-DOS, darkroom-tinted, pre-Google days of journalism. I could already feel the chalky newspaper print on my fingertips.

I was a vision of dumbfounded excitement, normally referred to as a stunned mullet! Writing for a living! In Perth, away from the small, isolated mining town my family called home!

I finished my last Year Twelve exam and flew down to Perth to stay with my grandparents in the regional town on the outskirts of the city where I would begin work. I didn't even stay for my Year Twelve graduation ceremony, or to accept the Year Eleven/Twelve runner-up Poetry Award (a book of Henry Lawson poems that's also still languishing in my bookcase).

My life had taken an opportunistic turn, and it was no accident. It was persistence.

Take this approach to your writing. Just be pushy. Especially with yourself.

FAKE IT UNTIL YOU MAKE IT – DON'T LET DISASTROUS BOSSES SQUEEZE THE LIFE OUT OF YOU

I'm still faking it. That's what you do all your life if you are constantly learning new things, isn't it?

In my own inimitable way – we each have our own – I knuckle down and do my best work at all times, all the while feeling like a beginner. It's a delicious juxtaposition, but one that keeps me on my toes, never contemptuous and always ready to learn something new.

I learnt to soak up the positive influences, too. There were a few bad ones that left me reconsidering if I really did want to be a writer, if I even had the ability to do that, but eventually I learned to push those bitter pills to the side of my plate.

In the media industry, hierarchy is almost everything. You start at the bottom of the bottom heap. You prove yourself to every superior level above, and only then can you approve of yourself.

Assume there will be snags, in the shape of bosses who believe every first 'par' should contain a cliché, that every story follows the same formula, and that you need to collect their dry cleaning and takeaway dinner and scratch their back because they can't reach that itchy spot themselves. Oh. Okay, that was just my boss …

Don't be disheartened by those threatened by the new, talented kid on the block … a council rose-picking dreamer capable of being named a highly commended cadet in the WA Media Awards.

As weird as it sounds, after hitting a particularly low period professionally, and personally, I dug in my heels and became the quietly determined little cow I am today. I did it on the back of something my father told me, something I didn't understand for some time. 'Give her enough rope and she'll hang herself,' he said.

She did and I went on to another company where a fantastic editor became a great role model and friend, and where I took on some awesome responsibility that had me faking it big time. And no one could even tell.

Lie to yourself until it becomes your truth.

NEVER STOP WRITING. EVER

From childhood to death, aim to write every day. Or at least read. Or better still, both.

I had pen pals all over the world, friends who left our transient town with their families that became my writing muses, grandparents in various locations; the Queen was even a lucky recipient, and a reply from her lady-in-waiting just inspired me further.

I've written diaries (spurred on by a habit drilled into us at primary school), gratitude journals, daily entries in diaries I wrote for my children during their gestation and first year of life, letters of protest, letters of love, poetry, short stories, university assignments, birthday cards, thank-you notes, painful personal writerly outpourings of raw emotion, children's stories, dreams, blogs, social media rants, shopping lists and others of pros and cons, and thrillingly, the first 14,500 words of the 'coming of age' novel that I can no longer keep inside. And these are just the personal scribblings.

Professionally I've written front page articles, back page sport reports, opinion pieces, news features, real estate, restaurant, film, music and theatre reviews, human interest yarns, travel features, articles for coffee table hardbacks, home decorator magazines, government department reports and media releases, speeches, newsletters, video scripts, funding proposals, communications plans, job applications, and so much more. And I've received awards for my achievements.

But I've also been rewarded for my efforts. Writing is who I am. It's how I express myself. I would be woefully incomplete without it, without the practise of wrangling words, old and new, into arrangements that please my sensibilities, as socialist and bleeding-hearted as they may sometimes be.

So. If this resonates with you, just give in to writing. Let it weave its palpable spell through the lives of you and yours.

Rest assured. If I know you, I will write about you. Somewhere. Somehow. Some time. That is what it means to be a writer, and the friend of one.

Write on, sisters. And brothers. Write on.

FIVE TIPS FROM MICHELE NUGENT

1. Identify your strengths, then lovingly nurture them.
2. Accept and seek help and advice – especially if it kills you.
3. Be persistent.
4. Fake it until you make it. Don't let bosses squeeze the life from you.
5. Never stop writing. Ever.

I Never Wanted to be a Journalist

by Teena Raffa-Mulligan

I NEVER wanted to be a journalist. When a career counsellor pointed me in that direction during my final year of high school I dismissed the suggestion outright. I wanted to be a 'real' writer.

The vision I had for myself was far more literary than writing news reports. I was going to write novels that had meaning and would change the way their readers thought. Beautifully crafted poetry. Inspirational works that would touch hearts and souls. Words that would linger in the minds of readers long after the pages of my books had become tattered from overuse. An apartment in Paris. A bohemian lifestyle. It was the 1960s after all and I had quite an imagination. How little I knew of myself and the way life works.

My story wasn't to be chapter and scene as I'd planned it. It wouldn't be a direct path to publication, a smooth road from A to B, but a meandering route that would take me on unexpected detours and lead me in a few unlikely directions.

Along the way I'd meet wonderful fellow travellers and inspirational mentors. And I'd learn so much. About writing. How to shape my words to suit a market. How to edit and rewrite and tame my innate creativity to behave occasionally in a way that fit in the world I found myself.

Above all though, I'd learn about myself. My expectations and ideas around the practise of writing would be put under the microscope time and again. The role of ego and self-importance. My concept of success as a writer. The biggest lesson of all would be to let go. To surrender and allow creativity to flow through me in its way, not mine.

We are all merely channels for creativity. We bring our minds to bear on how and when it will be expressed.

Many writers, particularly today, can do that extremely effectively. They set goals and targets, plot and plan, produce novel after novel on time and to order.

I am in awe of their process and productivity.

It is not my way as a writer and I'm fortunate to now be at a stage in my life where I can accept that and allow it. Yes, I write regularly, and I advise everyone who wants to be a writer to do this.

I know that 'turning up at the page', as Julia Cameron describes it, works. The way I understand the process, by picking up the pen or sitting at the keyboard we give the creative aspect of ourselves a clear message: I am here, I am ready, I am willing.

For me, it triggers a switch that doesn't usually flick on when I choose but at other, and often less appropriate, times. While hanging out the clothes, walking along the beach path, travelling by car or on the train, watering the garden. The words that wouldn't come when I wanted them to will fill my head, tumbling over each other in their urgency to be expressed. That's when I do my best writing. Bit by bit, from random scenes, phrases and sentences that I can later piece together to form a cohesive whole.

So writing for me can be unpredictable. Do I sit at the computer and work with conscious intent to tell a story? Of course I do. One of the most important lessons journalism taught me was that I can write to order and do it well. When I'm heart heavy or heart broken. When I feel there isn't a word left in me worth writing. Through everything else that is going on in my life and the family who share it.

At the time my first middle grade novel had been accepted for publication, my wonderful Dad was dying of cancer. I had six weeks to do the rewrites and, 'Oh, by the way,' the publisher added, 'we need you to expand the length from 17,000 words to between 30,000 and 40,000.' The novel is a light-hearted slightly quirky tale about a kid who sells his dad and has to get him back. I wasn't in the right creative or emotional space for writing. My heart felt like it was breaking. I was losing Dad and I ached with the pain of it. I was in no mood for fun and games, fictional or otherwise. Yet I did that rewrite. And I came up with some entertaining scenes. No one reading it now would be able to tell what was happening in my personal life at the time.

But is a writer's personal and writing life ever separate? They are merely different aspects of the one living experience.

Writing — or storytelling — has been a vibrant thread so closely interwoven throughout the fabric of my life that to remove it would be to create an entirely different pattern.

I grew up surrounded by an extended family of natural storytellers and listened enthralled to their tales about their lives. My English grandmother told me how my grandfather fell over on the ice and she helped him back on his feet. They married and came to Australia in 1926 to start a new life as part of the Group Settlement Scheme in the south west of Western Australia. When that venture failed, the growing family travelled from place to place while my grandfather built roads through the bush before becoming a poultry farmer and later working at Kwinana's first oil refinery.

In the early 1900s my Italian grandfather, who had gone to sea at the age of nine, came to Fremantle and was involved in establishing the crayfishing industry. He eventually returned to Sicily to find a wife and his mother suggested a respectable friend of the family, who accepted his proposal and left home and family to come to a place she knew little about. My parents told me their stories and I'm sure that rich cultural background was a strong influence on inspiring the storyteller in me.

From the time I discovered the wonderful worlds I could enter through reading I knew I wanted to be a writer. Even an early dream of becoming a ballerina included the plan to write novels in the dressing room between performances. And while reality put paid to the dance fantasy, the writing ambition persisted.

I didn't do a university degree or undertake formal studies to achieve it. My training as a writer was unconventional. That's not to say I didn't study writing, because I did. In those pre-digital days, I borrowed every relevant book about writers and writing from the library, and read fiction voraciously.

I began submitting short fiction and poetry to magazines and journals from the age of eighteen, without success. Marriage, pregnancy and motherhood barely interrupted the flow of words. I wrote all the time – while breastfeeding, keeping a watchful eye on toddlers playing in the bath, and waiting for dinner to cook. My daily to-do lists included 'Finish short story' and 'Organise submission', along with the routine household chores. I wrote first drafts in longhand in small notebooks and on scraps of paper, and typed the final versions on a portable Olivetti typewriter on a corner of the dressing table in our bedroom.

The idea of writing for children rather than adults had been born not long after our first child. For the next couple of years, I peppered publishers with picture book manuscripts and attracted one rejection after another. When the latest rejection was accompanied by some rather brutal feedback I was devastated and gave way to floods of tears. Writing was my passion, my vocation. If I wasn't a writer, what was I?

Mr Practical, who wasn't to set out on his own creative path for another decade, was somewhat bemused by this dramatic reaction.

'Find another hobby,' he said. 'Paint pictures. Make pots.'

There was something in me that couldn't abandon the writing dream. I'm told 'fire' was the first word I ever said. According to Mum, she was nursing me on her lap in front of the blazing fire at my English grandparents' place, where we were living at the time, and I pointed at the flames and said the word clearly.

Best-selling novelist Anna Jacobs says writers need to have 'fire in their belly' to succeed. Perhaps I had that. Some might have perceived my refusal to give up as stubbornness. I called it persistence. I picked myself up and forged ahead … in a different direction.

I set my fiction ideas aside and began writing and submitting magazine articles on spec, operating from the naïve assumption that anyone with basic written English skills could succeed in that field. I must have done something right because my stories sold. At last I was published. One editor even phoned to ask what else I was working on and after buying what I had on file, began to commission articles.

I used my earnings to buy an impressive timber double pedestal roll top desk, which took pride of place in what had been the meals area of the kitchen before we extended our small three-bedroom home to include a dining room. Its drawers soon began to fill with copies of manuscripts, efficiently kept in triplicate. I loved the pigeon holes where I could store envelopes, staples, postage records, income and expenses notebook and the box of file cards where I diligently noted every submission. I'd graduated to a full-size manual typewriter by then and the babies had grown into young children who often left a calling card of sticky fingers or additional words or letters on partly written manuscripts still in the machine. Although I was Mum first and foremost, I was treating this writing business very seriously.

When we received a free local newspaper in the letterbox, I had no hesitation in responding to an ad that caught my eye. I'd never heard of a 'stringer' (a paid contributor), but I was confident I could cover local news in my area. Fortunately, the editor agreed and considering our youngest was only two, it was a bonus that I was expected to work variable hours from home.

So, the fifteen-year-old who had turned up her nose at journalism as being a boring job, found herself doing just that. As well as being interesting and intellectually stimulating, journalism suited my temperament far better than I ever could have imagined. Working for local newspapers and continuing to freelance for magazines gave me the opportunity to turn my natural facility with language and innate curiosity about all manner of subjects to advantage.

Yet always it felt like I was in one place while wanting to be in another. I was writing and being published, but not as the writer I wanted to be.

Throughout my career as a journalist I never lost the desire to be what I perceived as a 'real' writer and continued to write picture books, poems and children's novels in what little spare time I had in between juggling the demands of family and work.

My first published book was the twenty-seventh picture book manuscript I wrote. That stranger danger tale about an elephant and a tiger inspired by a community policing talk at my children's primary school brought me five minutes' fame due its safety topic. There was a flurry of media interviews when the book was released and it was endorsed by the State education and police departments of the day and used in schools around the country. I thought I'd finally made it as an author.

I was wrong. My next two children's books weren't published for another fifteen years, despite me writing and submitting continuously throughout that time. It never occurred to me to give up my author dream. I'm sure the wonderful feedback from some publishers and occasional sales of poems and short stories to magazines helped, though I'd be lying if I didn't admit to feeling on occasion that there must be something wrong with me to keep pushing against that publication brick wall. If I weren't such an optimist I might have given up. I didn't and eventually some of my children's book manuscripts landed on the right publisher's desk at the right time.

Sometimes I've wondered how different my life as a writer would have been if I'd found it easier to get my children's books published from the start, if I hadn't taken that detour into journalism following those early manuscript rejections. Then I'm reminded of the role writing for magazines and newspapers has played in shaping me as the writer I am today.

I placed so little value on all the news reports, feature articles and interviews I wrote during my years as a journalist, celebrating only my publications as an author. Only now can I see all that productivity as simply another outpouring of my creative expression as a writer, no less or more important than my publications for children. And while my childhood vision was for quite a different writing life, I realise I've been living my writing dream all along.

FIVE TIPS FROM TEENA RAFFA-MULLIGAN

1. Write in the way that feels right for you. Measuring yourself against how or what others write is a waste of creative energy.
2. Remain open to possibilities instead of having a rigid mindset about the kind of writer you want to be.
3. Start writing your story wherever it's easiest. If you're stuck on the beginning, start with the end, the middle or anywhere else in between.
4. When the words won't come, walk away from the computer; close the notebook. You might think you've stopped working on your story. It's an illusion. Taking a break gives your creative mind the space it needs to work without the interference of the conscious mind. You'll return to the screen or the page with a fresh perspective.
5. Words are your currency but not every word you write is precious. A manuscript is crafted as much from the words you choose to lose as those you save.

Hard Travelin'

by Guy Salvidge

WRITING THE DREAM

I CERTAINLY wrote stories before the age of fifteen, but it was on April 30, 1996 that I first thought of myself as a writer. I wrote a science fiction story, "Contact", for a composition test in my Year Ten English class. The story scored 95 per cent and a comment reading, 'Excellent in both creativity and expression.' "Contact" is now the oldest story of mine I possess; it's #1 in my story file. #52, the newest story in the file, is "Frank", which recently won the 2015 City of Rockingham Short Fiction Award and has since appeared in *Westerly: New Creative* and *Award Winning Australian Writing 2016*. Fifty-two stories in twenty years doesn't strike me as being an awful lot, but that's because my heart was set on writing novels.

I expanded "Contact" into a 6000-word story I called "The Maklorian Encounter". My English teacher entered this and two other stories I'd written into the Roy Grace English Scholarship, which I ended up winning. The prize money was $600 and it helped me to buy my first car. I expanded "The Maklorian Encounter" into a 40,000-word novel, *Maklorian*, and that won the Children's Book Week Make Your Own Story Book competition in 1998. In 1999, I won the Young Writers category of the Katharine Susannah Prichard (KSP) Writers' Centre Short Fiction Award. At the ceremony I met Nathan Hobby, whom I'd bested on this occasion but who would later decisively best me by winning the 2002 TAG Hungerford Prize for his first novel, *The Fur*. I had my final writing success as a teenager by having a story Highly Commended in the 2000 KSP Speculative Fiction Award. I even persuaded judge Van Ikin to read the manuscript of what was by then my fourth novel, *Shield*. He told me that I had great promise but he didn't think *Shield* would be the first of my novels to be published.

If I could go back in time and speak to my nineteen-year-old self, I wouldn't tell him to give up writing, but I would tell him to rein in his expectations. Without knowing it, I'd been a big fish in a small pond to this point. Now I was a minnow in a wide, cruel ocean.

My twenties, the 2000s, are thus best forgotten. I thought I was a big shot, but I wasn't. I thought my novels and stories would be published, but they weren't. I even had to go to work full time once I'd finished my university studies, first in a series of liquor stores and then, after I completed a Diploma of Education, as a teacher. I entered my eighth novel, *The Kingdom of Four Rivers*, into the 2008 TAG Hungerford Award, but it didn't get a look in. The book was finally published by the now-defunct Equilibrium Books. Barely selling one hundred copies and attracting no critical attention whatsoever, it nonetheless became a limited success in its meagre way.

I'm not particularly superstitious, but when one toils a road as lonely as the road of the obscure writer, a little superstition can be of great comfort. I had the notion that I might fare better in my thirties, the 2010s. When I received a Commended certificate in the 2010 KSP Speculative Fiction Award, it wasn't lost on me that this was the first writing acclaim I'd received in ten years. There was more to come in the form of the 2011 IP Rolling Picks Award for my ninth novel, *Yellowcake Springs*. The novel was published by Interactive Publications and in 2012 it was shortlisted for the Norma K Hemming Award. A sequel to this, *Yellowcake Summer*, was released in 2013. All ten of my novels thus far had been science fiction, but now I thought to turn my hand to writing crime fiction instead. I wrote my eleventh novel, *Thirsty Work*, in part during two Emerging Writer-in-Residence stints, at KSP in 2013 and at the Fellowship of Australian Writers WA in 2014. Despite my best efforts, *Thirsty Work* remains unpublished. This was a blow, of course, but it hasn't prevented me from starting work on a twelfth novel.

My first love in both reading and writing was, is, and will always be, the novel. However, writing and not being able to publish novels can be the most gruelling and unrewarding work imaginable, and while writing short stories often isn't very much more rewarding, at least the whole process happens much quicker. It usually takes me the best part of two years to gestate and birth a novel, whereas a 3000-word short story might take me a week. Since 2010, I've generally written two or three short stories per year and I've had some modest success in publishing these. Three stories in my Tyler Bramble post-apocalyptic detective series have appeared in various publications, as have a handful of other works.

If a novel is like a child you've carried step by painful step to its two-year term, then a short story is like a cousin you only see at Christmas.

If something unfortunate happens to it (like, for instance, it doesn't win the award you've entered it into), then *que sera sera*.

FINE READING

I read about one hundred books per year and for the most part I don't think about writing while reading, but you can't help but be influenced by what you imbibe. My intention is to be a purveyor of fine reading but, like anyone, I have particular tastes. In the past decade I've read and enjoyed plenty of crime fiction. The exemplar par excellence of the genre is Raymond Chandler. To read his novels *The Big Sleep*, *Farewell, My Lovely* and *The Long Goodbye* is to sit at the feet of the master and marvel. A modern Australian near-equivalent is Peter Temple, especially his novels *An Iron Rose* and *The Broken Shore*. Likewise, the crime novels of US author Megan Abbott. For insight into the mind of the psychopathic killer, you need look no further than the works of Jim Thompson, particularly *The Killer Inside Me* and *Pop 1280*, the paragon of what the French call *Série noire*. Nor will you go wrong with the novels of Derek Raymond, James Sallis or West Australian author David Whish-Wilson — that is if you like your fiction served dark.

Down the other end of Genre Street, I discovered exemplary works of literary fiction. Here I heartily recommend the novels of English author Pat Barker, especially her Regeneration trilogy set during World War I. Another very different but equally evocative author is Mikhail Bulgakov, who has the honour, in my mind at least, of being the bravest of all writers in that he wrote to Stalin asking for permission to leave the Soviet Union at the height of the Great Terror. He died in 1940, but not in the gulag. Bulgakov's magnum opus is *The Master and Margarita*, but just as good and more accessible is *A Country Doctor's Notebook*, which is the subject of a recent and very enjoyable BBC series. Other literary authors I can recommend include Ken Kalfus, Zoe Heller, Ma Jian, Alan Warner, J.M. Coetzee, Raymond Carver and Michael Chabon. My favourite work of Chabon's, *The Yiddish Policemen's Union*, is the best alternate universe crime narrative set in an Alaskan Jewish state I've ever read. It's also among the very best novels of any kind I've read.

Then, somewhere between literary and crime fiction, lies the muddy hinterland of what is variously called Southern Gothic or Grit Lit or Country Noir. Most, but not all, of this type of work is by American authors and my introduction was by way of Harry Crews's incomparable *A Feast of Snakes*, still the only book I've ever finished reading and started reading again on the same day. The now-deceased Crews is a fairly obscure writer and most of his work is out of print, but I highly recommend not only *A Feast of Snakes* but also *All We Need of Hell* and his memoir, *A Childhood: The Biography of a Place*, which is about his dirt-poor youth in Bacon County, Georgia. Cormac McCarthy is the most celebrated contemporary author in this field, even though many people only know him as the author of *The Road*. I've now read almost all of his work, although I will admit to having been defeated by the ponderous excesses of *Blood Meridian* and *Suttree*. More to my liking are the works of William Gay and Daniel Woodrell, and then there's Larry Brown, Vicki Hendricks, Donald Ray Pollock and the grandmammy of them all, Flannery O'Connor. All are fearsome – fierce – and all are worth reading.

I haven't even mentioned my earlier influences in J.G. Ballard, William Burroughs, Graham Greene, M. John Harrison and, my biggest influence of all, Philip K. Dick. If you asked me who my favourite author was, I wouldn't be able to tell you. But if you asked me to name twenty, I could do it. My point here is that, to paraphrase Duffy Deeter from *All We Need of Hell*, you gotta have a little enthusiasm.

Stephen King has a line about how if you don't have the time to read, then you don't have the time or the tools to write. This is of course true. Writing stems from a love of reading. It is a consequence, a by-product, of all that reading.

FINE, WRITING

Writers need routine. Almost every writer can agree on this. What they seldom agree on is what that routine ought to consist of. What I've learnt from teaching creative writing at high school and occasionally adult level is that you can't force someone to be creative in a particular time and place. We all work in different ways. What writers need, then, is a routine that works for them. This routine needs to take into account work and family commitments, but it needs to prioritise writing, or writing will never happen.

WRITING THE DREAM

Almost everything is easier than writing and almost everything offers more lucrative financial rewards, so you have to really want to do it or you never will.

Conventional wisdom says we ought to find time each day for writing, even if it's only twenty minutes. The idea is that this way you'll chip away at your project gradually, no matter how busy you are. I've long eschewed this 'write every day' mantra. The way I've rationalised this to myself is that, as I have twelve weeks' holidays per year from my job as an English teacher, I can produce a year's work during those twelve weeks if I use my time effectively. If I write one thousand words per writing day, I can produce 84,000 words a year. In theory, anyway. Since 1996, I've recorded the quantity of the words I've written. A quick glance at this document informs me that I've only hit 84,000 words five times in twenty years and all but one of those times was before I started teaching. In fact, I've only written 461,000 words of fiction in the past ten years – 46,100 words per year. Not bad, I suppose, but I could do better.

Harry Crews says you should put your ass in the chair for three hours per day, but William Burroughs says writing you do when you don't feel like writing 'ain't worth shit'. It's hard to know who to believe, but what you should never do is let others dictate how, when or what you should write. The writers I admire most are fiercely individual. They're iconoclastic, idiosyncratic and they may also be irascible. These writers didn't accept anyone else's definition of who they ought to be, as writers or as human beings. Not only does Cormac McCarthy not use quotation marks for dialogue, but his Border Trilogy contains whole swathes of dialogue in untranslated Spanish. His books contain English words I haven't even seen before. McCarthy was an obscure writer for decades, but it seems not to have bothered him unduly. He just kept plugging away.

My writing routine works like this. During school terms I don't write at all. Not one word of prose fiction for ten weeks at a time. Once the holidays begin, I try to get myself into a daily writing regimen. The most important factor is A Good Night's Sleep. Factor #2 is Nothing Scheduled for the Morning and #3 is Lots of Coffee. When my children were younger, I used to get my long suffering (now ex!) wife to take the kids out of the house for two hours each morning, even (as she was fond of saying) in the middle of summer. Yes, let's admit it: factor #4 is Selfishness. With these prerequisites in place, writing can commence, ideally for me at about 9 a.m. I like to sit in my study, in the dark, with my second cup of coffee. I even have the idea that a sugar hit is good for cognitive function, so chocolate can even be justified.

Then, finally, the mysterious part.

What we talk about when we talk about writing often isn't the actual composition, but everything surrounding it. The writing process itself is enigmatic. It usually takes me around two hours to produce one thousand words of fiction, which is far slower than my typing speed. Thus I must spend a lot of so-called writing time staring into space. One thing I've noticed is that as I've gotten older, my writing speed has slowed down considerably, but I believe this to be a good thing. The only website I allow myself access to while writing is dictionary.com. When I'm in the groove, I might consult the dictionary four or five times an hour as I strain against the boundaries of my own vocabulary. When writing is working as it should, it often occurs in a kind of fugue or hypnotic state. Many times I've emerged from this state to find that an hour or even two has passed. When I'm enjoying writing, I often feel like I'm playing the piano, that my keystrokes have resonance.

Writing fiction costs nothing. It's a means of expressing your emotions in a creative way and I'm certain that it's good for your cognitive functioning. It's a craft that introverts like me can pursue in the confines of their homes, by hand or on computer, sober or otherwise, by day or night. Writing fiction means committing oneself to the longest of hauls. One way or another, you have to make it work for you, but when it does it'll make you feel like there's more to life than just living.

FINALLY, PUBLISHING

Traditionally, big publishers were the gatekeepers. If they published your work, well and good. If not, you were completely obscure. The rise of the Internet, print-on-demand, self-publishing, social media and eBooks have altered this landscape. Publishing is no longer the problem for writers, per se. The main problems faced by smaller publishers and their authors today are distribution and visibility. Established or traditional publishing companies like HarperCollins or Penguin have extensive distribution networks, ensuring that their printed titles appear not only on the shelves of (admittedly dwindling numbers of) bookstores like Dymocks, but also at discount retailers like Big W and Target. You'll also find these publishers and titles dominating the field at airport bookshops. Smaller publishers find it difficult if not impossible to break this stranglehold and most subsist on tiny publishing budgets, relying on the promotional efforts of authors themselves to spread the word. Social media campaigns are inexpensive to run, but are sadly often ineffective at generating sales in today's content-saturated Internet world.

The situation with eBooks is, if anything, worse. In theory, an eBook produced by a small publisher can compete equally on eBook platforms like Amazon Kindle or Kobo against titles from the big publishers. In a virtual medium, distribution problems don't exist, which ought to be a good thing for independent publishers. On the other hand, regional advantages that small publishers might enjoy, such as Australia's soon-to-be-repealed parallel importation laws, don't exist either. An eBook uploaded to the Kindle store quickly finds itself in competition with more than four million titles, many of which are heavily discounted and/or extensively promoted by the big publishers. The indies simply can't compete and, with occasional exceptions, their titles remain invisible.

For Australian authors trying to 'break out' in this landscape, having realistic expectations and a sense of perspective is key. Diehard optimists frequently invoke the name of J.K. Rowling in this context, pointing to her many rejections and eventual total victory. But even J.K. Rowling couldn't break out a second time, as her Robert Galbraith/*The Cuckoo's Calling* experiment indicated. Australian authors can and should try their hardest to win acclaim through literary competitions such as The Australian/Vogel's Literary Award or Text Prize for Young Adult and Children's Writing. There are dozens if not hundreds of writing prizes on offer in Australia each year and the diligent author should keep track of and enter as many of these as possible. Joining a local writers' centre can help, too. There are several such centres to choose from in Western Australia, including the Rockingham Writers Centre, Katharine Susannah Prichard Writers' Centre, Fellowship of Australian Writers WA, Peter Cowan Writers Centre and Out of the Asylum Writers' Group. Each Australian state and territory has its own writers' centre and thus authors can call on the services of the Queensland Writers Centre, New South Wales Writers' Centre, Tasmanian Writers' Centre, Northern Territory Writers' Centre, ACT Writers Centre, SA Writers Centre or Writers Victoria.

Then there's social media. We're told to build our author platforms as a means of gaining a foothold in the online world. It certainly can't hurt, unless you spend all your time building your platform and none honing your writing craft. Most published writers have a Facebook author page, although Facebook's increasingly hermetic internal algorithms means that your posts may never be seen. Unless, of course, you pay. Blogging platforms such as Wordpress are free, easy to use and may help you to raise your online profile, but don't expect miracles from them.

Social media can be inspiring and enriching, but you attempt to monetise it at your peril.

For the vast majority of us, i.e. those who don't strike it rich self-publishing E.L. James-style, those who don't win national or international prizes, those who aren't plucked from publishers' slush piles, we must commit ourselves to a longer game. We must build our profiles, but without recourse to gimmickry. We must grow, but not by way of get-rich-quick schemes. We must be visible online, but not by throwing ourselves at the feet of passers-by on every virtual street corner. In short, we must work at incremental change rather than dreaming of the transformational.

BE THE TORTOISE

I often feel like I'm running out of time. There will only be so many mornings, so many coffees, so many words I can write. Naturally I want to seize the day, but it isn't always that simple. Writing fiction seems to me to be an activity inimical to the living of ordinary life. And yet it seems that just about everyone wants to do it, as those four million titles on Amazon will attest. Those who persevere with writing fiction are those who are unfazed by numbers like these. They are the people who know that there might be seven billion people on the planet, but there's only one of *them*. Their idol is the tortoise, not the hare.

It's taken me twenty years of writing fiction to get to this point and I figure that if I live for another fifty, then it'll take me another fifty years to get to that point. Not everyone finds their calling in this life, but I found mine at an early age and there's nothing much else I've ever wanted to do instead. I've been lucky like that.

FIVE TIPS FROM GUY SALVIDGE

1. Prioritise writing. One way or another, you need to make room in your life for writing to happen.
2. Find a routine that works to you and stick to it. As Harry Crews says, 'Put your ass on the chair.'
3. Read! Writers are readers first and writers a distant second. Be a connoisseur of fine reading.
4. Don't accept anyone else's definition of who you ought to be. Writers make their own rules for living.
5. Be the tortoise and not the hare. If it takes you twenty years to achieve your dream, it will only taste that much sweeter when you do.

Rocky Road to Publication

by Jennifer Scoullar

THIS is the first post of a series about getting a novel published in Australia, based on personal experience with my first book with Penguin Books Australia, *Brumby's Run*.

WRITING YOUR NOVEL

First, you must finish your story. Agents and publishers will usually only consider completed fiction manuscripts. It is enormously useful to join your state writing centre. They also offer great online support, which is particularly important for regional writers. I completed two novels through the Year of the Novel program at Writers Victoria. I honed my craft, networked and gained invaluable friendships. Writing a 70,000 to 100,000-word manuscript takes single-minded dedication, and nobody understands this like other writers. It also helps to have a routine. I aim for a thousand words a day.

It's vital to keep reading, in and out of your genre, fiction and non-fiction. Reading fills up the creative well, and is just the tonic for a mild case of writer's block. (I don't believe in writer's block per se. It is a malady that generally strikes when you've written yourself into a corner, and don't know where the story is going next.)

There are an infinite number of ways to construct your manuscript. Some people write the end first. Some people write chapters out of order and tie them all together later. Some use programs like Scrivener to help keep the threads together. I begin at the beginning and write in a linear fashion, with only a vague plot outline to go by. This allows the narrative to surprise me, and is a lot of fun.

But whatever method you choose, writing a novel takes time and hard work.

Finally, after a great deal of hair-tearing, wine, chocolate and some sublime moments of inspiration, you type "The End" on your first draft. You put it aside for a few weeks to get a bit of distance. You celebrate. Catch your breath. For the real work is about to begin.

You have your painstakingly manufactured canvas. It's time to create some magic. The legendary Peter Bishop, former creative director of Varuna, the Writers' House, once said to me that the first draft is the *writer's draft*. It is essentially the writer telling himself the story. You need to revise it within an inch of its life – cutting, adding, polishing and shaping, until you have a *reader's draft*. Only then should you contemplate launching it into the world.

LANDING THAT ELUSIVE AGENT

A couple of years ago I decided I wanted a literary agent. I read everything I could on the subject, lurked on agent blogs (Kristin Nelson's *Pub Rants* was a favourite), and pored over the acknowledgement pages in my local bookstore, searching for likely candidates. I completed a third draft of my manuscript, and launched into an organised campaign bearing all the hallmarks of a military operation.

Firstly, I purchased an up-to-date copy of the *Australian Writer's Marketplace*. Each country has its own version, containing current details of every contact you could ever need in the publishing industry, including agents. This is also available online, but there was something very satisfying about highlighting each suitable listing, and then ticking them off as I made submissions. Australia is a small market with a correspondingly small number of agents. After carefully reviewing them all, it turned out just eighteen agents were accepting submissions for adult fiction.

I listed them in order of personal preference, agonised over a query letter, and then in October, I queried the top twelve all at once. I received six requests for chapters. Of those, I received four gracious rejections and two requests for the full 80,000-word manuscript. One of these was from Curtis Brown, my *first* choice! Trying to remain calm, I sent off my submissions and waited. Finally, in February I received a phone call from Curtis Brown requesting a meeting. It turned out I was already heading to Sydney that week for an Australian Society of Authors course. That meeting was a great success and I was offered representation.

Hurray! I thought all my troubles were over. Surely it was only a matter of time before my manuscript found a home. Nothing could have been further from the truth. My agent submitted to six publishers and got knock-backs. 'Write the next one,' she said, and I did, while my old manuscript languished. By the time I'd finished the next one (about a year) the agency had lost interest in me in a major way. They couldn't even find the time to read it. A cold stone settled in the pit of my stomach. If I didn't do something soon, I felt sure they'd drop me. What I needed was a plan B!

THE CONFERENCE PITCH

I'd found my dream agent. Problem was, I still didn't have my dream contract with a major publisher. Maybe my agent could use a little help? A writer friend of mine, fellow rural author Margareta Osborn, had asked me to go with her to the Romance Writers of Australia Conference in Melbourne.

'I don't write category romance,' I said.

'You don't have to,' said Margareta. 'All sorts of writers go. It'll be fun … and you get to pitch face-to-face to editors. Not just any editors, but key industry professionals like Beverley Cousins of Random House, Annette Barlow of Allen & Unwin, and Belinda Byrne, a commissioning editor at Penguin Books.'

'Really?' I said, my ears pricking right up. 'Editors?' Now, all I needed was a novel to knock their socks off. I already had two manuscripts with Curtis Brown. Maybe I needed something fresh, something that fused my passion for the land with an equally passionate love story. It was January, and the conference was in August – eight months away. I could only try. Thus *Brumby's Run* was born. I wrote and wrote, revising as I went, and had a polished first draft just in time for the conference.

I scored pitch sessions with Bernadette Foley of Hachette and Belinda Byrne. I agonised over my pitch, practised *ad nauseum* and was sick with nerves. The five-minute pitches were reduced to three-minute pitches. Not much time to impress anybody. Then the moment arrived for that long walk into the room, and *I* was the one who wound up being impressed. Both editors were so friendly and natural, and did everything they could to put me at ease. And best of all, *both* of them took my three chapters and synopsis.

Ten days passed without word, so I sent out polite reminders. Far from being annoyed, they both asked for the full manuscript. Then, after several encouraging emails from Belinda, she asked to meet me, and in October I received an email headed "Penguin Letter of Offer for *Brumby's Run*". At last! I printed that letter out and carried it with me for weeks, looking at it occasionally to check it was real. My agent was happy too, cheerfully returning emails once again and launching into contract negotiations with great gusto. And the rocky road to publication was suddenly an easy, downhill run.

(Reprinted from jenniferscoullar.com with permission)

FIVE TIPS FROM JENNIFER SCOULLAR

1. Use adverbs sparingly. During revision, I go back and question every single one. If in doubt, I take it out.
2. Stick to a simple *said* as your main dialogue tag, or use a beat of action instead. *Said* becomes invisible and won't intrude on the reader. And don't modify tags with an adverb. '*He said,*' not '*He pondered ruefully.*'
3. Avoid the passive tense, and don't use two words when one will do.
4. There is no such thing as great writing, only great re-writing. Revise, revise, revise.
5. Finish what you start.

Creativity and
Courage

by Melinda Tognini

WRITING THE DREAM

***'There is going to be a point in your life
when you have to decide
Am I going to play it safe,
Or am I going to navigate new territories,
And become a Brave One?'***
Cate Williams

I WANT to be a Brave One. But I often feel anything but courageous. Until recently, I shied away from telling people I was a writer. I dreaded meeting new people and being asked those automatic questions accompanying any introduction. 'What do you do?' and 'Where do you work?'

I'd open my mouth, then hesitate, running through the possible responses in my head.

A Teacher. Not strictly true these days.

Depends on the time of day. Too flippant?

I'd usually play it safe and reply that I was a stay-at-home-mum or I worked from home, which were both partly true, but not the whole story.

What was I afraid of? That I would be exposed as a fraud? That my passions, goals and dreams would be belittled or dismissed? Or that I'd simply discover I had no talent anyway? I know I'm not alone. Apparently even Pulitzer Prize winner Maya Angelou has suffered the effects of the Imposter Syndrome. She once said, 'I have written eleven books, but each time I think, "Uh oh, they're going to find out now. I've run a game on everybody, and they're going to find me out."'

But when did claiming our creativity start requiring courage, rather than simply being an extension of who we are?

As a child, I was naturally creative. On any given day, my imaginative play might include acting out a drama with my dolls and teddies, building a house in the scrub beside our grandparents' beach shack, living on the moon with my LEGO spacemen, or climbing the gum tree in our backyard and pretending I was sitting with Moon-Face and Silky in the Magic Faraway Tree.

I took to reading and writing the way some people take to kicking a footy, or are born performers, or have a knack for numbers. Certainly by the time my family spent a year travelling around Australia in a Toyota LandCruiser the colour of the sun, I was constantly scribbling stories and maintaining a daily journal. If I wasn't writing, I'd escape into the worlds created by others. I suspect I spent as much of that year living through the eyes of imaginary people as I did through my own.

Then we moved to a remote mining town in the country's north where everybody knew everybody, and it was decidedly uncool to be the new kid with not just one, but *two*, parents who doubled as teachers. I did eventually make friends, although residual insecurities remained and I continued to find refuge in fictional worlds, either those of my favourite authors or the ones I created myself. In my imagination, I *was* the protagonist, who was usually strong and capable, combatted bullies and found acceptance for simply being herself.

Yet, I can't say I dreamed of becoming a writer. Somehow, it never came up on the list of viable career options. Instead, I aimed to be a doctor or veterinarian, which wasn't a problem until I realised I didn't want to study science for another six years after graduating high school. With the loss of direction, my grades slipped and I almost left school altogether. At the eleventh hour, however, I discovered a university course that offered creative writing and theatre. Finally, I'd discovered something to aim for, although I considered it to be a stepping stone *while I worked out what I really wanted to do*. I still didn't view 'writer' as a potential career.

So I became a teacher. Despite years of claiming I'd never follow in my parents' footsteps, I discovered I enjoyed it, although it was an all-consuming career which left little room for anything else. My writing was sidelined for several years until one of my classes was required to write a short story based on an autobiographical incident. Deciding the best way to demonstrate the process was to lead by example, I drafted and edited a short story based on a dramatic incident from my teenage years.

I don't know whether I inspired any of my students, but the experience did succeed in reigniting my creative passion. The short story developed into a full-length young adult novel and I won a mentorship to work with an established author. With his encouragement, I now dared to dream of becoming a published author. I edited, and re-edited, and finally submitted my manuscript to six publishers. I waited with a mixture of anticipation, hope and fear, until gradually I received six replies. All rejections.

Refusing to give up, I reworked the novel, even after my son was born. I preciously guarded his afternoon nap time, not simply because he'd be a nightmare without sleep, but because it was the only writing time available to me. I didn't clean, cook or socialise, although I often had to fight the urge to take a nap, too. I'd often trick myself into writing by saying, *Just ten minutes. You only have to do it for ten minutes.* Usually, that was enough for me to be on my way, but there were times I wondered whether there was any point, given my time was so limited. Something about my process must have been effective because several shorter pieces of work – travel articles, personal essays and feature articles – were accepted for publication not only in Australia, but in the US, too.

Then our world disintegrated. During my second pregnancy, doctors diagnosed our unborn daughter with severe heart defects, with no certainty as to life expectancy or quality of life. After her birth, I abandoned my novel, banishing it to the top shelf of a cupboard. I gave myself permission *not* to write for at least six months – to simply concentrate on mothering my seriously ill child. However, when she was about four months old, I had the opportunity to contribute a personal essay to an anthology, and as I drafted the piece, something came alive in me. I realised I could no more give up writing than I could survive without food.

Thus, when a friend suggested I return to university to undertake my Honours in creative writing, I applied. In retrospect, I must have been slightly deranged, given the course started two months after our daughter underwent life-saving open heart surgery. However, my thesis arose out of that experience, with my short stories and accompanying essay focusing on motherhood and disability. Significantly, I also completed a biography unit in which I wrote about a friend who'd grown up under Pinochet's military coup and dictatorship in Chile. Her story is powerful and fascinating, and yet she'd never shared it with anyone, primarily because of the culture of secrecy and fear she'd been forced to endure. Not only did she lack the confidence to tell it herself, she was surprised that anyone else might be interested in hearing it.

I simply set out to tell her story, to convey the experiences of a teenage girl surviving a traumatic time in her country's history in the most vivid way I could. But what blew me away was her reaction to reading her story through my words – many of which were actually her words, which I'd transcribed. It wasn't just that she felt the narrative accurately conveyed that time period in her life. The process appeared to bring with it a certain level of healing for her, something I had not anticipated. Her response welled up in me a passion to help others tell their stories, particularly those I consider 'invisible stories', ones that have traditionally been sidelined, or omitted altogether, in the dominant narratives of our country.

In late 2007, as I was frantically finalising my Honours thesis, a 'sliding doors' moment came, when a writer friend emailed me a copy of a small advertisement: the War Widows' Guild of Western Australia wanted a writer to document the story of its organisation. The project had been initiated by Marjorie Le Souef (formerly Learmonth), who was the inaugural State president of the organisation in 1947 until her remarriage later that year. Remarkably, Marjorie returned to the same position some fifty years later, after the death of her second husband. She believed it was important to tell the Guild's history before it was too late, before the stories of these war widows were lost forever.

Despite having no idea the War Widows' Guild even existed, I immediately recognised the dearth of war widows' perspectives in existing war histories. And so I dared to submit a resume and sample writing. I was short-listed and attended an interview with the Guild's executive committee, but self-doubt ruled me out of the running. Imagine my surprise when the Guild's executive officer, Jenny Knight, phoned to say I was the one they wanted to take on the project. I immediately said yes, then hung up the phone and wondered what I'd agreed to. I was excited about the possibility of writing the story of the Guild, of bringing the war widows' stories to the centre of the narrative, but I also felt completely overwhelmed.

I still wonder whether I would have said yes if I'd known in advance the enormous task ahead of me or how long it would take. The Guild executive and I naïvely anticipated a two-year time frame. In reality, the publishing process took almost that long and the entire process lasted eight years. Numerous times I doubted if I would ever finish the manuscript, let alone see it published.

The moment I received news that Fremantle Press had accepted the manuscript of what is now *Many Hearts, One Voice: the story of the War Widows' Guild in Western Australia*, remains one of life's highlights, albeit a rather surreal one. From signing the contract, to editing the manuscript, viewing the layout proofs to holding the advance copy, it felt as though I was drifting through someone else's dream rather than realising my own. It was only as I stepped to the podium and looked out across the crowd gathered to celebrate the launch of *Many Hearts, One Voice*, that I accepted I was a published author.

The month following the launch was filled with speaking engagements and interviews for newspaper, radio and television. If you're an introvert, you will understand that much of this was way out of my comfort zone, and at times exhausting. Fifteen years ago, I would have laughed if you'd told me I could go on radio without completely flipping out. Back then, I couldn't even call Telstra to pay my phone bill without my heart pounding. But this wasn't just about me; it was about the women I'd come to know over the past eight years, and the courageous women who'd paved the way before them. They deserved to be acknowledged and honoured, and so I made a conscious decision to continue daring to say yes to these opportunities to tell the wider community about the war widows who had existed on the margins on history for far too long.

I imagined the writing life would suddenly become easier once *Many Hearts, One Voice* was published. I thought it would become natural to call myself a writer, to claim the time, space and motivation required. Yet I still struggle to resist the requests and demands of others, the distraction of email and social media and the baskets overflowing with dirty washing. Some days, I feel very much an imposter, and would prefer to snuggle under my doona and sleep. Ultimately, though, creative courage is a choice.

Courage must be taken and worn and owned, and the only one who can do that is me.

As Cate Williams says in the opening quotation, I can play it safe or I can dare to navigate new territories and become a Brave One.

When I think about bravery, I think of heroic deeds, of saving a life or surviving a natural disaster, daring to cross rough seas to seek refuge, or facing life-saving heart surgery. Perhaps in those circumstances, courage isn't really a choice. At least, the cost of doing nothing is greater than navigating new territories. When contemplating courage, I need look no further than those tenacious and determined members of the War Widows' Guild. Women such as Jessie Vasey, who was widowed when her husband, Major General George Alan Vasey, was killed in a plane crash off Cairns while en route to New Guinea. Marjorie Learmonth lost her husband Charles when his plane crashed into the sea off Rottnest. Gwen Forsyth was widowed with two young sons when her husband was killed in New Guinea. Gloria MacDonald's husband was killed while stationed outside Darwin when a runaway truck ploughed down a hill and into his tent. And Winifred Fowler welcomed her husband home only to watch him succumb to a war-related illness.

These women could have played it safe, maintained the status quo and remained silent, but under Jessie Vasey's leadership, they founded a nation-wide organisation. This was at a time when married women, many of whom had joined the war workforce, were expected to return to full-time domestic duties, and the traditional roles of wife and mother. War widows did not have that option. With the war widows' pension well below the basic wage, many, especially those with small children, now lived in near poverty.

The only way to make a difference was to step out of their comfort zone. And they did. In the aftermath of the devastating news they received, many of them still raw with grief, they reached out to other widows to offer emotional and social support. They initiated training courses, established a business and transformed the War Widows' Guild into a powerful lobby group. These women influenced the government on issues such as pensions, educational benefits and health care. They fought for public recognition and expression of their loss. They aimed to have a war widows' pension seen as compensation for their husbands' lives rather than a government handout. They campaigned for subsidised aged-nursing care and built affordable housing. They wrote letters, met with politicians, and long before Twitter and Facebook, used the media to their advantage. They may have been sidelined in the history books, but these women ensured they were far from invisible in those post-war years. Many of the benefits that war widows have today are a result of the determination and tenacity of those early Guild members, as well as the ongoing work and advocacy of the Guild today.

When I contemplate whether this writing life is too challenging, and I consider giving up, I will think of those war widows who demonstrated such courage despite everything they faced. When I'm tempted to play it safe and retreat into the shadows, I will remind myself of Marjorie and Gwen and Gloria and Winifred and the many others who refused to accept their lot, who persevered when faced with hurdles and dared to navigate new territories. I will to choose to create, to write even – especially – when it leads me out of my comfort zone.

And if I can, so can you.

Dare to say yes. Dare to become a Brave One.

FIVE TIPS FROM MELINDA TOGNINI

1. Just start. Focus on the time you *do* have, rather than the time you think you need; connect pen to paper or fingers to keyboard, and begin writing.
2. Give yourself permission to write rubbish. You can edit a badly written page; you can't edit a blank one.
3. Dare to say yes; know when to say no. We all have a finite amount of time and everything you say yes to involves saying no to something else, even if the connection is not immediately obvious.
4. Don't do it alone. Search out other creative people to walk beside you, preferably ones who don't want to play it safe at the same time you do. In that way, you'll be able to encourage each other to persevere instead of giving up.
5. Choose courage. Regardless of the support you receive from others, the courage to be creative is ultimately up to you.

Carving out your writer's niche

by Sandi Wallace

UNTIL relatively recent times, writers didn't think about author platforms, and they weren't the primary marketers of their works. Back then, while many books competed for the attention of agents, editors and publishers, and publication was still never guaranteed, if you scored a book deal, chances were it was for two or three books straight up. Now, we generally start with a one-book deal, and the debut needs to go quite well for the publisher to consider further titles. Advances are also largely a thing of the past, but earning out an advance comes with pressure, so perhaps that's not a negative, if royalties are good. There is also much competition from talented self-published authors, and an ease for readers to obtain books. So, it is more important than ever for an author to carve out his or her writer's niche.

Your writer's niche is your fit in the marketplace. It's generally not prudent to write to current trends, as by the time your book is planned, written, revised, polished, submitted and published, that trend could be declining. Rather, it's better to focus on finding your specialty as a writer with staying power. So, the following three questions are key in finding your niche. *What is your X factor as a writer? What makes you and your stories stand out? What makes you the best person to tell those stories?*

I have a confession. At a very early age, as a shy, imaginative, bookworm dreamer, I became hooked on crime fiction in print and film. My love for the genre, and particularly series books, started with the Enid Blyton adventures, and was fortified by the Famous Five, the Hardy Boys and Nancy Drew, to name a few. Later came crime, romantic suspense, adventure, romance and some horror, through classic, historical, and contemporary series and standalone books, but all the while, crime gripped my heart – and it seems to be increasingly so. And for about as long as I've loved reading crime fiction and watching crime shows, I've loved writing, and dreamt of being the author of crime books.

Before I started writing my first novel *Tell Me Why*, I had a rough idea that it would be an authentic, gritty, crime story with a touch of romance, set in country Victoria, and the spearhead of a series. And now I'm living the dream, with one book out in my Rural Crime Files series, the sequel to be released this year (2016), and the third book written.

So, I *get* how you feel about writing (as does every author who has contributed to this anthology). You love it and you can't not write. By extension, you would like to share your stories, but if publication never came, you'd still write. Ultimately though, whether or not you've told friends and family yet, you want to be a published author, to be validated as a writer and able to reach an audience of readers that enjoys your work.

You may be like me and already clear about what type of writer you are, whether it's of non-fiction, literary fiction, or genre fiction.

Or you may be a writer who dabbles in many forms of storytelling, and unsure of which style you should focus on for your novel, perhaps even unable to label your work-in-progress until characters, themes and part of the narrative takes shape. Many writers cross genres and diversification makes some sense, as it may avail you to a broader readership, and you may simply love writing that way. But take care that it doesn't result in a lack of coherent identity. The use of pseudonyms and separate author platforms is worth considering.

But even once you've worked out a category or genre for your work, you are still to establish your niche.

Does the phrase 'slush pile' make you cringe? Well, it does for me. I instantly visualise an enormous number of unsolicited manuscript submissions, sitting on editors' desks or in their computer in-boxes from writers who aren't yet in their publishing house stable. All these submissions need to be assessed for suitability for publication and there are numerous factors involved, but even great stories could be overlooked, if the writer's niche doesn't stand out.

Various pitch opportunities invite the submission of a synopsis, the first three chapters or hundred pages or 3,000 words of your manuscript, and your author's biography. There is particular emphasis on any previous publishing history, and receipt of awards, or residencies. These publishers often ask: 'What book would you see as a comparison title to yours?' Sometimes they also want to know who you see as your competitors or whose style you emulate.

What they are looking for is a tag, something that draws a comparison to an established author, highlights your special expertise as the author, or differentiates yours from other books, to make it easier to entice booksellers, librarians and readers.

Basically, they want to know what your writer's niche is.

And this can be the credentials or background of you as the author – something that makes you knowledgeable in the subject and more marketable – or elements of your storytelling that set you apart from others.

WRITING THE DREAM

An example of the former in crime fiction is Katherine Howell, a crime-writing ex-paramedic who released her final book in an excellent contemporary series featuring paramedics in February 2015. The standout information on the home page of her website is: 'Katherine worked as a paramedic for fifteen years and uses that experience in her books.' Her prior occupation gives her books authenticity and makes her easily marketable to a publisher and booksellers. It also shines off each page of her thrillers for readers.

Meanwhile, Honey Brown is best known for her psychological thrillers set in rural Australia. In 2000, a farming accident resulted in a lower spinal injury that confined her to a wheelchair at the age of twenty-nine, but Honey's X factor isn't her disability. Instead, it is the ongoing impact of the accident – the ensuing deep, lingering depression and lack of identity, which in turn led to her using writing – something she'd been good at but never considered as a career – to re-centre her life and reconnect with herself. Honey has had a lifelong fascination with 'what if', and the accident and its repercussions inevitably influence her ability to take 'what if' scenarios to terrifying or dark levels, as she weaves stories that feel realistic, believable, and their setting in small-town Australia familiar. Each book is beautifully written and varies thematically, and so, Honey's storytelling skill is her X factor.

It's been a winding path to achieve my writer's dream, with stints as banker, paralegal, cabinetmaker, office manager, executive assistant, personal trainer and journalist along the way. I don't see my 'writer's apprenticeship' as time wasted, however, as it intensified my writer's dream; it continues to provide inspiration and fodder for my stories, and it gives me maturity as a writer. All that aside, prior to publication, my greatest claim to fame was *almost* signing up for the police force several times – if I hadn't been driven to be a crime writer, I would've been a police detective. Because I'm not famous, infamous, or a cop, in order for me and my manuscript to stand out for a publisher, and subsequently for my book to engage an audience, I needed to develop an X factor that revolved around my storytelling.

A lot of this evolved in my subconscious, with hindsight making it seem obvious. I was actually many drafts into *Tell Me Why* before I really thought about my writer's niche or brand identity.

As a reader, I love character-driven, strongly set, contemporary crime novels, preferably in a series. My life dream was to write a crime series (or several) and some standalones. So it was a given that I should write a character-driven, strongly set, contemporary crime series. As for the primary setting of my series, Daylesford seemed just as obvious. It's a place I'm familiar with, and being only a few hours' drive away from our home, it's easy to revisit for research. It is pretty, romantic, and atmospheric, and has an inbuilt tension with regular influxes of tourists to the country town. I had my female protagonist worked out – Georgie Harvey, a writer from Melbourne – and when it came to my male lead, it had to be a local cop, didn't it? And so, along came John Franklin.

Thus, carving out my niche came in a gradual and instinctive way. As I grew more determined to achieve publication, I probed who I was as a crime writer, information which aided my pitches, and later, the development of my website and other branding. This understanding feeds into interviews and author talks now, and also helps me continue to write on course and with the same passion.

My niche combines my love for country Victoria and the characters who live here, with my overall respect and awe for our police, in believable, character-driven, contemporary crime fiction. Yes, there are bad eggs in the police. No, I won't always have sympathetic, good coppers in my stories. But overall, they do an amazing job of juggling – just as my cop Franklin does – dangerous situations and sad or horrific cases, with general duties and personal pressures.

I'm not recommending a meandering approach towards carving your writer's niche; hopefully, the benefit of my experience and hindsight, will help you early on. (But if meandering works for you, that's fine, too.) And although I found mine quite intuitively, it was also somewhat educated.

I've been a lifelong student of crime fiction through my addiction to it on screen and in print. This equipped me with various skills and tools through my subconscious, but with my growing determination to achieve my writing dream, I expanded on that, by becoming an informed reader. I kept a journal of books read. For each, I noted title, author and year of publication, an overall enjoyment rating, a brief summary, and what I most liked or disliked about the book, along with publisher and agent details (the latter being information that might be useful in targeting my submissions). I was never going to imitate my favourite authors or books, but understanding what made me tick as a reader helped me cherry-pick facets of writing to develop into my unique style.

Likewise, as someone who probably would've joined the police after leaving school if I hadn't failed the height requirement, which has since been abolished, I have a solid interest in policing. I talk to coppers and ask questions. I've had tours of police stations – including the old Daylesford one – and at the Homicide Squad and Victorian Institute of Forensic Medicine. I follow cases in the media, and subscribe to the

Victoria Police magazine. So there are a lot of ideas, facts and impressions about policing and being a cop stored in my memory bank.

This brings me back to the three key questions I mentioned earlier. *What is your X factor as a writer? What makes you and your stories stand out? What makes you the best person to tell those stories?*

The further crucial question that will help you find your writer's niche is: *What books do you want to read?*

Most writers are book buffs; we always have a book or two on the go, and try to read every day. (By the way, if you're not an avid reader, and want to be a good writer, you should take it up … now.) Through a lifetime of reading, we have established our taste. We're drawn to books based on having enjoyed that author's work previously, and to new books by their cover art, title, a little symbol on the spine at the library revealing the genre, or its position in the bookshop. The blurb has to grab us. Sometimes we'll read the first page before we commit to buying or borrowing the book. We get that being a published author is no easy feat, so we're pretty open-minded and give books a go, but mostly we know whether we're going to like them within the first chapter.

We know what we like, even if we haven't analysed it.

So, it follows that if we're going to write a book, it should be a book we'd want to read as a qualified audience, doesn't it?

I read across the sub-genres of crime all the time. But I don't read or watch a great deal of horror, although I enjoyed it quite a bit as a child and young adult. So, would I – should I – write a horror novel? No, because how could I truly understand what works for readers of that genre? How could I hope to have soaked up the skills to master such a book, if I haven't recently read at least dozens of respected works in the genre?

Your niche is about effectively using your unique, special skills or interests, whether they've been gained on the job or through experience in your ordinary life.

Write about what you know and what you want to know. Where necessary, research the gaps. You can draw upon significant experiences in your life – a love affair, marriage breakdown, car accident, failed exam, trip abroad, house move, new job and more – adding texture to your writing. This is part of your uniqueness and adds to the angle of your story. Be an informed reader, understanding what you think makes a good story and good storytelling, and where you fit in the marketplace with your books.

Of course, what is fundamental to all this, isn't just *knowing* what you want your writer's niche to be. It's *putting it into practice* – time and time again – until you've honed it, then never becoming complacent to your craft.

I wrote a complete first draft of *Tell Me Why* in first person, present tense, then realised it didn't work for me. The point being, it is only through experimentation that you start to grasp what is your style. It's then, through much practise, probably some tutelage and definitely constructive feedback, that you will improve.

To succeed as a writer, take the positives out of each setback. In my journey, first, a literary agent, and then, Clan Destine Press, the publisher who eventually gave me a book deal, both showed good early interest in my manuscript, although they didn't take it up at that stage. My book simply wasn't ready then, but rather than being a fatal setback, it was a speed hump that I could get over. I obtained the tools for doing that by working with a mentor.

So, while you have a growing appreciation of what will be your writer's niche, and you're busily penning your novel, it's also important to set a number of other elements into play.

Establish a network with fellow writers at all levels, across genres, but definitely including a number that write in your genre, as there is much to be learnt through the experiences of others, and everyone benefits from a mutual support system. Get among events and online with authors. Attend writer and reader conventions, with notebook in hand. Develop a set of expert contacts you can call upon with research questions. Be an active member of relevant writer associations. Be a valuable member of the writing community.

Contribute stories or articles to community newspapers or magazines. You may not be paid but you will learn a great deal. Additional benefits include the support for your journey from other members of the team and readers, as well as giving back to the community, even with just a story here or there. Be sure that your by-line appears with your work though.

Enter short story competitions, which helps promote your skills in crafting plots, working to deadlines and making every word count. If you get longlisted, this is strong encouragement; achieve a shortlisting or win a prize, and it boosts your writer's biography.

It was on the night that I won the 'Best Investigative Prize' in the 2013 Scarlet Stiletto Awards for one of my short crime stories, that the publisher sidled up to me, tapped me on the shoulder and said, 'I want your book. Well, the series, but starting with book one next year.'

The stars had aligned. Both the short story and book were in my niche. My skills had improved with practice to the level of achieving recognition for my short fiction, and evidently, this flowed into the quality of the manuscript I had resubmitted to the publisher. Added to this, I was now a prize-winning author, which may have made the publisher take more note and expedite her decision on my novel, and/or it may have appealed to her in a marketing sense. I don't underestimate that win or those which came later in cementing where I am as a writer today.

You should also consider enrolling in a writers' course or joining a group to workshop plot and story, and learn the art of giving and receiving critiques. If you don't belong to a writers' group, it is essential that you at least have a small support team of trusted readers who will give you honest and constructive feedback because you can't be truly objective about your stories alone. This group need to be readers/fans of your category or genre. Say you write romances, would there be much point seeking feedback from someone who reads only literary fiction or biographies? And your mum will love the story just because you wrote it, so let her read it later. Also consider a writing mentor – doing that took my *Tell Me Why* manuscript from being 'almost there' to 'under contract'. It showed just how close it was to being of publishable standard. In fact, if the publisher was larger and allowed for a structural edit stage, rather than copy edit only, it may have been accepted at that point. My mentor's feedback on my strengths and weaknesses, some things to tweak, and a structural query were brilliant.

Polish, polish, polish. But once it's ready, get it out there. Then start your next book.

All the while, keep your writer's niche in mind. Let it ground you and remind you what your purpose is: to engage, entertain, explore and perhaps educate, through painting pictures with words. And to paint those words so beautifully and uniquely that your story resonates with readers so they connect with your characters and care about their journey and the outcome. To be the best person to tell the story and yet not to intrude upon it. To hook readers with the first page of your book and make them want your next book with the last page.

FIVE TIPS FROM SANDI WALLACE

1. Surround yourself with positive, inspirational people, including other writers, to support and learn from each other.
2. Be patient, as little about writing and publishing a book happens quickly, while maintaining belief and resilience.
3. Carve out your writer's niche, understanding what books you want to write, how you and your books will stand out, and what makes you the best person to tell those stories.
4. Learn and practise your craft, getting your work out via competitions, courses, a writers' group, and submissions to magazines, agents or publishers. Seek and be receptive to constructive feedback, although you may sometimes choose to ignore it.
5. Writing books is not a race or destination. The journey will come with ups and downs. It will bring amazing people and experiences into your life. Just remember to maintain some sort of balance between the crazy life of a writer and the rest of your world. Slow down, do your best work, and enjoy every part, even the rocky bits, of living the dream.

Against the Odds

by Karen Weaver

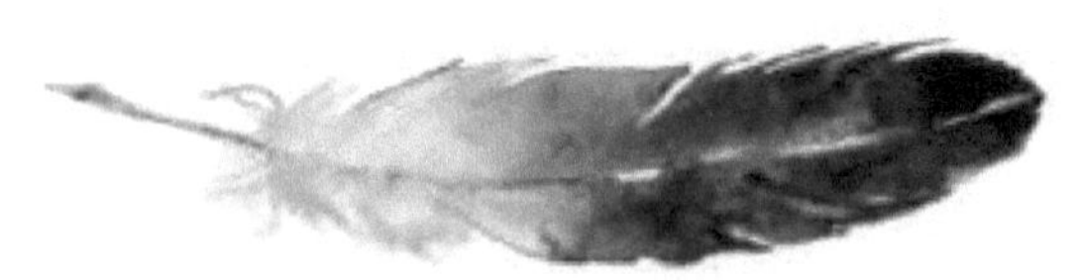

I DISCOVERED my love for story quite late – I was thirty. I often wish I could say I was well read, but that is not the case. I know that I would be a better writer having read more during my lifetime, but to be honest reading was not something that found me.

My earliest memory of books is of quietly observing my mum as she sat on her tan corduroy chair, totally engrossed in her new book. We lived in country Ireland and she didn't drive, so I don't know how she got the books. However, I do remember a subscription she had for red leather-bound Barbara Cartland books, and the postman was a welcome visitor on those days. I remember the unfamiliar feeling these books stirred in me – they were beautiful to behold. Eventually, reading became something my mum enjoyed doing, but I didn't feel that I could connect to this pastime. Mum would be lost in her book until she finished it, and I was happy that she had something she loved, because life was not easy for an isolated mum of six. I know now that reading was her form of escapism.

I did not enjoy English at school, but I have grown to realise that it was not the actual subject I disliked, rather, my experience of learning it. I attended an all-girls grammar school in Enniskillen, Northern Ireland, after passing the Eleven Plus exam. I often ponder whether I would have been best suited being top of the class in the lower-class school, or invisibly mediocre in the upper class one I attended.

My most vivid memory of English was in my third year of grammar school when the mid-life English teacher, who alternated between brown and blue suits every single week for the whole time he taught me, forced me to read aloud in class. The fact that I had, before class, asked him not to choose me to read, only seemed to have placed a 'Pick Me' sign above my head. I was mortified; my cheeks glowed and my head felt like a volcano about to erupt. It was a scary feeling, one that I was to endure repeatedly throughout my English lessons.

I do not have many memories of being read to, or being encouraged to read when I was growing up, so I was really behind in class and I felt it. I began to rebel.

I left school as soon as I could and got a job working in a factory. A few years went past. I had a son at nineteen; at twenty-three I left my well-paid supervisory position to go back into education. This was a whole new ball game; I never knew that learning could be so interesting. I had finally caught the learning bug. I passed an Access course and was accepted into university to study media, but I chose a more sensible path that was more home based, which was humanities.

English and English Literature were a big part of the course. In this different learning environment, I discovered a love for these subjects. I had the best teacher. Something he said to me when the course was complete has stuck with me since: 'Karen, I have to say I have always thought that you just winged it through these courses, getting your work in just on time and scraping through on Cs and Bs, and then I read your final assignment. Where the goodness has that Karen been? You blew me away. What was so different?' My answer was, 'I really enjoyed writing it – I loved the topic.'

Big writing lesson number one. Write about things that intrigue you and it will shine through your words.

I was also studying community drama at the University of Dublin, as well as the humanities diploma (yes, I know I had a five-year-old son), and I had two part-time jobs to keep things ticking along. Needs must! Each month we would arrive at the most spectacular locations in Ireland and Northern Ireland for an intensive weekend of learning and roleplaying. It was a cross-border initiative and I secured a place through an application and interview process. Everything was paid for and every month we learnt so much. However, one thing that came up in a role-play workshop was how I'd felt in my English class when my teacher had forced me to read aloud, especially on the day I ran out. It was all staged by yours truly and led to a powerful connection with the rest of the group. I healed from my blushing that day.

Big writing lesson number two – through writing we set the scene for readers to feel our words and connect with our characters.

Over the next few years I worked on a home-based writing course through The Writers Bureau. Personally, I endured a lot during those years, having worked through post-traumatic stress and then enduring a miscarriage that shook me to my core. I had a lot of healing to do. Then in 2008, we – my husband, myself and our two boys – moved to Australia for a new life and this was when my passion for writing really kicked in.

I was learning new things about myself and I wrote articles that were published on a website called Building Beautiful Bonds. I healed a lot by expressing myself through words. Many of these articles were picked up by a print magazine called Universal Mind. One called "The Power of Love" was re-blogged by a German blogger.

I have since discovered that writing is more than the craft of sitting down and putting pen to paper (or finger to keyboard). Writing is an all-consuming way of life – a lovely life for those who embrace it with passion. The dream of being a writer is often, in reality, not the same for any two authors. Similar to the dynamics of a snowflake, no two writing dreams and experiences are exactly the same.

This has become more apparent to me as I immerse myself further into this wonderful, whimsical world. Writers work damn hard. It's not just about sitting down writing your heart out, although that is very important.

Writing is about consistently learning new things, growing, and most importantly, creating a platform of readers and fellow authors who are kind of like your tribe.

Publishing has changed and if you already have a readership in place and can sell books you have a greater chance of landing a book deal. I have done things differently to the 'norm' but then, is there a normal way of being an author? I think not. Each journey is fascinating and there is so much to learn from the inspirational, creative path each author travels.

I have written books and published them. One thing that has been highlighted again and again throughout the publishing process is the importance of editing. All great books are edited and edited and probably edited again, and this is often where self-published authors fall short. Their budget cannot match those of the already established high-performing editing teams in big publishing houses.

Your first book may feel like your best work ever, but in hindsight, if you are dedicated enough to write more than one book, you may very well discover that your first book wasn't the best it could be. Knowing when to publish and when your book is ready, or *you* are ready, is the key to welcoming success when it comes knocking.

I remember reading an article written by a well-known Australian author around the time I published my first book. Her first three books, she wrote, were not publishable, but they had to be written anyway because doing so taught her about the writing process. While she accepted that these early books would never see the light of day, this was disheartening for me to read at the time. But as I write my fourth novel I now understand what she meant. Sometimes learning to write well comes not from being taught, but is something that is learnt by going through the motions.

My novel writing journey began like this: One day while in my living room with my children, the television show *The View* was on instead of the usual daytime children's programmes. Whoopi Goldberg was chatting with a celebrity couple who had experienced a miscarriage. I could see that it was still very raw in the woman's heart. Whoopi told the couple they had experienced a Visitor who came to say, 'Hey you guys, I am on the way so you had better get yourselves ready.' My own miscarriage was still a very tough thing for me to comprehend; even three years later, my heart was still mourning the loss. I craved a 'why' and Whoopi's words gave me the reasoning my heart longed for.

I felt compelled to write about this 'Visitor'. Other women needed to know how to heal grieving hearts, too. I have never felt an urge as great before. It was like a calling and so for the next thirty days I wrote 1,667 words a day during National Novel Writing Month (NaNoWriMo). I do not know where the words flowed from, but they did. I had never written a book before and 50,000 words was a great personal achievement. I sent it to my mum and she loved it. *Wow*, I thought, *I wrote something that my mum liked.*

I did not know what to do next. I was not in a writers' circle; in fact, I did not know many people as I had been quite isolated since moving to Australia. I was writing for the Building Beautiful Bonds website at the time, and my friend (the website owner) read my novel, and then offered to publish it. I did not expect such generosity to come my way, but I was becoming increasingly aware of how the things we desire often come from unexpected avenues. It felt so right and I was so grateful.

The self-publishing journey was not as smooth as I had hoped. Once my book went into publication I was advised to have it edited. There are different levels of editing and costings differentiate drastically. I learnt that my manuscript needed a content edit and it was going to cost more than the publishing deal. This was a big shock to me and to our family bank account, and it took away a lot of the goodness from my experience. But I did not know that my manuscript was not ready, because I did not know the process. *The Visitor* was eventually published and it became a finalist in the 2011 Readers Favorite book awards in Miami. This was a wonderful thing to happen for my first book, but it did give me a false sense of security about my writing. I still had so much to learn and I didn't realise it at this point.

Writing the second book in the series wasn't as productive. The words didn't flow as fast or smoothly. I had a brief plot line, but the 'Aha' moment wouldn't come. I thought I had writer's block, but I know now that it was not the case. There was another book that had to come *before* the one I was trying to push.

I sat down to write *The Wish Giver* during NaNoWriMo 2012. When I hit 30,000 words, I began a part-time job and so the novel went down my priority list. And then, all of a sudden, the words flowed. I got up every morning and committed to a thousand words, and before I knew it I was at 80,000 words and the story was finished.

How? I had discovered the process that worked for me. It goes like this: I write down a brief outline of an idea, and then write the name of the book in the middle of the page with lines and bubbles coming from it, and the names of characters and possible experiences they might have. I then write a twenty-chapter outline and give each chapter a title. Then I get a little more detailed and outline what *could* happen in that chapter, and if my inspiration allows, I write a little more detail. This is not a set-in-stone process, but it gives me guidance and focus to fall back on should I need to. I also like to put together a mock cover as it helps me to visualise the end product. I never know what the ending is going to be until closer to the finish, which keeps me excited because my characters often surprise me.

Book three, *The Memory Taker*, was finally ready to be written when I had my fifth child. I always get very inspired when I have a baby and magic things always seem to happen. The ending was nothing like I expected; it was pretty dark, but had a happily ever after (HEA).

Did I set out to write three books? No, not at all. My writing journey just evolved that way. Each of my three books were spiritual, and they took a lot of energy to write. My first book touched on the taboo subject of miscarriage, and my plan was that each new book would deal with a different issue. *The Wish Giver* focuses on a 'Be careful what you wish for as you may get it' theme, whereas *The Memory Taker* has characters who deal with Alzheimer's. One day, I will write a fourth that shares my reasoning for cancer, and it will be called *The Shadow Keeper*. I lost a dear friend to cancer last year and my mum has had half of her lung removed because of this disease, so I know that I will, when I can.

Novel number four is currently underway. It links Ireland and Australia, my two loves, and it is a love-swept romance about an Irish-dancing law graduate who finds herself in Australia.

I have also written for four collections of short stories. *Journey to Inner Light* was a collection compiled by Inner Light Publishing; *Living a*

Positive Life was published by Serenity Press; and *Writing: The Powerful Healer* was published by White Light Publishing house. My fourth published short story was called "The Whale Whisperer" and it was part of the *Rocky Romance* anthology of love-swept romance stories. This collection, published by my own Serenity Press, was launched at the Rockingham Book Fair in 2015. We had such wonderful local publicity for this book, even making a local newspaper's front page on launch day.

I have also discovered that writing non-fiction is much easier for me. My collection of musings shared on the Building Beautiful Bonds website during my time of enlightenment were published in a collection called *Heart Writer* after I learnt they had been read more than 56,000 times on the website. (I was blown away by that.)

There is another element to my journey, which I alluded to when I mentioned short stories. In 2011, I was co-founder of Inner Light Publishing, which published inspirational stories and journals. This was a heart-driven project that was embraced by many wonderful people. I worked so hard on it, fully aware that what I was doing took away from my already limited writing time, but it was like a calling and I had to see it through.

In 2013, Inner Light Publishing called it a day. We had several authors on the books waiting for their publishing deal to be fulfilled, so I couldn't walk away (I didn't want to, even though I was a little scared), and I chose to move forward by bringing all of our authors with me to establish Serenity Press.

The initial Serenity Press vision was to share as many inspirational stories with the world as possible, by offering authors the opportunity to publish their books in a positive way. As the founder of Serenity Press, I am passionate that our authors will *never* feel negative about their book. The book publishing experience deserves to be a positive one.

I have always known that Serenity Press would be an inspirational story in itself; I know this because we have the truest of intention in every endeavour. Serenity Press is still very young, but through persistence, passion and affiliations with wonderful people, it is growing, and the only way is up. We are a publisher with heart and, as we grow, our authors' profiles will grow, too.

Serenity Press is a family and I am proud of what we continually achieve with our wonderful authors. I have a clear vision of where Serenity Press is going. My co-director Monique Mulligan and I are powering through each year making amazing things happen. Each one of our books is a story in itself. Serenity Press has successfully transitioned from a vanity press for self-publishers to traditional small publishing press which acquires stories. We are gaining respect in the writing community, and thinking big for our future and the future of our authors. I have written more about my journey to becoming a publisher in the article "Accidental Publisher".

Authors, begin establishing your author platform as soon as possible. Be bold, brave and confident. Establish a positive connection with fellow authors, especially in your genre. Authors have an amazing way of supporting and lifting each other, as well as promoting each other.

Being a busy mother-of-six inspires me more each day. I love life and it seems to love me back. I don't have much time to waste, so being home-based allows me to focus on my family, as well as what I need to do for Serenity Press and my own writing commitments.

I know lots of authors who are working to deadlines for their publishing houses. I love deadlines, but my busy family and business life does not always allow for them. I do think of it as a bonus for me that most of my writing deadlines are self-imposed, because I can still enjoy the freedom of writing at my own pace, of letting my characters and the storyline grow organically in my mind. This is how I work best, and I am grateful to have created an environment that allows this. My hope is that by reading my writing and publishing journey, you are inspired to create your own.

FIVE TIPS FROM KAREN WEAVER

1. Write about something that interests you.
2. Find time to write every single day. Help it to become second nature.
3. Know the importance of editing. Self-editing and then professional editing.
4. Be prepared to work hard to pursue your dream of becoming published. Even self-publishing takes a lot of effort.
5. Build your author platform from day one.

Faith, Trust and a Little Pixie Dust

by Tess Woods

MY writing journey began in January, 2009 as a thirty-six-year-old. Well, my writing journey actually began as a brand-new baby when Mum read aloud to me. I was raised with a love of literature and at school my favourite subject was always English. I wrote volumes of poetry that are stored somewhere in the shed these days. I wrote short stories about children with unlikely pets such as elephants and walruses, and when I was seven I wrote a moving piece told in the first person point of view of an ant right up until his death via a foot stomp. My teachers raved to Mum and Dad about my stories and more than one teacher told me I should become a writer. But I didn't. Why? Because I'm Egyptian.

I may have migrated to Australia when I was nearly five years old, but with me came my very big, very traditional Egyptian family. And Egyptians who do well at school become doctors or dentists or physios or pharmacists, or if you really don't want a career in health, you become a lawyer or a teacher. No exceptions. Literally none. Ask my cousins!

I wrote for pleasure until I was about sixteen, but then doing all those difficult science subjects at school kind of killed any creative instinct in me. I was too bogged down memorising the periodic table. I gave up writing.

When it came time to put in university preferences, mine were all health-related. I got accepted into physiotherapy, so that's what I did. Luckily, I loved it, I really did. I thrived on the warm and fuzzy feeling of helping others and the job stimulated me.

I got married and became a mum and a mum again, and with my husband being my business partner, we moved interstate where we knew nobody and grew our business to become three physiotherapy clinics around Perth and we were busy-busy! No spare time to write a book that was for sure. So there I was, going along my merry way, quite happy to be a bookworm who devoured stories written by others. The thought of writing my own story was nowhere on my radar.

And then I read Stephenie Meyer's *Twilight* and that was the end of me! I'd always loved tragic love stories; they were the ones that stayed with me for years afterwards, stories like *The Horse Whisperer* by Nicholas Evans, *Tully* by Paulina Simons, and my favourite ever book *The Bridges of Madison County* by Robert James Waller. I had always loved stories where it's a love that's just not meant to be, just like Romeo and Juliet.

And I thought the concept behind *Twilight* was amazing – the man Bella loved was also the one who would most likely kill her. She had perfectly good candidates for boyfriends right in front of her but she only had eyes for her one soulmate, Edward, and he was the one who'd destroy her and effectively end her life. I read *Twilight* in one gulp and then raced out to Dymocks the following morning and bought the rest of the series. I read all four books in less than a week.

I literally couldn't sleep until I found out what was going to happen. Soon after I finished reading the books, the movie *Twilight* started showing at the cinema and I dragged my best friend to come see it with me. That night after watching the movie, I dreamt about someone I didn't know, someone who didn't exist except in my head and her name was Mel Harding. That's when my real writing journey began.

The next day I couldn't get Mel out of my head. I told my husband that there was this woman in my mind who was talking to me and she was trying to tell me her story. He thought I might have had too much sun! I decided he was probably right and Mel slipped from my mind.

I was going about the day as usual, hanging out with our kids, but after lunch I was at the sink doing the dishes, looking out over the back garden and the most bizarre thing happened. I saw a scene play out in my mind's eye that couldn't have felt more real.

Here was a woman walking into my back garden and she was completely heart broken. She'd just ended an affair with the love of her life and she'd made the decision to do the right thing by her family and stay in the marriage. But as she walked into the garden she looked over and there was her husband sitting on the back porch; he looked a mess and in that moment she knew that *he* knew she'd cheated on him.

I remember going into a trance staring out the window, waiting to see what would happen next between these two, but then one of the children called out to me and, just like that, the scene disappeared. So I left a sink full of dishes, ran and got pen and paper and started writing. I called out to my husband, 'Watch the kids please, I have to go write a book!' And it honestly happened that quickly. I'd had no musings or day dreams about becoming an author at all up until that day.

The first thing I did when I picked up pen and paper was to write that scene exactly the way I had seen it happen between Mel and her husband, Adam, in the back garden.

Then I had to work out what had gone on before that to lead up to that scene, so I started writing from the start and the story wrote itself. The whole thing poured out of me – I had no writer's block. Writing it was the easiest thing in the world. I wrote for hours upon hours, and three days later I had forty-five-thousand words and the bones of the story from start to end.

What I came up with was that Mel, a thirty-seven-year-old married mother and GP from Perth, hopped on a plane and met Matt, a twenty-eight-year-old, soon-to-be-married physiotherapist from Melbourne, who turned her world upside down. The story dealt with the lead-up to their affair and its aftermath.

And I was so thrilled with it because I'd taken that Romeo and Juliet tragic love from *Twilight* and brought it the suburban middle-aged wife. It wasn't teenagers and vampires, it was a woman I could relate to and who I felt married mothers would have much in common with.

When I finished that first draft, I sat back in bed and thought, *Oh my God, this is the best book anybody ever wrote! I'm going to be the next Marian Keyes, they're going to make a movie about this and Angelina Jolie will star in it and we're going to be rich!* The next day I re-read that first draft. And in the cold hard light of day I could see that it was an absolute piece of rubbish!

It took me a month of writing every single night to get to draft two and this draft was typed, rather than hand written like the first draft was. But typed or not, it was still a piece of rubbish! That's when I knew I needed help. So I googled, *Who can make my crappy book better?* and Google introduced me to manuscript assessors, experienced writers who you pay to read your story and they tell you how you can improve it.

I sent my piece of rubbish off to a manuscript assessor in Perth. Three hundred dollars and six weeks later she sent me a one-page letter pretty much telling me that it was a piece of rubbish and not to give up my day job. She didn't give me any pointers on how to improve it because she thought it was too far gone to be improved.

My husband encouraged me to get a second opinion, so this time I really researched manuscript assessors well to try and figure out who would best be suited to read and appraise the story. And I struck gold. I found an award-winning published author called Meredith Whitford. She was so clever and insightful. She cut straight to the chase.

She wrote, 'It's quite obvious you've never studied writing. There is lots of polishing that needs doing, you haven't developed any other characters except for the main ones, you've got no back story, and your descriptions of settings well and truly suck.'

But she also wrote, 'This book has the X factor that many people who have studied writing for years don't have. This book is going to be picked up for publication, I know it is. It's one of the very best manuscripts I've ever seen.'

I was over the moon! Meredith gave me a forty-point list of things to work on. I spent six months writing draft three and then I re-submitted it to her.

She got back to me with, 'Mmm, it's getting there, but not quite.' She gave me another list of points and I spent the next six months working on draft four. And then she liked it!

When I got Meredith's email saying she felt confident the story was now ready to submit to publishers, I was ecstatic for about oh, five minutes, before I started stressing out – what if she liked it but nobody else did?

So I decided to get a third opinion and I sent the manuscript to yet another manuscript assessor, who was also an author but, as well as that, she was a well-known book reviewer.

I read through her book reviews in magazines and she was really harsh on authors so I figured that if I sent it to her and she liked it, then that must mean something. Her name was Nicki Davies.

When I sent my enquiry email to Nicki, she'd actually stopped taking manuscripts to appraise and had forgotten to update her website. But I had decided that nobody else would do, so I totally stalked her and I think I sent her about six emails begging her to read my work. Rather than seek a restraining order against me, she finally said yes. And, hooray, Nicki loved the story, but she had one big issue with it. She thought my characters weren't raw enough and that they were hiding in the pages. She said, 'Give me more from Matt and Mel, I want more.'

Three months later I'd written draft five and handed it back to Nicki. She wasn't impressed with the re-write one little bit. She wrote, 'Stop being so scared to put yourself out there, I'm still not feeling you. Stop hiding! Are you afraid your grandmother will read this book and disown you or something? Is that it? Because I can't figure out why you have so much to give and you're not prepared to give it. Your writing isn't brave, be brave!'

After I rang my mum and cried that the writer lady was mean to me, I did what Nicki said.

I pushed myself way out of my comfort zone and ended up with some really intense scenes and that's when I started to believe, for real, that I finally had a good book.

I decided I was ready to submit it to publishers, but when I looked at the statistics for how many manuscripts were picked up by publishers when they were sent in by first-time authors, I knew I didn't have a chance in hell unless I had a literary agent to represent me. I'd never written a single thing as an adult before this book, not even a letter of complaint to a local paper, so I had no CV to speak of. I had no writing credentials whatsoever, I'd never done any kind of writing course, and I thought that my work would either sit in a slush pile forever or that publishers who read my letter of introduction would laugh me out of town.

So, I looked up literary agents and I spent the next two years being rejected by every single commercial fiction literary agent in Australia. Every last one of them. Some of them wrote 'return to sender' on the envelope without opening it, some read it and hated it, some read it and said they loved it but it would be impossible to find me a publisher because I'd never written anything before that and I'd never entered, let alone won, any writing competitions.

After opening the front door to find my rejected manuscript sitting on the porch from the last remaining agent I'd submitted it to, I slid it, still in its envelope, under the bed in the spare room and closed the door on it. I figured I had no chance with publishers if none of the agents wanted it. I thought, when we have money to spare one day in the future, I'll self-publish a few copies just for me.

I moved on with my life and kind of forgot I'd written a book. My friends who'd read it kept asking me about it, but for the meantime, I wasn't interested any more. Around that time, we had a lot of work and family stress going on, so the last thing I was thinking about was my unsold manuscript.

Then out of the blue, in 2013, came an email from literary agent Jacinta di Mase. This was not just any literary agent, but the president of the Australian Literary Agents' Association and the woman considered by many people in the know around the country to be the best, most committed and most influential agent in Australia.

Jacinta had read the book nearly two years earlier but decided she didn't want it. In her rejection letter, she'd said how hard it was to reject it because it was one of the best unsolicited works she'd ever read. But she hated the ending and I loved the ending, and she wanted a major change made to the plot that I just was not prepared to make. We both stuck to our guns and she said no to representing me.

I was particularly devastated when Jacinta had initially turned down my story, because I was convinced she'd be the one to take it. It was a really strong gut feeling I had that she would be my agent. I'd even printed out her name on a sheet of paper and had it sticky taped on my bathroom mirror two years before. The note said: *Jacinta di Mase will love my book and become my agent.* I remember my friends using the bathroom and laughing at that note. Who's laughing now, hey?

Jacinta's next out-of-the-blue email went something like this: 'Hey, I still have that book of yours in my mind even though it's been two years since I read it. Every time I get on a plane your book pops into my head and I look for Matt and Mel. I get thousands of enquiries from authors each year but here I am still wondering about your book. So, did you sell it yet? And if not, are you prepared to make the changes I want done to the story? If you're prepared to work hard on improving your manuscript, I'll go in and bat for you with the publishing houses.'

By that stage, it was four years since I had first written the story. I was prepared to sell her one of my children or give her my right kidney let alone make some changes to a manuscript. So I said, 'Yes, yes of course I'll make the changes!' and I set about changing the ending that she hated, but when I went to re-write the major plot change she wanted, I just couldn't do it.

For six months I tried different ways to write it and I simply couldn't. I was too embarrassed to tell Jacinta that I couldn't make the big change she wanted after all the grovelling I'd done, so I hoped that if I just kept a low profile and kept silent for long enough, being Australia's best agent and getting those thousands of other emails, she would just forget me and move on.

But she didn't forget. She sent me an email saying, 'So, where's the book? It's been nearly a year since I heard from you.'

I replied saying, 'I'm really sorry Jacinta, but I'd rather not be published than make that change you want. I'm sorry I wasted your time but I can't do what you want me to do to Mel's story.'

Jacinta replied straight away and said, 'I'm so happy Mel stood up for herself! Send it to me anyway and let's see if I like it.'

So I attached the manuscript as it was, hit send on the email, and the next day we headed off to Europe with the kids. I forced myself not to think about it anymore. If Jacinta wanted it, great, if not, I would self-publish it one day and sign the inside cover for my mum. I was completely worn out by it all by then.

Four weeks later, my family was in Cornwall on our 'book tour of the UK'. We were visiting all the places based on books we loved. Cornwall was my choice because of my love of *The Shellseekers* by Rosamunde Pilcher which was set there. We'd arrived the night before from London where we'd done all things Harry Potter.

Anyway, I checked my emails that morning and I had an email from Jacinta saying she loved the book so much, that without me even signing a contract with her yet, she'd already started sending it to publishers and that there had been an outstanding response to it! It is still amazing to me, to this day, that it was while I was in Cornwall, purely because of a book I loved, that I received the email about getting my own book published.

The next eight months was the unspeakable trauma of submitting to publishers. We had editors from the big five publishing houses saying they stayed up all night to read it but they couldn't get the backing of their teams or finance departments. It went to acquisitions at one of the biggest publishing houses in the world, acquisitions being the very last step before you get offered a contract, but it was rejected at the last minute. It was pure torture.

I was a hot mess through all of this, but Jacinta was as cool as a cucumber and she just kept on wheeling and dealing. And then along came an editor called Anna Valdinger at HarperCollins. Oh my goodness, let me count the ways I love her! When Anna couldn't get me a print deal, she offered me a digital deal instead, with the idea of going to print down the track, but to start with an eBook to at least get my foot in the door. In the previous year, HarperCollins had only taken on a handful of new Australian authors out of the tens of thousands who submitted to them so this was a huge victory for me.

Once I signed with HarperCollins, there were two more huge edits to get through until we all agreed the book was perfect! The best bit was that when I was reading through all the changes my structural editor had suggested I thought to myself, *Geez, this editor is a really clever writer, I wonder who it is?* And then I found out that my editor was none other than Dianne Blacklock – who just happened to be one of my favourite authors of all time. What a surreal moment that was, discovering that someone whose books were on my bookshelf and who I had loved for years, had been sitting there reading and working on *my* book.

So, after nine re-writes and almost six years from the day I first put pen to paper, I got there in the end and the book was published in April 2015 as an eBook. HarperCollins changed the title from the one I had given it of *Flight* to *Love at First Flight* which was a title my friend Emma had casually suggested over lunch one day. And they also gave me a beautiful cover that made me cry when I saw it for the first time. That was one of the most magical moments of my entire life, when I saw a book cover for the first time with my name on it.

My thought process after signing the contract was that I was published with HarperCollins, so now I could swing in a hammock and sip Pina Coladas all day for the rest of my life while I waited for the money to roll in. Wrong! So very, very wrong! What I found instead was that I was thrust head first into the steepest learning curve of my life.

These days, digital authors do ninety per cent of their own marketing. And as far as marketing was concerned, I had prepared nothing! I wasn't on Facebook, I didn't know anyone in the book world except for the few women who'd worked on my book, I didn't know what a book blogger was, I had no website, I literally had nothing.

Thank goodness I quickly found some Perth authors who became my mentors along with already published HarperCollins authors who reached out to me. These authors, both the ones I met in person and the ones who I connected with online, made time for me, held my hand and soothed and comforted me when I felt overwhelmed. Joining Facebook, joining the Romance Writers of Australia and joining a group called Chick Lit Chat Headquarters were the three things I did that gave me a writing community and an endless amount of support.

And those book bloggers I never knew about ended up being my biggest supporters who created lots of buzz about my novel and to whom I now owe the world. Together, this band of incredible women made up of authors and bloggers helped me navigate the insane world of being a published author.

The stuff I thought would happen when I got published, didn't happen. I have not undertaken any hammock swinging, I'm way too busy! So much of being an author isn't actually writing your novel.

These days I have an active website that takes much of my time, I do a monthly blog and publish a newsletter that goes out to hundreds of my subscribers, I have Goodreads and Amazon profiles where I review books, I do loads of interviews, I write articles for other publications and I've got a Facebook page that I spend hours each week on communicating with bloggers, writers and readers. Not to mention Twitter!

All the stuff I thought would happen, didn't happen, and the stuff I never dreamt would happen, *did* happen. When I was trying to get published, it was all just about landing a book deal. But becoming an author brought writers and readers into my life who have enriched it in ways I could never have imagined.

The Australian writing community is very tight-knit, especially the romance-writing community. I finally found a tribe of people who are as crazy as I am, who – just like me – have conversations with the voices in their heads, and I love them to bits. A few writers have become some of my closest friends, but the most special thing of all is that I've connected with readers around the world and that has hands-down been the most rewarding part of this whole experience.

To have someone in Romania email me that my book moved her to tears, to have someone in India tell me that my book has inspired her to become an author, to have someone in America say that she bought ten copies for all her friends, to have someone in Perth tell me that my book

is the most powerful she has read since she was married and had kids —
moments like that are what we writers live for.

Before I was published I had never thought to contact an author
after reading their book, even my favourite authors — it just never crossed
my mind to do that. But now, being here on the other side, I've seen how
important that connection with readers is and how much it means to us
when they do contact us. I've got my fair share of crazy Internet people
sending me all sorts of weird stuff too, but the few loonies aside, the
connection with people has moved me and motivated me in ways I could
never imagine.

I look back on the last year as the craziest, hardest and best year of
my life. Just before Christmas 2015 I won my first-ever award, getting
Reader's Choice Book of the Year at AusRom Today and then, in the
most exciting phone call I ever had, Jacinta called me with the news that
HarperCollins would be taking *Love at First Flight* to print. It is the very
first HarperCollins digital book to score a print deal, too. I launched the
print version in August 2016, seven-and-a-half years after I first dreamt
of Mel.

Oh, and a couple of things before I leave you. Remember that
scene I saw unfold in my garden on that very first day of my writing
journey? Despite nine re-writes it remains unchanged, virtually word-for-
word in the published version as to how I wrote it when I saw it. And
remember that plot twist that Jacinta insisted on and I refused to do?
During the edit for HarperCollins it hit me all at once that she was right
all along, and I wrote the twist in which ended up being the part that
readers loved the most!

So let's recap —
Did I study writing? Nope.
Did I enter lots of competitions and write poetry and short stories
and attend writing festivals and conferences? Nope.
Did I have a Twitter account, a Facebook account and a huge social
network? Nope.
Did I sit and write a book and write it again and again and again
until I had the best book I could possibly have? Yep.
And that last point right there is my tip for getting a publishing
contract! I'm not giving you five tips, I'm giving you one solitary tip. Go
and write and write well. With hard work (and in the words of Tinkerbell,
throwing in some faith, trust and a little pixie dust) you'll be unstoppable.

Russian Spies and Compost Piles

by Felicity Young

I OFTEN get funny looks when I tell people I'm a crime writer. A few years ago, a couple of authors and myself were visiting our local institute for the blind to watch our books being recorded for audio. While we were waiting in the foyer, one of the institute's executives approached our group. Before we could be introduced he said, 'Wait, don't tell me. Let me guess who you all are.' He pointed to my young, glamorous female colleague and said, 'You must be the children's writer.' To my other colleague, a burly, shaven-headed man dressed in black, carrying a brief case that could have deflected bullets, he said, 'And you are obviously the crime writer.'

He stamped me as the romance writer.

And I wasn't even wearing pink.

Well, he couldn't have been more wrong. The attractive young woman was the romance writer, the Mafioso-type was the children's writer and I was, of course, the crime writer.

So, what makes a crime writer? This is obviously one book you can't judge by its cover.

I guess I do have the kind of background often associated with writers. I was an only child and I was born in Germany in a British Army camp. Every morning tanks rumbled down cobbled streets near our house and the sky was always grey. My mother hated it. During my childhood we moved between Germany, Canada and the UK. Some of my earliest memories are of learning German songs from a local 'hausfrau' and singing Beatles songs between bites of a large green apple with Mum at the Liverpool docks.

My British Army parents never lived in any one country longer than two years, which meant long-term friendships could not be formed. I had to learn to amuse myself, usually by reading or retreating into my imagination.

At the age of nine I was sent away to board at a convent on the Sussex coast. When I was ten my parents were posted to Australia while I remained at school in the UK. These were the most miserable years of my life and I missed my mother desperately.

In retrospect though, it was the best thing that could have happened to me. An only child from a loner mother and a father who wasn't often home, I suddenly had three hundred sisters. I learnt how to socialise, how to fit in and how to make friends. It wasn't the kids I had problems with – it was the nuns. I was terrible at maths and I had no desire to learn French, two subjects that seemed to make or break a junior school career in those days. I was, however, a voracious reader who wrote 'wonderful' stories. This might have put me in good stead had anyone been able to read them, but this was an almost impossible task due to my abominable handwriting and atrocious spelling. Not surprisingly, I was put into the lowest stream for everything.

And gave up.

I became a rebel. I drank cherry brandy from my hot water bottle after lights-out and played football with the boys who jumped over the school walls at night (and was almost expelled for it). Fortunately, the nuns never found out about the porn the boys had also been showing us.

Once I found a 'grown up' book in pieces in the school compost pile. I stuck the leaves together and hid it under the dormitory floorboards and read it at night to my friends by torchlight. I'll never forget *Calamity Jane* – 'He gazed down the valley of her breasts' – and the hysterical giggles it promoted. This was hot stuff for a nine-year-old child.

It was then that I discovered I loved to entertain almost as much as I loved to read.

There was no inflight entertainment on the long trip home to Australia except for audio. During my thirty-hour flights home, once I'd got tired of listening to Charlie Drake's "My Boomerang Won't Come Back" or John Williamsons' "Old Man Emu", or mixing up all the Elizabeth Arden potions in the loo, (the scent of Blue Grass still makes me feel sick), I would read unsuitable books and magazines such as *Cosmopolitan*, and write unsuitable stories.

My stories were often about airport disasters or terrorist attacks. I was always the hero who saved everyone on the plane, of course. When I was older, the plane crash left me stranded on a desert island with the handsome co-pilot. I was then able to put into practice everything thing I'd learnt from Cosmo. Once, disaster did almost strike in real life when the plane's outer window cracked and the loss of air pressure caused us to plummet toward the Alps. I was making my potions in the loo at the time and hit my head on the ceiling. We had to make an emergency landing in Rome. I can't remember feeling frightened at all, only fascinated by the machine guns the soldiers were carrying at Rome airport.

As many of you might remember, the 1970s was a scary period of air travel, arguably even worse than it is now. Now I realise these scenarios I created were probably the only way I had then of controlling my fear.

Once, during a night-time fuel stop in Bahrain, I was frogmarched from the plane by a non-English speaking couple and locked alone in an airport office with a view of the runway. This time I was genuinely terrified. The wait seemed to take hours. I was sure that each plane I watched take off into the night through teary eyes was the one I was supposed to be on. Years later I realised the surly pair were just looking after the unaccompanied minor. At the time I was convinced they were Russian-spy-kidnappers. Lucky for them I wasn't carrying a stiletto under my school cloak. I have no doubt that I would have used it.

Due to one thing or another, there was a lot of fear in my childhood.

Things improved when I moved on to the senior school. I became involved in almost every extracurricular activity offered: hockey, drama, fencing and the choir. My dream was to audition for the Royal Academy of Dramatic Art (RADA), but the reality was that I would probably go into nursing.

My marks improved when I was allowed to study the subjects that interested me. My O level results were good enough for the headmistress to remark, 'Felicity, you've surprised us all!' A late developer, I was suddenly on a roll: hockey captain, fencing captain, the lead in the school plays, and house vice-captain.

Then I was told I had to move to Australia, where my parents had decided to settle.

These days, I don't think a sixteen-year-old would have accepted this move so well but I responded dutifully. I said goodbye to the friends I'd planned on studying nursing with in London and boarded the plane. For the first time in my life I had tears in my eyes during the trip *to* Australia.

I was sent to a local convent to do an exam called the Tertiary Entrance Examination (TEE). This was a two-year tertiary admissions course that I was given one year to complete. Compared to the liberal school I had just left, this convent was like something from Victorian England. It was like my miserable primary school all over again. I was threatened with expulsion for wagging softball. I didn't know what softball was.

When Dad left the army he worked as a labourer in a rose nursery. I always admired him for that, for following his passion. Unfortunately, the job paid so poorly that he had to find another. Aware of my bookish ways and having always enjoyed my letters home, he urged me to choose journalism as a career. But the move to Australia had caused me to lose most of my newly found confidence and I didn't think I'd cope in the tough world of newspapers. Although I'd gained university entrance, I chose to continue with my nursing plans. Inside I still yearned for a career on the stage, but I knew I needed a paying job. My parents didn't have much money (the army had paid for my schooling and flights home) and I didn't think they could support me at uni, let alone during the unpredictable course of an acting career.

I chose nursing because I thought it sounded exciting and romantic. I would either nurse a rich old man who, after falling in love with me, would die and leave me all his money. Or, it would be Prince Charming that I nursed back to health. I'd mop his brow and soothe his fevers and give him sponge baths, after which we would fall in love and live happily ever after.

I met my future husband in a pub.

We were married when I was nineteen, just as my parents' precarious marriage was shattering. I loved my nursing, I loved the camaraderie – it was like boarding school without the angst – but I couldn't cope with the shift work once we started having children. I took the opportunity when uni was still free to enrol in an Arts course at the University of Western Australia (UWA) to stop myself from going mad. It took me ten years to get my degree in English literature, but it was worth every second.

Nursing taught me about life; the Arts made me question it,
and appreciate it in all its textures, richness and diversity.

As the children grew, so did our menagerie and no block seemed quite big enough. A few years passed and the neighbours began to complain about the sheep in our suburban garden, especially when they began wandering around the neighbourhood with our two big dogs.

In the early nineties we opted out of city life and moved our family of pet sheep, ferrets, rabbits, mice, horses, cats and dogs to a small farm in the hills. My husband commuted to work and I established a Suffolk sheep stud, studied music, raised orphan kangaroos and began to write books.

Writing was something I always knew I'd have a shot at one day. I think that's a given for an avid reader – it was just a matter of timing and circumstance for me.

But studying the classics and learning literary criticism is not necessarily the way to kick-start a career in creative writing. If anything it put me off. What could I write about? How could I ever expect to write anything worthwhile? They say write what you know, but as far as I was concerned I didn't know much about anything except rearing children, animal husbandry and husband husbandry.

The catalyst was a trip to East Timor just after the trouble in 1999 when my husband was commissioned by the United Nations (UN) to help rebuild the destroyed city of Dili. In the compound where we were billeted I mixed with the UN police and local people, and found myself transfixed by their heart-wrenching stories, especially from those who lived through the Indonesian occupation. With nothing else to do while my husband was at work, I sat in the donga behind a barbed wire fence, the generator grinding out power in the background, and put together my first fiction manuscript, *A Ticket to Timor*.

('Ah,' an old uni friend exclaimed after discovering that I had become a crime writer. 'So *that's* what you do with a lit major.')

I realised then that you didn't necessarily have to 'write what you know' as long as you had access to people who could tell you what you didn't know. I also realised that while I couldn't write to change the world, I could still write to entertain … that word again.

The manuscript was terrible. I never attempted to have it published, but I did have it assessed by several professionals. Taking on board their comments, I soon realised where I had gone wrong and started again with a totally different book, a crime novel set in Western Australia.

But why crime, you may ask? There are a few answers to that question. Firstly, I've always enjoyed reading crime fiction. Without realising it at the time *A Ticket to Timor* was mostly a crime novel. I say *mostly* because it was a bit of a mish-mash of genres, and that was my biggest mistake. Publishers like to pigeonhole and this manuscript was not definable as anything in particular.

I decided that my next novel would be a crime novel only. As my brother-in-law was a recently retired police superintendent, I had the 'write what someone you know, knows' box ticked.

But what about the inspiration? No problem there, I thought, as I settled into our tiny country town and looked around – crime was everywhere!

Twenty-five years ago our rural neighbourhood was a pretty interesting place. Among other things, it was the officially declared marijuana capital of Australia. Only an hour's drive from the Perth CBD, it attracted an odd assortment of people – people who weren't quite country but couldn't fit into city-life either: Bikers, petty thieves, paedophiles, hard-core junkies, and snow droppers. I caught a snow dropper in the act once and it was one of the most frightening experiences of my life – even more scary than my kidnap by Russian spies.

Oh, and there was also a murder on our property too, but that's another story. The murder and the capture of the snow dropper were woven into my first novel, *Flashpoint* (aka *A Certain Malice*), as well as my sometimes-terrifying experiences as a volunteer with the local bush fire brigade.

I was very lucky with this novel. It hadn't received many rejection slips before it won first prize in a UK-based crime writing competition. The prize was to be published and admitted into the stable of a new publishing house. The publishers liked the novel so much that they asked me to write another. I spent a year writing a sequel. When that was finished they said they 'didn't have time to read it'.

New authors beware: Don't accept any proposal that is not in writing!

Despite that setback, writing became a compulsion. Our children were almost independent and I had at last the chance to put the stories that had been spinning around in my head for years on paper. Before I found out that I'd won the publishing contract with *Flashpoint*, not dreaming that I would get anywhere with it, I started another book, consciously making it as different to *Flashpoint* as I could. While *Flashpoint* featured a male cop in a country setting, *An Easeful Death*, featured a female cop in a city setting. I named my new protagonist Stevie Hooper.

Because of my moderate success in the UK I caught the attention of Fremantle Press, for whom I wrote three more Stevie Hooper novels: *An Easeful Death*, *Harum Scarum* and *Takeout*.

My agent then suggested a change of tack and I began writing historical mysteries for HarperCollins. History has always been a passion of mine, the Edwardian period being my favourite. While it might not be in my living memory, it was in the living memory of people I once knew. For example, my protagonist's background is based on the life of my grandmother. Her unpublished memoirs have helped immensely with the writing of the Dody McCleland series.

My fifth historical mystery, *A Donation of Murder*, is set for release in 2016. Also due out at that time is the never-before-published sequel to my very first novel, the one the UK publishers did not have time to read, now titled *Flare-Up*.

Once this year is over I will have published ten books in eleven years of writing. But whatever I have written, whatever I have read, I know that deep down nothing will ever be so thrilling, so daring, so influential as that first 'grown-up' book, steaming and fresh from the compost heap, *Calamity Jane*. Thanks 'C'lam' – you taught me to entertain, and that, after all, is what crime fiction is all about.

FIVE TIPS FROM FELICITY YOUNG

1. Give yourself headspace; time to dream.
2. If you can't write what you know, write what someone else knows.
3. Establish a writing routine.
4. Write in a comfortable environment.
5. Seek out the advice of experts.

Contributors

LOUISE ALLAN
Louise Allan is a former medical practitioner who now writes full time. In 2014, her first novel, *Ida's Children*, won a Varuna residential fellowship, and in 2015, it was shortlisted for the City of Fremantle-TAG Hungerford Award. She is currently revising it in preparation for publication. A few of Louise's short stories, memoir pieces, and articles have been published in journals and anthologies.

Louise lives in Perth, Western Australia, and is married with four children and two dogs. Her website is www.louise-allan.com.

SONIA BELLHOUSE
Sonia Bellhouse grew up in England, where the cliffs and coves of the Cornish coast remain as treasured memories. Writing is Sonia's lifelong passion, inspired by Enid Blyton's comment, 'One day you might write a book'). In 1973, she embraced the beautiful coastline of Perth and the chance to start life afresh. She has been published in multiple magazines both in Australia and the UK, and won two major awards in short fiction contests. Sonia is currently writing her third contemporary women's fiction novel, the first in a series, based in Herons Bay provisionally titled *Starting Over*.

SANDI BOWIE
Sandi Bowie is a writer, a librarian and a bookseller with an eclectic taste for fashion which combines a clashing blend of primary colours and pop culture. Sandi denies any and all allegations that her behaviour was responsible for turning her husband's hair grey. She does admit to being guilty of singing along (badly) to Cyndi Lauper songs.

Sandi lives in Western Australia with her husband, a disgracefully behaved blue heeler called Pepsi, and a 'To Be Read' pile of books so high that they frequently threaten to cause a book-a-launch. Her website is www.sandiwrites.com.au

ANDI BREMNER

Andi Bremner is a romance writer who is lucky enough to live by the beautiful Indian Ocean in Western Australia with her husband and three teenage sons.

Andi grew up with her nose in a book and her head in the clouds. Her favourite books were the ones that transported her away to another world full of dashing heroes and damsels in distress set in faraway time periods. Romance, and in particular, *complicated* romances, soon became her favourite novels to read and write, and she now writes angst-ridden tales of first love with some steamy interludes thrown in for good measure.

Trinity, the first in the Moonstone series, was released in April 2016 with the second book, *Drummer Girl*, due June 2016 with Evernight Publishing. *Star Struck* and *First You Were Mine* are due to be published later in 2016 with Liquid Silver Books. Her website is www.andibremner.com

DEBORAH BURROWS

Deborah Burrows was born in Perth, Western Australia, and is a proud Sandgroper. When she is not writing she is a senior government lawyer. Her fascination for history led her to complete a BA in History, an MPhil in Medieval and Renaissance Studies and an MSc in Medical History. A firm grounding of historical research and legal common sense underpin her flights of literary imagination. She is the author of three novels set in World War II Australia: *A Stranger in My Street* (2012), *Taking a Chance* (2013), *A Time of Secrets* (2015). *Ambulance Girls*, to be released in 2017, is set in the London Blitz. Her website is www.deborahburrows.com.au

DEBORAH DISNEY

Australian author, Deborah Disney, practised as a litigation lawyer prior to finding her true calling in the school pick-up line where she started typing a little story on the notes app on her iPhone one afternoon. That little story turned into a book, and before too long that book turned her into a published author with HarperCollins.

Deborah's first novel, *Up and In*, hit the Australian bestseller charts on both Amazon and iBooks and has enjoyed international acclaim. Deborah is currently working on her second novel, which is about in-laws.

You can connect with Deborah on Facebook – her page is creatively called 'Deborah Disney Author'.

SARA FOSTER

Sara Foster is the bestselling author of four psychological suspense novels: *All That is Lost Between Us*, *Shallow Breath*, *Beneath the Shadows* and *Come Back to Me*. Her books have been published in Australia, the US and Germany. Sara lives in Western Australia with her husband and two young daughters, and is a doctoral candidate at Curtin University. Find out more at www.sarafoster.com.au

MONIQUE HALL

Monique Hall is an author of small-town contemporary romance and a member of Romance Writers of Australia. Her first manuscript, *A Place to Belong*, is currently being considered by a number of publishers. It is a novel inspiring hope, acceptance and belonging and will become the first in a series.

Monique lives in the southern suburbs of Western Australia with her husband and two children. Her website is www.romancingmonique.com

ANNA JACOBS

Anna Jacobs has had more than seventy novels published in the genres of historical, modern and (formerly) fantasy fiction, as well as short stories and articles. She is one of Australia's most successful authors, but is published mainly in the UK.

Anna Jacobs lives in both Western Australia and the UK, spending time in each country every year. She uses her love of these areas to produce powerfully written modern and historical novels that span those countries. She receives numerous fan emails each week, and her readers most commonly tell her that they can't put down her novels! She doesn't mind at all.

Anna produces three novels a year, and is totally addicted to story-telling. She writes for two UK publishers, Hodder & Stoughton (one of Hachette's imprints) and Allison & Busby (a respected independent publisher). She was the fifth most-borrowed author of adult fiction in the UK library service in 2014-15 and is popular in Australian libraries, too. Her website is www.annajacobs.com

On a personal level, she's been happily married for fifty-three years, and has two grown-up daughters and a grandson.

KYLIE KADEN

Since being plucked from the Random House slush pile, Brisbane writer Kylie Kaden is now an internationally published author of women's fiction, and columnist at *My Child Magazine*.
Kylie was raised in Queensland and spent holidays camping with her parents and two brothers at the Sunshine Coast, where parts of her books are set. As the only female in a house of males, she stays sane by plugging away with her writing while her youngest naps (and the washing mounts).

Her second suspense novel, *Missing You*, was also published by Random House. Her website is www.kyliekaden.com.au

REBECCA LAFFAR-SMITH

Born to the magical beauty of her sunburnt country home in Western Australia, Rebecca Laffar-Smith always yearned to explore the wonders of this world and beyond. After twelve years as a freelance writer and editor, she gave up writing about the non-fiction world in favour of fantastical creatures and fanciful things. Now she writes in stolen moments between home-schooling her children and volunteering as an events coordinator in her local writing community. She dreams of running a writers' retreat and writing her stories in a detached, hexagonal room with floor to ceiling bookshelves and plenty of natural light. Her website is www.aulexic.com.au

T.W. LAWLESS

Thomas Bell writes under the pseudonym, T.W. Lawless. He is the author of the Amazon best-selling Peter Clancy series, which includes three books to date. A fourth Peter Clancy thriller is set for publication in 2016. T.W. Lawless is currently working on an outback noir series.

A registered nurse for many years, he always wanted to do something creative, so he studied film-making, screenwriting and creative writing. His passion is writing and when he's not writing a book, he's thinking about the next one. His website is www.twlawless.com

NATASHA LESTER

Natasha Lester's third book, *A Kiss from Mr Fitzgerald*, is out now from Hachette Australia. She is also the author of the award-winning *What is Left Over After* (2010) and *If I Should Lose You* (2012). *The Age* newspaper has described her as 'a remarkable Australian talent.'

She has been the recipient of grants by the Australia Council, and a writing residency from Varuna, the Writers' House. Her work has also appeared in the anthologies *Australian Love Stories* and *Purple Prose*. In her spare time, she teaches writing, and she loves yoga and playing dress-ups with her three children. Her website is www.natashalester.com.au

JULIET MARILLIER

Juliet Marillier was born and educated in New Zealand and now lives in Western Australia. Her historical fantasy novels and short stories for adults and young adults have been published internationally and have won many awards. Juliet's lifelong love of folklore, fairy tales and mythology is a major influence on her writing. She is a member of OBOD (the Order of Bards, Ovates and Druids). Juliet's next novel is *Den of Wolves* (Blackthorn & Grim series, book 3) and is due for release in October 2016. When not busy writing, Juliet is active in animal rescue. Find out more at www.julietmarillier.com

JENN J MCLEOD

Moving to the country in 2004 to escape the hectic world of corporate communications was like coming home for Jenn J McLeod. These days she lives the gypsy life in a fifth-wheeler caravan, travelling this beautiful country, her days spent writing heart-warming tales of the Australian country that weave intricate tapestries of friendship, family and love, contemporary human issues and small-town life.

Readers and reviewers alike enthusiastically received Jenn's debut, *House for all Seasons*, placing it at #5 on the 2013 Nielsen's Top Selling Debut Novel list. *Simmering Season* is book two, followed by *Season of Shadow and Light* and her fourth book, *The Other Side of the Season*, published by Simon and Schuster Australia in 2016. Her website is www.jennjmcleod.com

MONIQUE MULLIGAN

Monique Mulligan has loved words from the moment she could use them. She earned the title of family chatterbox as a child, and once she could read, she devoured books with gusto.

A former newspaper and magazine editor, journalist, children's curriculum writer, Monique has had a varied career in writing. In 2011, she created Write Note Reviews, a blog that celebrates her love of reading. In 2012, she founded the successful Stories on Stage program at Koorliny Arts Centre, which features authors being interviewed in a theatre setting.

In 2015 she turned to fiction writing, with the publication of "The Point of Love" in *Rocky Romance* followed by children's picture book *My Silly Mum* (2016). She is now working on a full-length contemporary novel, as well as with Serenity Press. Her website is www.moniquemulligan.com

MICHELE NUGENT

Michele Nugent is a former newspaper journalist and editor with thirty years' experience, a passionate communicator and listener, and a consumer and teller of stories. She now works as communications coordinator of a large West Australian not-for-profit care group.

Michele has been a regular blogger for several years, broaching subjects as vast as the challenges of being thrust into the solo world of parenting teenage daughters, her distaste for personalised number plates and the travesty of the cosmetic industry's vacuous endeavours to guilt women into giving their vaginas the Mona Lisa smile treatment.

A lover of stories since birth and a reader of them since before Kindy, she began writing as a youngster, and continues to successfully make a living from it. In her snatches of spare time, Michele is writing a coming-of-age novel for adults young and old. Her website is olsolomeoh.wordpress.com

TEENA RAFFA-MULLIGAN

Teena Raffa-Mulligan is a reader, writer and daydream believer who believes there is magic in every day if you choose to find it. She discovered the wonderful world of storytelling as a child and decided to become a writer at an early age.

Teena writes for children and adults and her publications range from poetry and short stories to picture books and a middle grade novel. Her writing life has also included a long career in journalism. She shares her passion for books and writing by presenting talks and workshops to encourage people of all ages to write their own stories. Her website is www.teenaraffamulligan.com

GUY SALVIDGE

Guy Salvidge is a Western Australian English teacher and author of the novels *Yellowcake Springs* and *Yellowcake Summer*. He is a member of the Literary Committee at the Katharine Susannah Prichard Writers' Centre and he's twice been Emerging Writer in Residence, at KSP in 2013 and at FAWWA in 2014. Guy's short fiction has been published in *The Great Unknown* and *Tincture Journal* and his crime story 'Frank', which won the 2015 City of Rockingham Short Fiction Award, has been published in *Westerly: New Creative* and *Award Winning Australian Writing 2016*. He lives and works in Northam and blogs at www.guysalvidge.com

JENNIFER SCOULLAR

Jennifer is a lapsed lawyer who harbours a deep appreciation and respect for the natural world. She lives with her family at Pilyara, a beautiful property in the southern Victorian ranges that has been in her family for generations. She writes rural/environmental fiction and has six published novels. *Wasp Season* (Sid Harta 2008) *Brumby's Run* (Penguin 2012), *Currawong Creek* (Penguin 2013), *Billabong Bend* (Penguin 2014), *Turtle Reef* (Penguin 2015) and *Journey's End* (Penguin 2016). Her website is www.jenniferscoullar.com

MELINDA TOGNINI

Melinda Tognini's feature articles, travel writing and personal essays have appeared in magazines and anthologies in Australia and the US. Her first book, *Many Hearts, One Voice: the story of the War Widows' Guild in Western Australia* was published by Fremantle Press in 2015.

Melinda is passionate about telling 'invisible' stories – those stories absent from or sidelined in the dominant narratives of our history – and empowering others to find their voice. After growing up surrounded by the bush, bauxite and beaches of North East Arnhem Land, she now resides in Perth with her husband and two children. Her website is www.melindatognini.com.au

SANDI WALLACE

Award-winning crime writer Sandi Wallace writes authentic, gritty, rural crime stories with romantic elements. Her debut novel *Tell Me Why* won the 2015 Davitt Award Readers' Choice and was also shortlisted for the 2015 Davitt Award Best Debut. The sequel and next book in her contemporary Rural Crime Files series, *Black Saturday*, will be released in 2016. Her website is www.sandiwallace.com

KAREN WEAVER

Karen Weaver is a heart writer who embraces the beauty in every day and hopes to share that with others through her writing. She embraced her passion for writing when she moved from Ireland to Australia in 2008. Karen writes romance, spiritual and self-help books as Karen Weaver, and children's books under the name Mamma Macs. She has a diploma in humanities and a background of tutoring drama. She hopes to continue to be a positive part of people's lives through writing.

As a busy mum of six and founder of Serenity Press, she lives by the quote: 'Where there is a will there is always a way.' Connect with Karen on her Facebook page or www.serenitypress.org

TESS WOODS

Tess Woods is a physiotherapist who lives in Perth, Australia with one husband, two children, one dog and one cat who rules them all. Her first novel, *Love at First Flight*, released by HarperCollins in April 2015, received worldwide critical acclaim, hit the best-seller charts in Australia and was voted Book of the Year in the AusRom Today Reader's Choice Awards 2015 where Tess was also top ten nominated as Best New Author.

Love at First Flight is the first HarperCollins Australia digital book to be given a print release in August 2016. Tess's short story, "Destiny in a Day", released in the anthology *Hot Stuff: Surfing Love* is set in beautiful Cornwall, where she dreams of living one day, and Tess is currently writing her second full-length novel, *Beautiful Messy Love*. When she isn't working or being a personal assistant to her kids, Tess enjoys reading and all kinds of granny-ish pleasures like knitting, baking, drinking tea, watching *Downton Abbey* and tending to the vegie patch. Her website is www.tesswoods.com.au

FELICITY YOUNG

Felicity spent her childhood years in the UK and moved to Western Australia with her parents as a sixteen-year-old. After finishing her nurses' training, she married, had three children, and completed an Arts degree at UWA. In 1991 Felicity and her family moved to a small farm where she established a sheep stud and began to write.

After having published several contemporary crime novels Felicity is now working on her sixth book in a historical mystery series for HarperCollins featuring Edwardian autopsy surgeon Dody McCleland.

Felicity is also an active member of her local volunteer bushfire brigade. Her website is www.felicityyoung.com

Thank you!

Thank you for reading *Writing the Dream*.

We invite you to share your thoughts and reactions on Goodreads and Amazon, and also to spread the word among your writing and reading community.

For more information about Serenity Press titles, please visit serenitypress.org

While you're there, we invite you to sign up for our e-newsletter so you can keep up-to-date with new releases and submission opportunities.

---

[1] The lyrics from Woody Guthrie's "Hard Travelin'" have been included after noting the following copyright notice from Woody Guthrie: *"This song is Copyrighted in U.S., under Seal of Copyright # 154085, for a period of 28 years, and anybody caught singin it without our permission, will be mighty good friends of ourn, cause we don't give a dern. Publish it. Write it. Sing it. Swing to it. Yodel it. We wrote it, that's all we wanted to do."*